Storytelling in
Contemporary Societies

ScriptOralia   **22**

Herausgegeben von
Paul Goetsch, Wolfgang Raible, Helmut Rix
und Hans-Robert Roemer

in Verbindung mit
Michael Charlton, Gunther Eigler, Willi Erzgräber, Karl Suso Frank,
Hans-Martin Gauger, Ulrich Haarmann, Oskar von Hinüber,
Wolfgang Kullmann, Eckard Lefèvre, Klaus Neumann, Herbert Pilch,
Lutz Röhrich, Hildegard L.C. Tristram, Otmar Werner und Alois Wolf.

Lutz Röhrich / Sabine Wienker-Piepho (eds.)

Storytelling in Contemporary Societies

gnⱱ Gunter Narr Verlag Tübingen

CIP-Titelaufnahme der Deutschen Bibliothek

Storytelling in contemporary societies / Lutz Röhrich ; Sabine Wienker-Piepho (eds.). –
Tübingen : Narr, 1990
  (Script Oralia ; 22)
  ISBN 3–8233–4475–7 kart.
  ISBN 3–8233–4239–8 Gb.

NE: Röhrich, Lutz [Hrsg.]; GT

Gedruckt auf säurefreiem und alterungsbeständigem Werkdruckpapier

Satz: Barbara Herrmann, Freiburg
Druck: Müller + Bass, Tübingen
Verarbeitung: Braun + Lamparter, Reutlingen
Printed in Germany

ISBN 3–8233–4239–8 (geb.)
ISBN 3–8233–4475–7 (kt.)

Zeichnungen: Claude Serre, Autos, Editions Glénat

CONTENTS

Lutz Röhrich

INTRODUCTION

This volume consists of some outstanding papers presented at the International Congress of Folk Narrative Research (I.S.F.N.R.) which was held in Budapest in 1989. Above all, it comprises those contributions which were especially elaborated by the members of the Theory Commission of the I.S.F.N.R., primarily dealing with "Theories of Modern and Everyday Narration". I am most obliged to the new President of this International Society for Folk Narrative Research, Prof. Reimund Kvideland (Bergen) as well as to the local President, Prof. Vilmos Voigt (Budapest) for all their helpful organisatorial assistance in preparing this publication. "ScriptOralia", the periodical of the Freiburg research program "Relations of Orality and Scriptuality" seems to offer an ideal platform for the presentation of the results from Budapest. Therefore, I have to express my gratitude to the general editors of "ScriptOralia", our Freiburg colleagues Prof. Wolfgang Raible and Prof. Paul Goetsch. Furthermore, my particular thanks go to my colleague Dr. Sabine Wienker-Piepho (Freiburg), for – given her editorial sensibility – she coped so successfully with many obstacles. It was her, too, and Peter Tokofski (Bloomington) as well as Prof. Tom Scott (Liverpool) who skilfully helped to translate many contributions into English, which is more internationally understood.

The themes presented in this volume cover a wide range of topics. The proposed framework has the advantage of being current while also looking to the future. It also extends the discussion to non-traditional genres such as autobiographical reports, narratives at work and in hospitals etc., rumor, jokes and so on. The topics include fictional as well as non-fictional narratives. And in particular, current needs and functions fulfilled by narration, such as providing information, teaching, eliciting sympathy, identification, etc. should be discussed. Consequently, this broad outline will provide an ample diversification of themes.

In a certain sense, this corresponds to the geographic heterogenity; the contributions come from northern, central, eastern and southern Europe, as well as from America and Asia. Thus they truly represent an international cross-section

10

of the I.S.F.N.R. Diverse phenomena can be described under the heading "Modern Story Telling":

1. The appearance of new genres, texts, forms, and narrative techniques.

2. The transformation of genres and contents, the adoption of traditional materials and contents by the media in the technological world (books, newspapers, radio, television), stages of disappearance, recasting of functions, and parodies.

3. The transformation of folkloristic methods and the future of folk narrative research.

The question of "narrative continuity" comes up repeatedly in the following papers: In the age of mass communication, where and how do people still narrate (or begin narrating again)? What are the relationships among reading, writing and narrating, between literacy and orality? How is the art of narration cultivated or even openly promoted? What are the intellectual conditions for the maintenance of narratives today; does memorization have any chances for survival?

The role of the mass media has already been frequently discussed. On one hand they contribute to the disintegration and disappearance of traditional orality; on the other, they have become an important part of modern folklore. The transformation of narration is not necessarily a new phenomenon. Folk narratives such as Märchen, legends and jests etc. have always adapted to their respective social and cultural environment. In principle, every traditional narrative can be modernized. Thus there has always been "contemporary storytelling". In this sense we can identify a few general trends in the corpus of modern narratives: for example folktales adapt to modern reality, requisites are modernized (airplanes, motorways, telephones, televisions), modern weapons replace swords, airplanes appear instead of flying carpets; we also observe a reduction of religious and supernatural elements. The same applies to the characters: robbers replace giants, a midwife appears in place of the witch or Schicksalsfrau, etc. From Perrault through the Grimms to the present, changes in the social milieu for narrators and the contents of their narratives have constantly taken place. Traditional narrative forms mutate into new forms of communication. The content of Märchen and legends appears in films, cartoons, comics, or in popular literature. Other elements, in contrast, seem almost timeless, "archetypical", always renewable. Certain elements can also move from one genre to another:

medieval humorous tales appear as modern jokes, Märchen still exist in atrophied forms ("Schwundstufen"). Almost every wellknown and frequently told narrative can become the victim of parody or joking. Thus in addition to established generic labels we must coin a new terminology such as "anti-Märchen", "anti-proverbs", "urban legends", and "phantom-lore". We might ask whether this new terminology is necessary or superfluous.

All of the papers essentially ask: what relationship do today's narratives have to "traditional" materials and genres? When must we speak of a "new", "modern" narrative or merely of a "transformation" of traditional materials? These questions are more interesting as far as the legend is concernced than the Märchen.

In current folkloristics these problems are most commonly discussed in regard to the so-called "urban legends": "Do legends of today and yesterday belong to the same genre?" In any case, there are ample narratives today that include the legend's characteristic claim to depict true events. These narratives are not only told in the present; they also depict present conditions and experiences. Yet what should we call them: "urban legends", "wandering stories of everyday life", or "folk legends in our time"? Bengt af Klintberg correctly points out the difference between "scientific and ethnic genres". He emphasizes the difference between the structure and content of "legends" and "personal experience story." Thus most authors see no reason to separate the modern legends from traditional ones. Most importantly, modern legends function as equivalents of older tradition (e.g. reports of UFO-sightings). Also, the legend can be adapted to any cultural context. Not infrequently, they contain grotesque or macabre humor, but this too corresponds to traditional legends. In any case, a historical perspective does justice to modern narrative forms as well.

But modern narration poses many other questions: Who tells these modern horror stories, rumours, and "haunted stories"? When and where does modern narration take place: at work, in school, at the university, in a train compartment, or in the bus, at parties, in the confessional, or in waiting in a queue? What needs do these narratives meet? What is their social function? Certainly many transport prejudices, fears and aggression towards strangers (refugees, foreign workers, minorities, etc.) in a given culture. Frequently, jokes too express a similar xenophobia. How are these stories collected? Through newspapers and radio shows? With the tape-recorder? On what occasions? What is the extent of the international distribution of such modern narrative complexes and urban legends? How do they diffuse? What role in this diffusion do folklorists themselves play? Certainly, striking titles of successful books by some of our colleagues have had a not insignificant effect on the spread of the stories about vanishing hitch-hikers and rats in the pizza. Radio, daily newspapers, and tabloids also have their share in spreading the stories. Yet the distribution process still needs to be investigated, and the effect of folklorists in these processes should be considered.

Other contributors consider religiously motivated reports. The very successful humorous parallels to the Bible published in Hungary are not the only items to be considered here. Narration can also be an information on miracles or a conversation with God in a prayer; and the entries in petition-books in modern highway churches, for example, in which drivers report about moving experiences during their travels (accidents, traffic, vacations, problems with love, exams, etc.) also belong here as something like a spontaneously "written-down orality".

Donald Ward appropriately draws our attention to a neglected category, namely "Idionarrating – Talking to the Self". He understands this phenomenon to be an important transitional stage that precedes "communicating these stories to others".

The "family anecdote" is a genre of autobiographical narration that has existed for some time, but it has not yet been investigated closely even though we all know such stories from our own families. The genre is introduced for the first time here (by Bengt Holbek). The genre most closely corresponds to what André Jolles once labelled "memorabile". For this genre we should ask: how and why are they performed and passed on? They consist primarily of stories about socialization processes, about conflicts between grandfathers, fathers, and sons, between siblings and between the sexes; they discuss authority and emancipation, norms and deviation from them. Although they seem to report very individual experiences, these narratives follow the structural principles, typological tendencies, and other "epic laws" found in traditional folk narratives.

Like the family anecdote, the joke also has an autobiographical background. The psychological connections between the individual and the joking narrative are particularly interesting. Although jokes elicit laughter, they have serious backgrounds and reflect social, technical, moral-religious, as well as political developments in society. Jokes are always psychograms of the society in which they are told, as well as of the individual who tells them.

Last but not least, the following papers also discuss the significance and loss of prestige of various schools and theories. For example Don Ward discusses the advantages and disadvantages of "performance theory". He accuses advocates of this very theory of sliding back into a Romantic view when they assume that folklore only exists in "oral performance", and thus of having a false conception of storytelling in the age of natural sciences, industry and technology. To show just how false this conception can be, he offers the example of the legend of the Pied Piper of Hamelin which is known around the world even though it never existed as an oral performance. Instead of subscribing to a single theory, Ward argues that in the future folklorists should examine folklore "in the light of issues such as class, gender, nationalism, community, institutions and economy".

What lies in the future for folk narrative and folk narrative research? How can the enormous amount of material be made available? Prof. Isidor Levin (Leningrad) tries to suggest a computer-aided solution here. What is the outlook for folk narrative in the next millenium? How will human memory develop in a world of "computer memory" and in the technical world of the machine? How will „orality" hold its own in a world of pictures and optic signals? How can individual fantasy develop in a world of mass communication?

No one is a prophet. Yet a look at the past and present teaches us one thing in particular which will certainly also apply to the future of folk narrative: "every form of culture belongs to a particular age." In an increasingly small and inter-connected world, folklorists have new problems: How successfully can the theory-commission of an international scholarly organization work if it only meets once every five years, and even on those occasions not as a whole? Are folklorists really still a family that speaks one language or do they frequently talk past each other? It is correctly pointed out (e.g. by Don Ward) that information deficits – mostly due to language barriers – obstruct international communication and the progress of our discipline. We surely need to listen to each other more closely and to take better notice of theoretical and practical developments in other countries.

Reimund Kvideland
(Bergen)

STORYTELLING IN MODERN SOCIETY

The title of this section can be understood as a program, it does not say "narrative tradition" but "storytelling in modern society". In other words, the title puts the stress on the activity. This is not a new perspective in narrative research, but from time to time it is necessary to point out that genres and content are not the only perspectives in narrative research.

A comparison with folksong research may be worthwhile. Repeatedly scholars have stated that it is important to study the singing, not merely the texts. The German musicologist Heinrich Besseler expressed that already in the 1920s.

John Meier, the founder of Deutsches Volksliedarchiv, claimed on several occasions that the musical activity is the basic entity: "Wirklich ist nur das Singen, (...) die Tätigkeit, nicht aber das Objekt, der Gegenstand."[1]

Naturally the Schwietering School has maintained similar ideas. Between 1970 and 1980 Ernst Klusen appears a strong representative of this research, followed by Wilhelm Schepping and Walter Heimann. Also in other countries such research is done, but it is still in its beginnings although it is as zestful as that of Klusen.[2]

Some years ago I proposed a Nordic project on singing as a cultural phenomenon. In the discussions about the proposal, Otto Holzapfel said that we ought to talk about storytelling as an activity, too. To tell a story is a social act. If we do not understand the act, we are unable to reach a full understanding of the text. Studying the act of singing is no more a new perspective in folksong research, than the study of storytelling in narrative reseach, but in both research areas we can note a tendency to forget this perspective.

---

[1]John Meier, "Volksliedsammlung und Volksliedforschung in Deutschland, in *Deutsche Kultur im Leben des Volkes*, 15 (1940), 190-210, p. 205.

[2]Cf. Wilhelm Schepping, "Lied- und Musikforschung," in *Grundriß der Volkskunde*. Einführung in die Forschungsfelder der europäischen Ethnologie, ed. Rolf Wilhelm Brednich (Berlin, 1988) 399-422.

16

For a long time it has been claimed that the narrative tradition has become extinct in modern Western society. This claim has been repeated so often that many people believe it to be true. But in later years more and more folklorists have discovered that people continue to tell stories, perhaps not the kind of stories folklorists wanted to be told, but people do tell stories. Recent American research has demonstrated this and thereby given impulses for a renewal of European thinking.

Recently, in Fabula 1987, Dorota Simonides has presented two thought-provoking examples of how genre-thinking decides what we collect and publish and what we leave out. The first example is a story about a voice from a new grave. This story was told over a wide area in the first half of the last century. It was collected, but since it was considered a true story, it was left out of the printed edition as nontraditional. Nevertheless, between the first and the second world wars the story became popular again – as a true story. The second example presents the negative responses Simonides received when she asked people to collect stories in a certain area. She was told that there was nothing to collect because everybody told only vampyre stories. In the first case it was the editor who made the selection, in the second it was the local collectors or informants.[3] The author concludes that we only know bits and pieces of the older narrative tradition, collecting was concentrated on clearly traditional narrative material then as it is today. We do not appreciate stories from everyday life or true stories, although these stories reveal modern man's creativity. She is right in saying that we do not know what will be 'real' legends for future generations. This is not the point, however. Taken as social activity or cultural expression, a far greater part of the narrative material than the fixed folkloristic genres is informative. To underline Simonides' conclusion: "Was für uns traditionell ist, bildet nur einen kleinen Teil des Erzählrepertoires früherer Zeiten"[4] – let me add: the same is true today.

Again we have to ask: what were the conditions of storytelling in older society and what are they today? Where are the possibilities for storytelling in contemporary society? It has been claimed that short forms like the joke are today's narrative tradition because we lead such hectic lives, and lack the time to tell and to listen to long stories. This statement is correct as long as we only think of that part of the day which is the most stressed. But neither did people in the older peasant societies have time or a chance to tell or listen to folk tales at all times

---

[3]Dorota Simonides, "Moderne Sagenbildung im polnischen Großstadtmilieu," Fabula, 28 (1987), 269-178, p. 277 f.

[4]Ibid., p. 278.

during the day or while working. People born in the last part of the previous century, often said that they never had time to play, there was always work to be done. It is easy to point to the most important changes: Both family life and leasure time have in many places become more private, centered as they are around the nuclear family. Factors like housing policies and television contribute to strengthening this tendency. This means that many of the occasions for story-telling known from elder society – kveldssete – have disappeared. Neighbour-hood relationships have become more superficial, the rules for social intercourse have changed.

It is also important that the communicative channels have changed, today we are far less dependant on oral transmission than earlier generations. We receive narrative material through radio, TV, dailies, magazines, books and xerox-copies. All these media fit well into the private sphere and its one-way communi-cation patterns.

We no longer depend on the fellowship between storyteller and audience. This means that the storytelling-activity becomes more and more professional-ized. Clear examples are storytellers in radio, TV, film and writers for the mass media. As watchers, listeners or readers, we have no or only very little influence on what the mass media have to offer.

(Semi-)professional storytellers have also gained a greater presence and in-fluence in many formalized situations. We find them in entertaining paying audi-ences or audiences based on membership, at company parties and courses, but also at private arrangements like weddings and birthday parties where a toast-master or master of ceremonies is performing. In these cases the host buys a complete product, if he wishes, he can and does arrange what is to be told.

Ernst Klusen has placed musical activity and passivity in a continuum ran-ging from immanence via immanent/emanent representative to emanence, that is from common interaction via delegation of musical tasks to autonomous musical performers. He does not see this as a purely historical development, but rather as an additive process.[5]

Narrative materials have yet not been analyzed this way, although certain basic work is done in an article on genres and interaction by Roger D. Abra-hams.[6]

---

[5] Ernst Klusen, "Zwischen Symphonie und Hit: Folklore?" in *Musikpädagogik heute*, eds. H Antholz and W. Gundlach (Düsseldorf, 1975) 79-91.
[6] Roger D. Abrahams, "The complex relations of simple forms," (1976) in *Folklore Genres*, ed. D. Ben-Amos (Austin, 1976) 193-214..

Traditionally, folklorists have been looking for texts, either through literary research or fieldwork. Eventually we learned that not only the text, but also its context is important. We always first looked at the text and then at the context. First at single data, then at more complex data until we almost had to admit that the entire culture was our context. Faced with the impossible task of mapping out this inclusive context, we escaped into group- and subcultures, where in many ways we still find ourselves today. But in narrative research this represents an important step ahead.

Nevertheless, we have to be cautious about our exclusive concentration on well-defined groups. Hermann Bausinger has drawn attention to the important fact that there exist cultural units today which are not units in the original sense of the term, i.e. fixed, unchanging groups, but "jeweils aktualisierte Gruppierungen, deren Konstellationen sich allerdings immer wieder ähnlich herausbilden."[7] Such groups do not possess stable traditions, they are rather characterized by an exchange of and an encounter with newly created cultural expressions.

Within one and the same cultural unit or microculture we find stories about the hiker with an axe in his bag, about God's miraculous guidance, and about erotic adventures. Instead of one unified narrative tradition groups reveal some criss-crossing fields of narrative, or perhaps more precisely, several strands of narrative traditions known only to a part of the population in each group. If parts of these traditions become generally known through publication, they may even threaten local culture. This recently occurred on the Finnish islands of Åland, where an unexpurgated edition of children's traditions was published with public support. According to plan the book was to be distributed to schools and kindergardens. But when the politicians saw the book they tried to stop the distribution of it. Its content was too obscene, erotic and impertinent to be distributed among the informants! The children's own tradition was dangerous for them! Or was it perhaps dangerous for the adults who were so far unaware of its existence?

The study of customs has shown that in a local community various customs have various performers. It would be a task for narrative research to demonstrate the same for narrative traditions. It is a paradox that even working with context research and performance analysis, it is always the text to which we turn. Text-context research and performance analysis would also tell us that perhaps we should first turn to the context in order to find what texts exist in a given context. Only by this approach will we be able to grasp the essentials of storytelling in modern society. I am not concerned about what might be future tradition.

---

[7]Hermann Bausinger, "Neue Felder, neue Aufgaben, neue Methoden," in *Deutsche Volkskunde – Französische Ethonologie*, eds. I. Chiva and U. Jeggle (Frankfurt, 1987) 326-344, p. 330.

I would prefer to turn to different groups and situations and find out what is told there, regardless of genres. If we discover new genres, so much the better.

American scholars in particular have pointed the way through studies of narrative traditions in various groups such as occupational, age, socially marginal and religious groups. I would also mention Gillian Bennet's fascinating study of older women's view on ghosts, premonitions and fortune-telling which brings out the factors that dominate the individual's relationship with the supranormal and death.[8] The study of childrens' own cultural expressions, give us greater insight into childrens' culture.

American folklorists have also studied specific Christian narrative traditions and their function in congregational and family life. In Norwegian folklore collections we would hardly find any traces of such stories, even though many of them, without any difficulty, could be classified as subgenres and narrative types. A quick glance at the literature produced by lay movements shows that there exists a rich tradition of edifying, memoir, or fictional literature. Today these traditions are used and spread through devotion columns in various media and radio devotions. But first and foremost they are told in the congregations and we must go to them to study their function and meaning.

I use these stories as an example of a narrative tradition that is unknown to Norwegian folklorists and also as an example of the vitality of contemporary narrative activity. Based on their supranormal content, the stories can be characterized as legends or memorates – depending on their form. Often they are told as personal experience stories to emphasize their actuality and truth. That the same stories occur as legends and memorates confirms that we are dealing with traditional narrative material. Parallels in older literature give evidence of the same.

Among the most popular types we find stories about a) Angel guardians who save a person from assault, b) miraculous rescues and events, c) prayer hearings, d) God reminding someone to do something for someone else, for instance give food or money, d) salvation experiences, f) visions of Jesus and Angels, g) healing through prayer. According to my material stories about h) revelation through dreams and i) near-death experiences with a religious explanations are less well known.

Analysis indicates that it is not the stories with the best plot or suspenseful action that are the most important. From the individual's and the congregations' point of view, it is the story which describes the salvation experience that is decisive. As action story, however, they are not particularly exciting. Typical motifs

---

[8]Gillian Bennet, "Traditions of Belief. Women and the Supernatural" (London, 1987).

are God's calling, sometimes a refusal to it, the realization that one is a sinner, the troubled mind, release through a word from the Bible, and an intensive experience of being forgiven and saved.

It is the testimony in the congregation, the recreation of the experience in story form which decides whether a person is accepted as reborn and consequently can become a member of the congregation without reservation. This means that the narrator has to provide this experience with a certain structure and content in order to be accepted. This indicates that the experience is dominated by a known narrative structure. An unambiguous model can be found in the New Testament's account of Saul's conversion, but there are also other patterns depending on the kind of conversion theology propagated in a particular congregation.[9]

This agrees with the view on personal narratives expressed by Richard Bauman in his book *Story, Performance and Events*: "Events are abstractions from narrative. It is the structures of signification in narrative that give coherence to events in our understanding, that enable us to construct in the interdependent process of narration and interpretation a coherent set of interrelationship that we call an 'event'."[10] As Bauman points out, the narrative structure and narrative process contribute to create 'the event' in the narrator's as well as in the audience's mind.[11] A competent preacher is of course highly esteemed in the congregations, but both for him and the person who gives his testimony, the right relationship with God is the important thing. Narrative competence, therefore, is not valuable in itself, on the contrary, it can become a negative factor in the evaluation of an individual by the congregation when the genuineness of his or her testimony is in doubt. Usually, members of the congregation prefer a testimony coming from the heart instead of the head. These factors become particularly clear in the stories about salvation experiences, but they are also found in other sub-genres.

In conclusion I believe it would be a mistake to focus just on personal experience stories or memorates. We have to bring to light all narrative forms, from

[9]William Clements, " 'I once was lost': Oral Narratives of Born-Again Christian," *International Folklore Review*, 2 (1982) 105-111, and Elaine Lawless, " 'The Night I Got the Holy Ghost...' – Holy Ghost Narratives and the Pentecostal Conversion Process," *Western Folklore* 47 (1988) 1-19, and Sandra K. D. Stahl, "Contributions of Personal Narrative Research to North American Folkloristics," *Fabula* 29 (1988) 390-399, p. 394.

[10]Richard Bauman, "Story, Performance, and Event: Contextual Studies of Oral Narrative" (Cambridge, 1986) 5.

[11]Lauri Honko, "Memorates and the Study of Folk Belief," *Journal of the Folklore Institute*, 1 (1964) 5-19.

short forms to longer ones, from the recognizable narrative types to narrative material in the form of a dialogue. We have to ask how the narrative material fits into the communicative pattern, and into which strategies various elements find their way. As a social activity storytelling is based on a given world view. It is our task on one hand to bring this world view to light through analysis, on the other to analyse the functions of storytelling, as for instance, the function of propagating its own understanding of the world. One intention could be to support the world view in the immediate environment, another to place oneself within a given world-view, or – and that is perhaps most important – to find one's place in a complex society characterized by many competing world views. In recent years we have seen many exciting studies written from this perspective, and I believe this area provides great possibilities to bring out important aspects of 'storytelling in modern society'.

Vilmos Voigt
(Budapest)

MODERN STORYTELLING – STRICTO SENSU

Storytelling is *per definitionem* always 'contemporary'. Even if we concentrate only on 'tales' in the proper sense of the term we could easily find stories that we can classify as tales in ancient Egypt and in the present day, and from Greenland to the Sahara and Taiwan. Within at least four or five thousand years of taletelling from five continents, there is always a place for 'contemporary' storytelling.

On the other hand, all serious scholars of folk literature are well aware of the fact that 'today's' tales differ from those of the 'past'. What is the main difference between 'old' and 'new' or perhaps, more specifically, between 'traditional' and 'modern' tales? We could give two different answers to the question.

If we stress the events of storytelling as being 'modern', we could admit that both 'old' and 'new' tales could serve the purpose of actual storytelling. New variants may contain modernization in some motifs (trains, telephones, televisions etc. occur in the tales). The whole motivation of the story may even change (as the tale loses its religious or marvelous character). Perhaps the actual setting of the storytelling (in nurseries, even for broadcast or TV) could also have been altered radically. Communication neglects or protects the channels: instead of illiteracy and orality, written or printed tales arise. In books of tales, illustrations gain great importance. Most recently home computers run 'tale programs'. Disneylands and fairylands grow everywhere, from the United States to Japan and from France to a common Austro-Hungarian attraction during the World Exhibition, projected for 1995. We know less about modern storytelling in Brazil, Cameroun or the People's Republic of China. Still there is no doubt that all over the world forms of modern storytelling flourish.

Still there is another way of understanding modern storytelling, if we focus on the modern 'tales'. At first glance it seems very difficult to find new tales. Tale type indices often suggest 'new' types or subtypes. In fact, however, the numbers with an asterisk do not refer to true 'new' tales, but only to a version, which has not properly been separated or acknowledged by previous researchers. When Ørnulf Hodne (Thy Types of the Norwegian Folktale, 1984) listed some 'unclassified narrationes lubricae', he could not find AaTh numbers e.g. for the stories 'The strange animal' (a well-known story of exposing oneself in tar and feathers) or for 'the maiden who pissed so far', which in fact is the most widely known international seduction tale.[1] Moreover, both tales were also first collected in Norway more than a century ago, i.e. are not 'younger' or 'later' as most of the Norwegian folktale collection items.

When, after World War II devoted communist folklorists wanted to show the superiority of the new folklore above the old, they tried to find 'new' tale types. Linda Dégh's famous Hungarian storytelling woman, Mrs. Zsuzsanna Palkó told her a tale in 1950 ('Német Gábor'), in which a poor lad is ridiculed by the rich village mayor. He moves to the capital, becomes a carpenter in a factory, and later is adopted by the owner. As a rich capitalist, he marries the village mayor's daughter.[2] A more 'actualized' tale, with indications of class differences and struggle, finally turns out to be a capitalist's career story, in which the hero is a devoted Roman Catholic. In one word: the 'new' or 'socialist' tale does not succeed at all.

One might suggest for 'modern' tales certain cases, in which written sources have been used as the basis for actual storytelling. The best known source for such retold tales is the Brothers Grimm's collection of German tales. In some cases, even during the shaping of the 'final' form of the tales, the first published versions have already influenced the greater public.[3]

Thanks to quick translations of the Grimm's tales into several other languages, their influence on world folklore is very considerable. Of course there are tales which more or less became known throughout the world because of literary sources (Snow-White [AaTh 709] from the Grimms' collection, The Cat as Helper, [AaTh 545] from Perrault's Le Maistre Chat ou le Chat Botté, etc.) and in such cases, the variants deriving from them can be very different. If a tale is adopted from a written source, both 'genuine' storytellers and professional writers tend to deal freely with the original text. Picture or mass media versions are also very common sources in such cases for generating modern tales.

Still we should not equate modern tales simply with tales from a literary background. The very complicated and intriguing history of the type The Offend-

[1] Ørnulf Hodne, The Types of the Norwegian Folktale, (Oslo etc., 1984), 343 f.
[2] Linda Dégh, Kakasdi népmesék vol. I. no. 48 (Budapest, 1955) 466 f.
[3] Cf. e.g. Hänsel und Gretel (KHM 15), Rotkäppchen (KHM 26), Von dem Machandelboom (KHM 47) etc. Notes by Heinz Rölleke, in Brüder Grimm, Kinder- und Hausmärchen 3 (Stuttgart, 1980).

ed Skull (Statue) [AaTh 470 A], better known as the Don Juan-plot,[4] has clearly shown that early literary sources do not explain the relative popularity of particular stories. Famous works of literature, however, tend to be reinterpreted from time to time, though 'eternal' Electra, Faust or Don Juan versions usually fall outside of the confines of the proper folk literature, and thus can be disregarded here.

In his seminal study on contrasted or distorted proverbs, Wolfgang Mieder emphasizes the fact that 'anti-proverbs' occur mainly in our century, when old fashioned ethics are vanishing: "Warum diese Vorliebe für Antisprichwörter in der Moderne? Der Hauptgrund wird darin liegen, daß die den meisten Sprichwörtern zugrunde liegende altväterliche Moral einfach nicht mehr in die gesellschaftliche Wirklichkeit paßt."[5] Of course, there are differences between 'modern' anti-proverbs and modern tales. A proverb can be as short as a sentence, and perhaps by changing only one word, or, in some cases, even one letter, the meaning turns into something ridiculous, opposite or funny. In tales, the entire structure must be changed: the hero is defeated, the princess becomes an ugly whore, technical gadgets are substituted for magic, etc. As the best examples of such a treatment I would refer to numerous 'tale-plays' by the Soviet playwright, Yevgeny Shwartz (1896-1958), in which he meticulously observes the structure and plot of old tales, whilst writing in a style which is grotesque, and presents a moral which is ironical or hostile. His best play, *Dragon*[6] once was directed against fascism, but is in fact a bitter satire on all kinds of dictatorship. It is a true anti-tale of AaTh 300. Shwartz labelled his works as 'tales', and many of them were also very popular in Soviet children theatres. Thus, from various points of view it can be called as an 'anti-tale'.

I still think the term 'anti-tale' for modern tales is suitable only in a number of restricted case, when the moral of the 'old' tale was questioned in an explicit way. More often the 'old' stories just appear in 'new clothes', as the Hungarian folklorist and Hebraist Alexander Scheiber used to say.[7] Scheiber quotes mostly literary variants or draws on Jewish tradition, the same phenomenon of 'putting into new clothes' is still generally apparent.

---

[4] Cf. Leander Petzoldt, *Der Tote als Gast. Volkssage und Exempel*, FFCommunications 200 (Helsinki, 1980).

[5] Wolfgang Mieder, *Antisprichwörter* I (Wiesbaden, [2]1983), x.

[6] Yevgeny Shwartz, *"Drakon. A Tale in Three Acts"* (Leningrad, 1944-1962).

[7] Alexander Scheiber, "Alte Geschichten in neuem Gewande," in *Essays on Jewish Folklore and Comparative Literature*, (Budapest, 1985), 307-397 (first published under the title *Old Stories in New Garment*, in *Fabula* and elsewhere, 1966-1983). – Altogether Scheiber gives about 80 stories, including also wellknown tale types, as e.g. AaTh 1645 "The Treasure at Home".

In one of his most quoted papers, Kurt Ranke had, in 1955, also written on 'Schwank und Witz als Schwundstufe',[8] stressing the fact that jokes and anecdotes express transitory or reinterpreted forms of traditional tales. Of course, not all 'old' tales are capable of undergoing such a transition, and not all jokes or anecdotes can be traced back to their original tale form. It is not by chance that Lutz Röhrich in his summarizing book *Der Witz. Figuren, Formen, Funktionen*[9] does not give a concordance in indexing AaTh type numbers. Equally G. Legman (who is definitely interested in indexing types and motifs) in his pioneering book *Rationale of the Dirty Joke*[10] does not present us with a list of types or motifs. Matti Kuusi, himself being another enthusiast for indexing and typologyzing of folk literature, in his anthology of 1001 Finnish jokes and anecdotes[11] does not attempt to give any type or motif indication to the stories. The largest typology of jokes and anecdotes was made by Sabina Cornelia Stroescu[12] including "3029 types de facéties et 199 types d'anecdotes" as contrasted with the international type catalogue by Aarne-Thompson, containing "692 types de facéties". Stroescu foud 307 Roumanian types parallel to international AaTh numbers, suggesting that others are of Roumanian 'national types'.[13] When fifteen years later she was reediting some parts of her catalogue[14] she gave slightly higher figures both for Roumanian types and variants in general but maintained her opinion about the proportion of 'national' versus 'international' types of Roumanian jokes and anecdotes. The aim of the Roumanian index was different, still I think we can draw a conclusion that at most one tenth of the stories (307 from 3029 + 199) could be ascribed to international distribution. In other words, one tenth of the jokes and anecdotes can be understood as new forms of international lore. As far as I think it is very important to mention that Roumanian material indexed by Stroescu is, in textual terms, as old as other genres of Roumanian folk narratives, dating back to classical (published or unpublished) collections from the 19th

---

[8]Kurt Ranke, (originally in *Festschrift für Will Erich Peuckert zum 60. Geburtstag*, recently better available in the volume of Ranke's collected essays *Die Welt der einfachen Formen* (Berlin-New York, 1978), pp. 61-78.

[9]Lutz Röhrich, *Der Witz. Figuren, Formen, Funktionen*, (Stuttgart, 1977).

[10]Gershon Legman, *Rationale of the Dirty Joke. An Analysis of Sexual Humor*, First Series (New York, 1968).

[11]Matti Kuusi, *Kansanhuumorin kuka kukin on*, (Helsinki, 1980).

[12]Sabina Cornelia Stroescu, *Typologie bibliographique des facéties roumaines*, vols. I-II (Bucuresti, 1969).

[13]*Op. cit.*, vol. I, pp. VIII-X.

[14]Sabina Cornelia Stroescu, *Snoava populars romaneascǎ*, (Bucuresti, 1984).

century too. Thus we cannot find any absolute difference in dating the collected stories.

A brainchild of American folklore research of the seventies, the 'urban legend' is in the eyes of their experts a very 'new' phenomenon. Jan Harold Brunvand in the preface to his first of the three collections (*The Vanishing Hitchhiker. American Urban Legends and Their Meanings*) lists all the key-words of 'new' stories: "This ist a book about *modern* American folk narratives, stories that most people have heard as *true accounts* of *real-life* experiences, and few except scholars recognize as an *authentic* and characteristic part of our contemporary folklore."[15] Brunvand, contrasting 'modern' and 'contemporary' versus 'traditions passed along' in the 'backwoods villages of bygone days',[16] stresses the new characteristics of the genre. Paul Smith and others from England, Bengt af Klintberg and others from Scandinavia, Leea Virtanen and others from Finland agree with that interpretation. In some cases we can see more precisely what the term 'contemporary' means in this case. When in 1975, a Swedish scholar, Bengt af Klintberg sent a questionnaire concerning 'modern urban legends' to his Finnish colleagues, the response was next to none. In contrast to that, 1985 and 1987 gave a rich harvest in Finnish collections of the genre.[17] As a matter of fact, the significant difference in a dozen of years makes it highly questionable whether Virtanen is right in naming the material in Finland as 'town's folk legend'. She also admits that mass media distribute the stories, which are very popular among school children. If we use the term 'urban folk' without any qualification, taking into consideration the international and rapid distribution of the stories, we focus on one characteristic feature of 'folk', neglecting others. On the other hand, the popularity of 'modern urban legends' is a fact, and thorough historical analysis can tell us the earliest known date of variants of legends which are so widespread currently. The first two Sheffield conferences on 'contemporary legends' in 1982 and 1983 have resulted in a proposal to develop a computer data bank for urban legend stories. I think both the more accurate description of recent ways and means of spread of the tradition and a more systematic search for historical antecedents or 'first noticed variants' may serve to provide a greater understanding of what modern stories are about.

---

[15]Jan Harold Brunvand, *The Vanishing Hitchhiker. American Urban Legends and Their Meanings*, (Glasgow, 1983), 11 (italics in the text by Vilmos Voigt).

[16]*Ibid.*

[17]Leea Virtanen, *Varastettu isoäiti. Kaupungin kansantarinoita*, (Helsinki, 1987), 208-210 – (with good bibliography).

As we can see in some of the most recent studies devoted to 'modern urban legends' (af Klintberg and Ward)[18] the risks of too hasty conclusions are clear to most of the folklorists who like to be very up-to-date in their researches.

Change in media channels, newspaper or broadcast (recently television, video etc.) variants have frequently been quoted as key factors in modern storytelling. If we leave the contemporary European or American tradition, we find entirely different circumstances as regards the sources of folk tales. Already, the type and motif indices of Japanese folk literature show the problem. The most striking material was included in Nai-tung Ting's *A Type Index of Chinese Folktales*.[19] As the subtitle says "in the oral tradition and major works or non-religious classical literature", in China the approximately 600 sources excerpted by Ting for his catalogue, are in fact printed works, in the main not for scholarly research, but more or less 'true' publications for greater Chinese audience fond of tales (and similar genres). The Chinese edition of the catalogue gives even more "practical written source material."[20] In the 'Introduction' Ting defines the limits of his material, excluding "modern literary works based on, and imitative of, folktales."[21] However, at least one third of his sources could be disregarded by European folklorists in their own country. Written books, journals, schoolbooks and the like are to some degree an inseperable part of a folk tradition. E.g. in China there is no way to make a distinction between 'old' = 'oral' and 'new' = 'written' sources. Still the problem of forced modernization of tales occurred.

In order to summarize, there are very few historical studies, of what we can refer to as 'modern tales'. In her interesting essay Marianne Thalmann (*Das Märchen und die Moderne*) analyses the German literary tales of great romantic poets like Wackenroder, Novalis, Tieck, Brentano and E. T. A. Hoffmann.[22] According to her final statement surrealistic and modernistic elements occur in the German literary tales from 1797 on (!), while in the tales there is a very explicit shift of world view from the old to the new.[23] But what does it mean "to destroy the old world and shape a new one?" German romantic writers gave up the classical world view for a fantastic, unstable one. The same disrupted tradition stands for all kinds of 'modern' tales.

---

[18]Cf. Bengt af Klintberg, *Do the Legends of Today and Yesterday belong to the Same Genre?* and Donald Ward, *Storytelling in Contemporary Sciences. Idionarrating and Social Change*, both printed in this book.

[19]Nai-tung Ting, *A Type Index of Chinese Folktales*, FFCommunications 223 (Helsinki, 1978).

[20]Nai-tung Ting, (Peking, 1986), 524-556 ff.

[21]Ting (cf. note 19) p. 11.

[22]Marianne Thalmann, *Das Märchen und die Moderne*, (Stuttgart, 1961).

[23]*Op. cit.*, p. 10.

Surely, all tales can be 'modern' ones. After the first edition of Marc Soriano's classical analysis *Les contes de Perrault* (Paris, 1968) a round-table discussion was organized among the French historians belonging to the so called *Annales*-trend.[24] Jacques Le Goff and Emmanuel Le Roy Ladurie (agreeing with
Soriano) spoke about two conceptions of folk tales. A traditional one, according
to which tales are timeless and are distributed without a greater change
("... quand nous regardons les classifications et typologie d'Aarne-Thompson,
etc., nous avons l'impression que le conte populaire est une espèce de réalité
intemporelle ... On n'a pas l'impression que l'histoire ait grand-chose à voir avec
cela, c'est une espèce d'échange perpétuel dans l'identité permanente").[25] A new
kind of approach, examplified by Soriano is a very closely historical one, stressing
even a year's events in Perrault's elaboration of the folk tales.

> Vous [= Soriano], au contraire, tout en amettant cette analyse, vous introdusiez dans
> tel conte populaire des faits très concrets de l'histoire contemporaine, et par example,
> avec une certaine raison, semble-t-il, la famine de 1693, en ce qui concerne *Le Petit
> Poucet*. Est-ce que finalement cette injection de l'histoire ajoute quelque chose
> d'essentiel au conte, ou s'agit-il simplement d'une sorte de mise au goût du jour, qui
> n'en change pas du tout la structure profonde?[26]

Soriano himself argues for a permanent recreation of the tales during storytelling
events:

> Ils nous apprennent que le conte, merveilleux ou facétieux, pour se transmettre et
> pour durer, devait être *assumé, recréé* par des artistes à part entière, ces conteurs et ces
> conteuses ...[27]

According to this view there is a stock of tales available to storytellers, and they
constantly reshape the variants. It is perhaps surprising that French scholars, who
do not have the habit to do fieldwork among living storytellers, stress the importance of the permanent artistic recreation by the formerly living storytellers.

As is well known, Russian and later Soviet folklorists concentrated their
attention on great folklore performers. Their publications, expecially Azadows-
ki's book on Siberian Russian storytellers, became widely familiar among comparative folklorists. Recently, Chistov's book on Russian 'storytellers' from Kare-
lia (1980) and Chicherov's book on 'schools of storytellers' from the Onega reg-

[24]Marc Soriano, *Les contes de Perrault*, (Paris, 1968); cf. *Annales*, issue Mai-June 1970; – better
available as "Preface" to the 1977-edition of Soriano's book (Paris, 1977).
[25]*Op. cit.* (1977), p. X.
[26]*Ibid.*, p. XI.
[27]*Ibid.*, p. XI.

ion (1982) have appeared, but in fact they deal mostly with singers of epic songs (Russian *byliny*), and mention storytellers of proper tales only occasionally. Thus we do not know how Russian taletellers reacted to social events in Russia during the last century or, rather, we do not know much more about the topic than we knew forty years ago. During the thirties 'communist tales' were propagated, and it would be very interesting to establish how the actual situation of contemporary (or 'modern') storytelling in Russia can be characterized.

Another obstacle for understanding 'modern' storytelling is that we do not know much about 'modern' tales from outside Europe. Excellent publications[28] describe the actual setting of telling tales, but fail to point out exactly what tales are innovations or definitely new ones. Without having an encompassing picture of modern folktales around the world, we are not able to offer a description of modern storytelling in general.

In the strict sense of the word, modern storytelling occurs when people tell 'modern' tales. In some of my previous papers I have tried to emphasize the difference between *meaning* and *sense* in folktales, according to wellknown principles in semantics.[29] By listening some forms of reshaping folktale variants, I was able, I think, to show various forms of modernizing tendencies in folk literature. By now we need to take only one more step.

A tale is modern when its *sense* (and not its *meaning*) becomes modern. In this context, modern stands for a change in world view, expressing something radically different. Because we can not change the entire text of a tale (without loosing its identity), and thus the meaning of the tale must be continuous to the previous meanings, only in the *sense* a radical change could occur. That is why in the title of my paper I used the expression "in strict sense".

A tale will be modern if there is a radical change as regards its sense: and it can occur in shaping new types (in a similarity to 'old' AaTh type numbers) or atypical tales. If tales are retold with a different sense (regardless of the fact that the original was written or oral, folk or literary product), including even the totally contrasting tales ('anti-tales'), or putting an 'old' story into 'new clothes', the same phenomenon occurs. Shifts in genres (from tale to joke, anecdote or else), shifts in social settings (from village to city, from adults to schoolchildren), shifts in communication system (from oral tradition to newspaper, broadcast, film, tele-

---

[28]E.g. Ruth Finnegan, *Limba Stories and Story Telling*, (Oxford, 1967), or Camille Lacoste-Dujardin, *Le conte kabyle*. Etude ethnologique, (Paris, 1982), etc.

[29]E.g. Vilmos Voigt, "Semantics and meaning in folktales," *Arv* 40 (1984), 153-161, and Voigt, "The Text of the Folktale and its Semantics," in *Le conte, pourquoi? comment? Folktales, why and how?* (Paris, 1984), 169-184 (with further bibliographical references).

vision etc.), shifts in world view (from magic to realistic, from religious to secular, from aesthetic to didactic *vice versa*) or similar changes are well known from around the whole world. Even without exact data, we can envisage a global theory of 'modern storytelling' based on the premises I have made above.

If 'to be modern' is a question of sense, one could ask, from what point in time we can speak about the 'modern age' in the proper use of the term? 'Modern time' is not a term of folklore research, its definition is a task of social historians, and it is not very difficult to understand that in different continents and countries the term 'modern' has various connotations. Still it is without doubt a very prominent characteristic of our time. In our culture, a 'new' world view instead of the 'old' occurs, thereby causing a shift in the sense of the tales too. This is precisely why we should refer to it as modern.

And, if I may make a final statement here, presently and without any detailed reasoning, I subscribe the term *modern* following to Jakob Burckhardt's works, or the famous *Introduction à la France moderne* by Robert Mandrou[30] or Peter Burke's *Popular Culture in Early Modern Europe*,[31] all of which start the 'modern age' in Europe at about 1500. I suppose modern storytelling and the modern tales in Europe have existed since about the same time, i.e. hundreds of years before Grimm brothers or Perrault. The overwhelming majority of European folktales available to us are 'modern' tales in this strict sense of the word. A statement similar to Albert Wesselski's (who considered the origin of folktales detectable from the shift of *Wahnmotiv* to *Wundermotiv*) could be proved perhaps on a different occasion. For the other continents the problem is an even more subtle one.

If, which is the case in regard to most of the historical sources of European tales, both the pre-history and the influence of Basile's, Straparola's, Perrault's, of the Brothers Grimm, the great 'first' national folklore collection in Europe from the 19th century contain hundreds of 'modern' tales. We even could go on and suppose that medieval *exempla, fabliaux*, fables and animal tales show an actual shift in world view, as contrasted with their 'earlier' or 'original' folklore versions. An uninterrupted tradition of European 'modern' tales has existed during the last five hundred years. Written texts, then printed sources, urban traditions versus village stories, learned rules against innate ones predominate through these centuries. In many respects all the history of modern European storytelling is the same as the entire dimension of storytelling as we know it.

[30]Robert Mandrou, *Introduction à la France moderne (1500-1640)*. Essai de Psychologie historique, (Paris, 1961).
[31]Peter Burke, *Popular Culture in Early Modern Europe*, (London, 1978).

Donald Ward
(Los Angeles)

IDIONARRATING AND SOCIAL CHANGE

American Folklore Theory: An Assessment. There is apparently little consensus among American folklorists regarding the state of the profession and its image in academia as we approach the end of the 1980s. In an address before the plenary session of the American Folklore Society at the meetings of its centennial celebration in October 1988, Alan Dundes proclaimed that folklore had acquired new stature among diverse academic disciplines while noting that, although it previously had derived virtually all its methods and theories from other fields, folklore could now boast that other disciplines were turning to it for fresh approaches and theories. Around this same time Gary Alan Fine expressed a view that was not only less sanguine, it was diametrically opposed to Dundes's observations:

> American academic folklore survives in perilous times. American folklore – as a theoretical approach – has lost its momentum. Related fields, such as anthropology, social history, and literary criticism seem to be thriving. It is increasingly worrisome that folklore as an intellectual, rather than a descriptive or applied, approach seems lacking in direction.[1]

Fine also noted that while there were many examples of "rich and significant research" in folklore that one could point to, they are lacking in a "meta-theoretical base:"

> American folklore has not always lacked focus. In the early 1970s, the discipline flourished. "Performance theory" dominated talk at collegial gatherings, and the *Journal of American Folklore* devoted a special issue in 1972 to the new perspective.[2]

Fine acknowledges that performance theory is so well established that it is today taken for granted by most folklorists, but its period of "fashion and fer-

---

[1] Gary Alan Fine, "The Third Force in American Folklore: Folk Narratives and Social Structures," *Fabula* 29 (1988), 342-353.
[2] *Ibid.*, 342.

ment" is past and that which was once an exciting new theory has now "run its course." In its place Fine proposes a "third force" in American folkloristics that will emphasize "the socially situated character of tradition – interpreting folklore in light of issues such as class, gender, nationalism, community, institutions, and economy."[3]

Performance Theory. The luster indeed seems to have worn off the so-called "performance-school" of American folkloristics. Indeed much of the work that came forth from the school remained of a theoretical nature and the number of documentations and analyses of performances in natural contexts were very few in number.[4] In its place there has emerged a myriad of methods and theories that, while maintaining an interest in performance contexts, have placed the main focus on other issues such as narratives of personal experience (Sandra Stahl), narrative memory and the stability of tradition (Elliott Oring), discourse analysis (Labov and Waletzky, Gillian Gennett), and many others.

Although performance theory has not by any means been eclipsed, it has certainly experienced a gradual demise. Although the theoreticians of performance were among the truly outstanding folklorists of the past thirty years, I fear that the theory itself was, from the outset, plagued by a number of almost insurmountable problems inherent in its very nature. Among these are the following.

Documenting Performance. The study of live performances of folk traditions in their natural contexts demands, in addition to expensive equipment, a great deal of time, energy, patience, planning, and dedication on the part of the researcher. Even after all these conditions are fulfilled, being in the right place at the right time often involves a certain amount of blind luck or even serendipity. Most academic folklorists are so burdened with their daily routines of teaching, committee work, administering examinations and directing theses, that they simply do not have the time to engage in thorough research of performances in context. Actually, even folklorists outside of academia rarely have the time and opportunity to engage in this kind of field documentation. By way of example, I cite the case of the California Folklore Society (of which I have been a member for thirty years). In its circa fifty-year history the society's total membership must

---

[3]*Ibid.*, 343.

[4]This is not the place to survey the many valuable studies that have been inspired by performance theory. It is interesting to note that the very theory has influenced folklore research other than narrative analysis as is the case, for example, in the recent surge in the documentation and analysis of children's lore. In the field of narrative research, Kirschenblatt-Gimblett's study of *A Parable in Context* (1975) was particularly successful, as was Dell Hymnes' *Breakthrough into Performance* (1975). This essay, however, is probably more important for discourse analysis than it is for narrative research.

number in the thousands. Yet, in all these years, there has been precious little systematic documentation of California folklore in performance situations. This record is certainly not encouraging for those who believe that folklore should consist of the analysis of performances in context.

There are certainly many opportunities for scholars to document oral performances of traditional lore. The influx of many thousands of Southeast Asians into the United States in the last twenty years alone has provided opportunities for documenting traditional forms of oral narrative as they are performed in their albeit it new, but nevertheless natural, contexts. Some of these peoples like the Hmong, a mountain people of Laos and neighboring countries, are non-literate thus insuring that oral forms of literature are still thriving among them.[5] Few professional folklorists, alas, have a sufficient command of the languages that would be necessary for one to engage in meaningful field investigation of these peoples and their lore. There are certainly other forms of oral performances that are prevalent that could be exploited by researchers interested in performance theory. Joke-telling sessions occur daily under our very noses; folklorists, however, perhaps still bewitched by a romantic notion of what folklore is, seem to be reluctant to investigate the commonplace, and seek out in its stead the more exotic.

This assessment does not, however, hold for those interested in the analysis of "narratives of personal experience," which has increasingly become a focal point of narrative research in the United States. The fact remains, however, that those engaged in this research have relied more heavily on new modes analysis and new theories that on performance theory.[6]

Oral Performance and the Romantic Vision. In my opinion, performance theory had, from its very onset, a burden to bear of which its foremost practitioners and apologists were never fully aware, and it was this lack of awareness that proved to be an obstacle in the path leading to the theory's goal. I suggest that performance theory, instead of being a revolutionary approach to narrative analysis as envisioned, was from its inception, firmly steeped in a romantic vision of storytellers who were conceived as the bearers of an exclusively oral tradition which they – in delightful storytelling events – passed on to others to keep the tradition alive. In other words, the model of the storytelling event itself was a fanciful image that simply did not correspond to the reality of folklore in the age

[5]Charles Johnson, ed., *Dab Neeg Hmon, Legends and Folktales from the Hmong of Laos*, (St. Paul, 1985).

[6]E.g. Sandra K. Stahl, "Contributions of Personal Narrative Research to North American Folkloristics," *Fabula* 29 (1988), 390-399.

of science, industry, and technology. In insisting that true folklore only exists in oral performance, researchers were forced to deny the very existence of the myriad modes of dissemination of narratives in the modern world. In Western society this "modern world" reaches back at least to the Middle Ages. One merely needs to look at the story of "The Pied Piper", a traditional tale that has roots stretching back to the thirteenth century and, although beloved around the world, would not qualify as folklore for the performance-theorists, because it had never existed as "oral performance."

Because Romanticism, since its inception in the eighteenth century, was largely a European intellectual and aesthetic movement, the reaction to it was also largely a European phenomenon. I suggest that the fact that this intense reaction largely missed North America has led to a perpetuation among Americans of a Romantic worldview long dead in European countries. I further suggest that much of American folkloristics, performance theory included, still reflects a somewhat naive and essentially romantic world-view that should have been abandoned decades ago. There are scores of examples of this lingering influence of the romantic mode of thought. One of these is Dorson's compulsion to divorce fakelore from true folklore.

Academic Provincialism. I certainly do not mean to imply that American scholars have not made great advances and significant contributions to the study of folklore. But I do insist that they have done so working under the handicap of their ignorance of the advances that have been made elsewhere in the world. Few American folklorists read foreign languages and thus have been led time and again into situations of having, as it were, to re-invent the wheel each time they seek to advance new methods and theories. Virtually every "new" theory advanced by American folkloristics in the last thirty years has already been "old hat" by the time it was proclaimed as divine revelation. Contextual studies that analyzed traditional lore within communal contexts have been commonplace in Europe for almost sixty years[7] as are the analysis of oral performances in their natural contexts.[8] European scholars have engaged in discourse analysis and personal experience narratives since the 1930s[9], and that the modern age of technology demands the recognition of a new kind of urban folk culture that has shaped its

---

[7] Martha Bringemeier, *Gemeinschaft und Volkslied*, (Münster i.W., 1931).

[8] Otto Brinkmann, *Das Erzählen in der Dorfgemeinschaft*, (Münster i.W., 1933).

[9] André Jolles, *Einfache Formen*, (Halle, 1930); Mathias Zender, *Volksmärchen und Schwänke aus der Westeifel*, (Bonn, 1935); Robert Petsch, "Wesen und innere Form des Volksmärchens," *Niederdeutsche Zeitschrift für Volkskunde* 15 (1937), 1-24; Hermann Bausinger, "Strukturen des alltäglichen Erzählens," *Fabula* 1 (1959), 234-254 (English translation: "The Structure of Everyday Narration," *Folklore Forum* 20, 9-37.

own new traditions was recognized and expounded upon in remarkable detail decades ago.[10] Similarly, the notion that folklorists should primarily be interested in processes rather than texts, that is, in singing rather than in songs, in storytelling rather than in stories, proclaimed in the United States in the 1970s as an example of a new trend, was explicitly called for in almost the same words in Europe in the 1940s,[11] and similar demands had already been expressed in nineteenth-century Europe.[12]

The topic chosen for this conference, "Storytelling in Contemporary Societies," bears with it, in my opinion, inherent problems that relate to the point that I have already discussed. The theme of "storytelling," in its apparent insistence on oral performances only perpetuates distorted notions about the true nature of popular narrative traditions. By focusing on only a relatively narrow part of the broad spectrum of tradition, scholars are forced to ignore the dynamics in the processes of dissemination via diverse mass media. There are, of course, scores of folklorists who recognize this fact and thus study the role of mass media in disseminating, and thus exploiting, traditional narrative lore.[13] This recognition, however, should not be interpreted to mean that oral performance is a dead issue. As outlined above, there are many forms of oral narrating that are prevalent even in pluralistic urban settings of industrial nations. Nevertheless, as Gary Fine stresses, it is difficult to discern just what the trends and directions of American folkloristics are at present. I am not presumptuous enough to try here to define the highway upon which narrative research should travel into the next millennium. Instead I merely wish to make a few observations of that which could eventually turn out to be important trends.

Homo Narrans. Today we take the ability to narrate for granted as if it were an inherent component of language itself. The emergence of language as the most efficient means of communication between the members of the species has been recognized as perhaps the most important "invention" in the history of mankind. Indeed the work of linguists in showing that all languages share a deep structure that is manifested in the transformational process by competent speakers into diverse surface structures has led to the notion that language ability

---

[10]Hermann Bausinger, *Volkskultur in einer technischen Welt*, (Stuttgart, 1962).

[11]Richard Weiss, *Volkskunde der Schweiz*, (Zürich, 1946).

[12]Wilhelm Heinrich Riehl, "Die Volkskunde als Wissenschaft," in W. H. Riehl, *Culturstudien aus drei Jahrhunderten*, (Stuttgart, 1859), 205-229.

[13]Rudolf Schenda, *Die Lesestoffe der kleinen Leute*, (München, 1976); Bausinger, *Volkskultur*; Jack Zipes, *Fairy Tales and the Art of Subversion: The Classical Genre for Children and the Process of Civilization*, (New York, 1983); Lutz Röhrich, *Wage es, den Frosch zu küssen: Das Grimm'sche Märchen Nr. Eins in seinen Wandlungen*, (Köln, 1987).

38

has become a phylogenetic trait among humankind. But language, for all its complexities of structure, remains by itself chiefly a means of communicating information to or directing the action of others. Humans, however, learned early in their history that they can do more with language than communicate, they can also create hypotheses, theories, and philosophies.

Language remains, of course, the *sine qua non* of complex human thought. But somewhere in the course of time, humans discovered that they could utilize language for more than communication, they could use it to compose and tell stories. In so doing humans acquired a tool that without which learning, ideas, experimentation, and science would not have been possible. The real world, in the chaotic splendor of its multifarious existence, is simply too vast for the human intellect to conceptualize in a meaningful way; in order for the human mind to grasp, understand, and analyze the world, one is forced to fashion limited constructs of reality. Only after humans learned the art of creating and playing with these meta-realities were they able to speculate, predict, experiment, and to draw inferences about the world. Physical science, for example, could not have brought forth atomic theory without the ability to make an imaginary construct of the atom, which in turn permitted the emergence of the periodic chart of elements. Science was thus able to visualize the atom, predict its behavior, and theorize about the nature of matter at a time when no human had ever seen an atom. I suggest that the first human who ever abstracted real events and fashioned them into a narrative sequence, took the first step in creating the intellectual conceptualization of the world. Today both "neurobiologists and linguists suggest that language is more important for telling stories than it is for directing action".[14] The ability to narrate, like language itself, has evidently become a phylogenetic trait of humans.

Narrating and Social Change. Although the ability of the human mind to create and exploit meta-real constructs for a multitude of purposes has progressed far beyond the act of narrating, the latter remains a vital element in maintaining and transforming human society. Society is itself, as Ernst Cassirer has observed, "a mediated and ideally conditioned reality".[15] The process of mediation and conditioning is achieved above all through religion and narration. There is a dynamic of reciprocal transformation between the individual and his society that constantly helps shape the individual personality but also serves to effect social change. This dialogue between the individual and his society is not manifested ex-

---

[14]Barbara Myerhoff, "Telling One's Story", *The Center Magazine* 13 (1980), 22-43.
[15]Ernst Cassirer, *The Philosophy of Symbolic Forms*, 2 vols. (New Haven and London, 1955), II, 193.

clusively in the social dialogue between a society's members; it often begins with the individual in solitude with his own thoughts.

Bronislaw Malinowski was one of the earlier researchers to recognize the importance of solitude in, paradoxically, such collective religious rites as initiation:

> The seclusion of individuals at initiation, their individual personal struggles during the ordeal, the communion with spirits, divinities, and powers in lonely spots, all these show us primitive religion frequently lived through in solitude.[16]

These moments of solitary reflection are, I suggest a vital element in the processes that ultimately lead to social change. It is in these moments that the narrative structures that later enter into the dynamic between the individual and his society have their genesis.

Idionarrating: Talking to the Self. A remarkable scholar by the name of George Herbert Mead, who taught in the 1920s at the University of Chicago, outlined in his lectures the significance of the dialogue with the self. Fortunately, one of his students kept detailed notes of his words and these were later published.[17] Mead noted that "the self is not so much a substance as a process in which the conversation of gestures" with other humans and with the environment becomes "internalized within the human form." The evolution of the self thus occurs through the world with which it is a part. Mead differentiated within each individual self elements which he labeled the "I" and the "Me." The "Me" was the "generalized other as internalized in each individual" that was both "conventional and habitual" by nature. The "Me" is characterized by "those habits" and "those responses" that reflect the communal view. The "Me" thus represents the "objectified conventional component" without which there could be no self, since "we cannot realize ourselves except in so far as we can recognize the other in his relationship to us." It is in the act of assuming the attitude of the other and in responding to it that the individual is able to realize himself as an entity that is both a part of a separate from the society.

These acts, taken collectively, exert a dynamic influence on society, for the individual's response to the collective attitude is frequently mediated to others and exerts its influence on the collective. Elements are introduced into society that were "not previously present in the experience".[18] The unpredictably respon-

---

[16]Bronislaw Malinowski, *Magic, Science and Religion and Other Essays* (New York, 1948), 56.

[17]George Herbert Mead, *Mind, Self and Society from the Standpoint of a Social Behaviorist*, (Chicago and London, 1934).

[18]*Ibid.*, p. 196.

sive "I" is "not only the token of individual differentiation within the society, but the agency of social transformation".[19] This process is possible because the narrations that began in solitude between the "I" and the "Me" later become the subject of discourse between the "I" and other members of society. Mead stresses that such a process is at the base of social change, for social discourses of this nature, are incompatible with notions of the fixed and immutable nature of society. The unique importance of the individual is "in his acting the role of 'I' to society's collective 'Me' and thereby bringing to actuality what remained potential before".[20] The man who "saw things that were and asked 'why?' and then saw things that never were and asked 'why not?' "[21] doubtless had to pose these questions first in a discourse with his "me" before he employed them to influence others and thus to instigate social change.

In a recent UCLA dissertation on the plight of homeless and maltreated women, Marjorie Bard (1988) has called attention to the need of individuals under duress to engage in discourse with the self, a phenomenon she labeled "idionarrating." These unfortunate individuals, forgotten and ignored by society, would probably never be in a position where their own viewpoints could directly promote social change. Nevertheless, they engaged in the kind of idionarrating that was poignant and even powerful and that asked why things were as they were and not otherwise.

Mistreated by their mates, forgotten by relatives and the community, these women found meaning in the meaningless by telling their stories to themselves:

> My head gets filled with what happened and I start to think about it like a book. I'll go over every bit of what happened as if it were a movie script, and I was the actress. I know all the lines, and if just one little thing isn't quite right, I'll start over again and do it just the way it happened.[22]

Bard observed how idionarrating is often "a deliberate prelude to sharing the experience with others"[23] when the need to tell others arises. How pressing this need can become is eloquently stated by one of these victims:

> I couldn't tell anyone what was happening at home, it was too awful – you know – embarrassing. But I'd go over and over everything that happened so I never felt like I

[19]*Ibid.*, p. 335.

[20]*Ibid.*, p. 275.

[21]I cite this from memory from Ted Kennedy's eulogy for Robert Kennedy; I assume he was quoting a known aphorism, but as of this writing, I have not located the original source.

[22]Marjorie Brooke Bard, *Domestic Abuse and the Homeless Woman: Paradigms in Personal Narrative for Organizational Strategists and Community Planners*, Diss. ULCA (Los Angeles, 1988), 60-61.

hadn't told anyone about the stuff. And then one day I just decided that I was going to burst, and I said out loud to myself, "I'm going to tell!"[24]

It is noteworthy that language usage itself reflects the necessity of the process of idionarrating. When a man, for example, survived a harrowing and life-threatening experience, people will frequently comment that "he lived to tell his story." Similarly, when a woman escapes from the brutal treatment at the hands of an abusive male to seek help from others, one will hear the comment, "she was finally able to tell her story." In using these expressions, the speaker is expressing the (unconscious?) recognition that there was a profound and intense need for the individuals in these cases to frame their experiences in the form of a narrative that was first told to one's self before it was narrated to others. Whenever humans are under duress, they feel the compulsion to tell "their stories" to others.

In analyzing the idionarrations of maltreated women, Bard posed a number of thought-provoking questions. Among these was whether the "basic stories which we tell to ourselves are possible antecedents to action; we may be consciously formulating a plan by depicting a situation in which we visualize specific activity, or unconsciously verbalizing situations which seem to be in need of action".[25]

It is, I believe, apparent in the cases adduced and analyzed by Bard how crucial it is for society to give to the oppressed the opportunity to voice their experiences and thoughts and thus mediate them to members of the collective. For it is apparent that victims of social injustice are the true experts on the solutions to social problems. The acquisition of the competency of narration, the ability to formulate one's encounters with need and distress occurs first in acts of idionarrating. This discourse with the self is a necessary step in the crucial act of communicating these stories to others. When these stories are finally told, they can provide the vehicle for needed social transformations.

[23]*Ibid.*, p. 63.
[24]*Ibid.*, p. 77.
[25]*Ibid.*, p. 79.

MODERN LEGENDS

Dorota Simonides
(Oppole, Poland)

CONTEMPORARY URBAN LEGENDS IN POLAND

Folklore is usually associated with tradition and old people. The older a text and a narrator of a story are the more valuable the story seems to be. The category of "Antiquity" has become the criterion of the greatest value in the science of folklore. Generally, folklorists were interested in everything that had already been recognized as "folklore", that researchers had got acquainted with well, and that had become a precisely defined subject of studies. On the other hand they were not interested in anything that was going on around them, though it was popular and widespread because it did not fit into any recognized literary genre.

The above statement is based on my successive review of mediaeval and later manuscripts which contain a lot of "pecularities", descriptions of uncommon events which, however, were not included in collections of folkloristic works because they were not regarded by either collectors or researchers as genres of folklore. And so, we have a nineteenth-century folkloristic collection which served as a source for an author, a collector himself, for a volume of stories. He did not include, however, one story (of a young mother, who had died in childbirth and was then burried. Some hours later people heard a call for help coming from the grave. The parish-priest declared, however, "let us leave burried what was once burried"), in spite of the fact that everybody in the village and sourrounding area was talking about it. We can imagine to what extent this event was retold, commented on, and consequently transformed. However, J. Lompa did not include it in his collection. As he writes himself in his book, it was true and authentic. It was not fiction, neither a fairy-tale nor Sage, nor an anectode.[1] Considering such explanations he came to the conclusion that it could not be included in the folkloristic collection.

The above example testifies significantly that it is folklorists who have set the limits to the possible kind of legends. It was not noticed that pursuing the

---

[1] Dorota Simonides, "Silesia Horror," (Katowice, 1985), p. 11.

46

"antiquities" and everything that is connected with "tradition" folklorists became a kind of archeologists of human memory and that some of them keep digging out of it everything that is time-honoured and sanctified by science.

Meanwhile, we witness the appearing of new modern stories around us but we do not pay attention to them because they do not differ particularly from the other utterances in their verbal level. They contain neither those special initial formulas "Once upon a time" and final "I was there, too" nor other characteristic features of the genre, which would make it easier to separate them from every day utterances of interpersonal communication. They are no longer repeated mainly by countryfolk which was a sine qua non condition of folklore in the past.

Nevertheless there is something so unusual and something so much intriguing about them that only are they able to interest all of Poland but also become part of the common repertoire of all social, professional, and age groups. They are known in industrial environment, in the country, among intellectuals, workers, and farmers, among students, and children.

The most amazing fact is, however, that those who tell the stories and maybe even invent them, do not want to realize that these are only "stories" about imaginary events that de facto never occured anywhere and, if they really did occur, the real events differ from the stories based on them. These "new" legends circulate as the stories about actual occurrences that happened to real people in definite place and time, and by no means seem to be fictitious. We know from the literature of folklore that quite a number of serious people were taken in by story tellers and believed in the stories authenticity.[2]

A folklorist knows this convention since it reminds him of "Sagen", old legends. The "truthfulness" of the stories which is defended, as before, by either authorities or our acquaintances as "my friend", "boss of my husband", "friend of my friend", "doctor of mine" etc., is the decisive factor which immediately makes the listeners subconsciously accept the event as being authentic, maybe a bit exaggerated and even unusual but still real.

After 30 years of investigation this phenomenon, together with my students, I may state that the term: "new legends" is inadequate here. Only a subject and realia of the stories are "new". Sometimes even the subject is not "new" but it is not this problem that is the most essential about these stories. A folklorist is, first of all, interested in the very fact that the progress of contemporary culture and civilization has only managed to change the mental structure of man slightly and

[2]Marja Boskovic-Stulli, "Zeitungen, Fernsehen, mündliches Erzählen in der Stadt Zagreb," *Fabula*, 20 (1979), pp. 8-17.

that horror and sensational stories still suit the immanent mental needs of man. On the other hand the researcher concentrates on the very message that is the purpose and for which a given event has been so quickly and widly circulated in all social strata.[3]

We conduct research of the phenomena of folklore according to five verified, recognized, and still relevant groups of questions. They are focused on the fundamental problems such as:

1. Subject of communication which is the main theme of stories about "real" events, rumours, hearsay, in other words, problem of the current alive, contemporary repertoire of various social groups,
2. the description of encoder and decoder, and their social groups,
3. circumstances of communication (sender, receiver) that determine exchange of an exciting and thrilling piece of information,
4. means of communications: verbal, written, and mechanical (phone, mass media),
5. the function of information, its purpose for which a given occurance is repeated.

Considering the above problems, our subsequent discussion will be based on a brief analysis of the material obtained from the above questions:

Ad.1. The investigation of texts collected over several decades proves that those unusual stories which make one's blood run cold and sound even incredible prevail. There appear both tragic and very humorous events in them. They also contain traditional stories which, if they only happen to occur in modern circulation, also become the subject of our interest.

The prevailing feature of the contemporarily transmitted stories is their location in the industrial environment which, as a result of almost absolute anonymity of its citizens, makes it impossible to determine the authenticity of an event. Whereas in the country where all inhabitants know one another it would be easy to prove the falseness of rumour. The example may be the story about the poisoned wedding gown worn by a young bride which results in her death on the day of her wedding. The house in which the tradegy took place and the grave in which she was burried both could be immediately located. It is practically impossible to do so in a city.

---

[3]Lutz Röhrich, "Was soll und kann Sagenforschung leisten? Einige aktuelle Probleme unseres Faches," in *Probleme der Sagenforschung*, ed. Lutz Röhrich, (Freiburg, 1973), p. 28.

48

We tried to come across at least one trace on the basis of one of the plots widespread in Poland since 1968. Our very active search, consisting of correrspondence which included constant contact with thousands of teachers, did not yield any results.[4]

In order to make the readers become acquainted with the themes of Urban Legends prevailing in Poland we mention some plots discussing only those stories occur in more than 100 variants. We are aware of the fact that those plots are not only of Polish origin and it is easy to find for most of them foreign equivalents:[5]

a) the story about an aunt that has been "drunk" by her family (a parcel from a Western country contained ashes of the aunt and her relatives mistakenly thought the contents of the parcel to be vitamines and drunk it with milk);

b) a limousine (laboratory), drivers of the car kidnap school children in order to take their blood and send it to the West in exchange for hard currency;

c) children are missing from home because criminals smuggle either jewelry or drugs in their corpses;

d) a hitchhiker, dressed in black in a car foretells dreary forecast for the world and then vanishes;

e) a hitchhiker, dressed in black, together with a driver, saves a child burried alive in a cementery. It turns out that the hitchhiker is the dead mother of the child;

f) a long-haired son, a hippy, murders his own mother because she has cut his hair;

g) a child eats a banana with vipers's poison and dies;

h) a young bride scratches herself while zipping her wedding gown and dies during the wedding ceremony. A doctor determines ptomaine poisoning to be the cause of her death. The wedding gown was bought from a gravedigger.

Ad. 2. The encoders and decoders of these stories are, in fact, members of all social classes and professional groups. They happen to be professors of universities, lawyers, policemen, judges, and journalists and each of the emphasizes that the heard about "it" from "an absolutely reliable person". In such a situation

[4]Dorota Simonides, "Moderne Sagenbildung im polnischen Großstadtmilieu," *Fabula*, 28 (1987), pp. 269-78.

[5]Jan Harold Brunvand, *The Vanishing Hitchhiker. American Urban Legends and Their Meanings*, (New York-London, 1981); Linda Dégh, "The Runaway Grandmother", *Indiana Folklore*, 1 (1968), pp. 68-77; Robert Dale, *"It's true ... it Happened to a Friend". A Collection of Urban Legends*, (London, 1984).

it is difficult for an investigator to keep proper distance because he himself is involved in the process of listening and transmission. However, it should be doubly emphasized that the main encoders and decoders are people coming from large industrial centres.

Ad. 3. There are different situations in which the stories of events are told. It takes place most frequently in places of employment, at school, and at university on a train or bus, in queue in front of stores, and also at parties and friendly gatherings.

Ad. 4. Generally, the main means of communication is direct face to face contact but it also happens that it is published in the press dementi which is very often understood by readers as a confirmation of the described events' authenticity. A lot of people cite the press as the source of the heard story.

The very headline itself forces one to read the contents of an article because the sensational character of an event is well presented, e.g. "Waxen Corpse of a Child", "A Nun in a Black Limousine", "Dead Mother Saves Her Child" etc. It also happens that those "shocking" pieces of information are transmitted by phone, from town to town which explains their extraordinarily rapid circulation.

A very characteristic feature of the transmitted stories is that they are so overfilled with details and so much set in reality that if we questioned their truthfulness the storyteller could be offended.

Ad. 5. A storyteller is not aware of the purpose he wants to achieve. Each story has some levels of meanings and several functions.[6] One of its functions is to satisfy archetypical needs of experiencing something extraordinary and shocking which would also satisfy archetypical need of fear, and needs of facing irrational and incomprehensible phenomena. On the other hand one may be influenced by the message carried by the stories which perform didactical functions. On the basis of some plots discussed above we have observed the didactical function of storytelling and must admit that it does not differ much from mediaeval exempla. Some of the plots were even transmitted both by priests in their sermons and teachers in school as either an example illustrating the corruption of contemporary teenagers (hippy murders his own mother) or as a piece of advice, e.g. one should not buy anything from unknown sources (the poisoned wedding gown); under no circumstances should a child enter a strange car (children kidnapped by strangers in a car), etc.

---

[6] Lutz Röhrich, (cf. note 3), pp. 18-21.

On the whole, it should be noticed that contemporary humans invent stories which fully reflect what interests, intrigues and suits them best. The inventor in this respect does not differ from his ancestors. It is only the ways of satisfying his needs which are different since they correspond to the state of mind and perception of the average individual at the close of the twentieth century.

Leander Petzoldt
(Innsbruck)

PHANTOM LORE

In December of 1981, one of the largest regional newspapers in southern Germany reported a rumour that had been alarming the population of Upper Austria for quite some time. The article, titled "the puzzle of the mysterious 'black lady'," reads as follows:

> An enigmatic "black lady" has, of late, been worrying the citizens of the Salzburg districts Pinzgau and Pongau, as well as the archdiocese of Salzburg. According to reports by automobile drivers, this uncanny woman appears at night on the Pinzgauer national highway and signals cars to stop. One distressed driver reported that, after driving a few hundred meters after he had picked the hitchhiker up, she told him: "If you hadn't stopped and taken me along, your would have had an accident." At that moment she disappeared ,without a trace". Going by the descriptions, many living in the area believe that the mysterious woman is the resurrection of a young waitress from St. Veit, who was killed in the previous year in an accident on the Pinzgauer highway. The car of the 23 years old driver had crashed off the road directly onto the traintracks running parallel to the highway and was hit by the train that came through in the next instant. According to police reports, the young woman was not immediately killed, and her ,piercing screams filled the air." The archdiocese also reacted to the rumours: this type of appearance is often the result of a deception of the senses, an overexcited imagination or hallucinations. Only a fraction of such apparitions, the archdiocese concluded, fall into the category of "true hauntings".

This is yet another occurence of the well-known "vanishing hitchhiker" legend, appearing here in a local version. It is remarkable that the Catholic Church should feel the need to comment on this matter, which mainly has to do with a peculiar quality of other versions of the same phenomena which I collected in Upper Suevia. In this area the stories revolve around a "hitchhiker" in the form of a black anger or "the Archangel Gabriel" himself. The Church, feeling its own staff so directly addressed, was compelled to reply, using the conspicious phrase "true hauntings".

The characteristics of this version which set it off from the mass of everyday tales are its numinous coloring and its external structure, which is nearer to a rumor than to a legend. Patrick B. Mullen has applied the rumor-theory to contemporary legend-formation[1] and Bengt af Klintberg confirmed this with his own observations.[2] It is distinguished by its open form and by the traditional morphology of the legend and its socio-cultural background respectively.

The "vanishing hitchhiker"-stories have undoubtedly become a prototype of this group of legends, which already has been the subject of several research programs,[3] the last of which differentiates between "phantom Hitch-Hikers of folk-narratives and the allegedly factual item".[4] It is obvious that the interest the Anglo-american folklorists show has not had an insignificant effect on the popularity and dissemination of these stories. At the same time however, these "road ghosts" definitely do have a long tradition, as Bennett determined, using Beardsley's and Hankey's investigations as a starting point. Above all, the results of these and other investigations make plain that "the legend can be adapted to any cultural context",[5] which studies outside of the US also have proven.[6] Still, these stories of the "Phantom-Hitchhiker", of "The Boyfriend's Death" and "The Philanderer's Porsche" and many others mentioned by Brunvand have become an "integral part of the white Anglo-American culture".[7]

If one elaborates the inner structure of these stories, and deliberates them from actual contemporary elements and oikotypical details, the core of the story is reduced to the presentation of one person's uncanny experience, of driving along after dark, stopping and giving someone a ride. Now, the passenger is either good-willed, in that he saves the driver from an accident, neutral, in that he or she just dissapears and in an after-effect proving to be a ghost or evil, in that the driver for some reason becomes afraid, gets rid of his passenger and later discovers, that the old woman, nurse etc. was in reality a thief. This is the

---

[1] Patrick B. Mullen, "Modern Legend and rumour theory," *Journal of the Folklore Institute*, 9 (1972), pp. 95-109.

[2] Bengt af Klintberg, "Folksägner i dag," *Fataburen* (1976), pp. 269-296.

[3] Richard K. Beardsley and Rosalie Hankey, "A history of the vanishing hitchhiker," *California Folklore Quarterly*, 2 (Jan. 1943), pp. 13-25; – Katherine Luomala, "Disintegration and Regeneration: The Hawaiian Phantom Hitchhiker Legend," *Fabula*, 13 (1972), pp. 20-59; – Jan Harold Brunvand, *The vanishing hitchhiker*, (New York, 1981) (Reprint London, 1983); – Gillian Bennett, "The Phantom Hitchhiker: Neither Modern, Urban, nor Legend?" *Perspectives on contemporary legend*, (Sheffield, 1982) (= MS-print, no pagination); – Michael Goss, *The evidence for Phantom Hitchhikers*, (Wellingborough, 1984).

[4] Michael Goss, *The evidence*, p. 55.

[5] Bennett (op. cit. note 3).

[6] Aliza Shenhar, "Israelische Fassungen des verschwundenen Anhalters", *Fabula*, 26 (1985), pp. 245-253.

[7] Brunvand (op. cit. note 3), Repr., p. 11.

53

whole spectrum of these stories in a nutshell. In the late 1970s I was able to record the following story in Upper Suevia:

> (Place near Wangen, source M. R., female student who heard the story from a neighbour, whose children she picked up from school. The mother of one of the children in class supposedly had the following experience):
> Story: Shortly before 11:00 p.m. a hitchhiker dressed in white stood on the road side near Wangen. The mother of the school child stopped and the man got in the car. He than gave the woman exact directions which way to drive: to turn right instead of driving straight ahead, because otherwise she was in danger of getting an accident. Then he disappeared. It turned out that at the spot the woman would have gone past, another car had an accident.

This story corresponds with the newspaper article already mentioned, especially because the teller of the story also related the same story, this time the hitchhiker appearing in the form of a "black angel", in a different social context, in the country milieu as the hitchhiker's warning of the threatening danger to the unsuspecting driver. The following story takes place in southwest Germany in the early 1930s (1933):

> A farmer was on the way home. He carried a purse full of money with him, the result of a good sale transaction. On the way he met a little old lady who wanted a ride, so he let her sit in the back of the waggon. As they came to a bumpy downhill road, he placed a "Radschuh" (in order to break and to lower the speed, L.P.) under one wheel. At the bottom of the hill he took it (the "Radschuh") from the wheel and threw it in the back of the waggon. He had completely forgotten the little old woman in thinking about the day's good business. At home he found her dead in the back of his waggon; the farmer had accidently hit her that hard with this "Radschuh" that he had killed her. Good or bad luck? As he looked more closely he discovered that the supposed little old lady was really a disguised thief.[8]

It seems this "rustical version" of the phantom hitchhiker is a version which shows all the characteristics of a legend and whose claim to be truth is unquestioned. Will-Erich Peuckert recalls a story often told during his childhood in Schlesien. An experience of his grandfather had become a part of his family's narrative tradition:

---

[8]Menzingen, Kreis Bretten (Baden), Zentralarchiv Marburg, No. 15 130.

The other story from his farmhand's and driver's years is the one about he was coming home from Bunzlau, and halfway between Liebichau and Töppendorf somebody was standing on the road, a wrinkled little old grandma. She asks if he couldn't take her along a little while. "Well, of course" he says to her and stops his horses. First she hands him up her basket then puts her foot on the running board and climbs in. Because she is such an old little woman he thinks to himself: "now you should help her", and as he takes the reins in his left hand and reaches down, the moonlight shines right onto her face and he sees – she had a woolen scarf on – just as she is climbing in, that she has a long beard. "Eh!" he thinks, and: "will you take a look at that!" and takes his whip and hits the horses. He normally never hurt any animal, but this time it really was necessary. The horses jumped and the robber, because that's what the little old grandma really was, fell over backwards and my grampa raced away with his team. As soon as he was a little way away, where the underwood clears a bit from the road, something whizzes by him and he hears a bang. The robber shot at him from behind. It was quite a little while before he let his horses trot again. But at home, when they opened the basket, it was full of knives and guns. He could imagine what the little woman's intentions were.[9]

When one counts back in time, his grandfather died when Peuckert was "six or seven years" old (thus around 1902), this "experience" can be dated approximately to the last decades of the 19th century. The decisive point is not if such stories are "true" or not. Important is that they are handed down as a memorate within a family or a community and that they are propagated in this manner, that they come to life again as "memorabiles"[10] and that one can watch their resurrection. Brunvand, the most zealous multiplicator of these stories, classifies this one to the category "The Hairy-armed Hitchhiker".[11] As Yallop established, this story existed in England as early as the middle 19th century.[12] But what scientific value does this proof have, which could also be determined for many of these narratives, which, seen structurally at least, reach back to older narrative types and motivs? Medieval merry tales may also be transported into 20th century America in this manner, as shown by the story-type "The Philanderer's Porsche". In this story a woman recently widowed sells a Porsche for 50 dollars that is worth approximately 100 times that amount, because in her husband's will the profit from the sale should go to his mistress.[13] This naturally reminds one of the anecdote of the pious miser, who leaves his widow with the task of selling a rooster and a cow. The money from the cow is to be donated to

---

[9] Will-Erich Peuckert, *Sage. Geburt und Antwort der mythischen Welt*, (Berlin 1965), p. 29.

[10] Otto Görner, *Vom Memorabile zur Schicksalstragödie*, (Berlin, 1931).

[11] Jan Harold Brunvand, *The choking Doberman and other 'new' Urban Legends*, (New York, London, 1984), pp. 33 f.

[12] D. A. Yallop, *Deliver us from Evil*, (London, 1981), p. 273.

[13] Brunvand (op. cit., note 3), p. 29.

the church, and the money from the rooster she is allowed to keep. What does the woman do? She offers the cow for five florins and the rooster for fifty, on the condition that both be bought only together. There is practically no structural difference to be observed between this anecdote and the Porsche-story, although such groupings are always difficult. Can we really assume, on the basis of structrual congruency alone, that they belong to the same type, the same motif? Besides the fact that often the connecting links of literary as well as of oral tradition are missing, the problem of narrative continuity is perhaps impossible to solve. In this manner the centuries-old ritual-murder legend of Rinn, Tirol[14] or of William of Norwich and Hugo of Lincoln wind up in the chapter "Restroom Legends".[15] Brunvand connects this odious story with modern stories in which black boys cut off a white boy's penis in the restroom of a supermarket and calls it one of the "modern horror legends with the best documented early histories ...".[16] It is difficult to establish a connection, even if both cases involve "culprits" who belong to a hated and persecuted or, at least, socially different and feared minority (Jews, Blacks). Although such stories in contemporary America could be attributed to a barely suppressed racial discrimination, the meaning of each is totally different. The ritual murder legends were purposely applied defamation, appearing in each case, in connection with an unsolved crime and almost always resulting in a pogrom on the Jewish minority. These stories had direct, often fatal consequences, whose religious, political, social and economic implications had wide-reaching results in the whole of Central Europe.[17] A structural similarity between the stories, however, is not to be overlooked. This similarity encompasses the following common elements: the physical aggression of a despised and distrusted minority against helpless members (children) of the ruling majority. The designed purpose of these stories, or the fact that they contain unprovable slander, is, however, not to be placed as a motif. The intended psychological effect can be only circumscribed and one asks if this truly concerns "characteristic traditional folk motivs".[18]

More important than the investigation of traditional motif-connections, or of the age of such narratives, appears to me to be the question of which functions

---

[14]Grimm, *Deutsche Sagen*, no. 353; – Leander Petzoldt, "Religion zwischen Sentiment und Protest. Zur Sistierung des Kultes um 'Andreas von Rinn' in Tirol," *Zeitschrift für Volkskunde*, 83 (1987), pp. 169-192.

[15]Brunvand (cf. note 11), p. 89.

[16]*Ibid.*, p. 87.

[17]Leander Petzoldt, "The Eternal Loser. The Jew as Depicted in German Folk Literature", *International Folklore Review*, 4 (1986), pp. 28-48.

[18]Brunvand (op. cit., note 3), p. 11.

do such stories have in modern society. Do they fulfill the same purpose as the legend in the 18th and 19th centuries? – whereby the legends function in socio-cultural context is nowhere near to being unequivocally explained. However, the contemporary ("urban") legends give us the opportunity to observe and analyze the process of legend generation and formation, so to speak, "ab ovo". Looking back upon the diachronic investigation of narrative continuity, that which is not to be made to us in the example of the European folk-legend, can, though under changed cultural conditions, made apparent and declared a goal for further research: analysis of the generation and dissemination of contemporary legend, its relationship to reality and the social milieu of its narrator, its transmission and (apparent) verification, the influence of mass media, especially that of the daily press, changes of the story elements and adaptation to different cultural conditions, the function of the supernatural in some of these stories, the reciprocal action between narrator(s) and listener(s) and the modification of the material (type) itself, for many narratives go through a "sociomorphic" change, as I would like to call it, on their way from one social class to another, or when they appear in a different cultural context.

First of all, the distribution processes of these stories should be investigated. As already established, "the massmedia themselves participate in the dissemination and apparent validation of urban legends".[19] But then what are the roles played by folklorists and pseudo-folklorists themselves in this process? It seems the interest of the university-folklorists in Anglo-America has not inconsiderably contributed to the spreading of "urband legends" and "hauted stories". The suspicion that research itself indirectly provokes these "phantoms" cannot be easily dismissed. Brunvand, for example, does not only encourage the readers of his books to send him such stories ("Have I missed your favorite urban legend? Please send your variants of these or texts of 'new' legends to me ..."),[20] but also leads a lively mail-correspondence with his readers. ("I got numerous letters from readers asking about the legends".[21] He describes the reaction of one mother to the above mentioned restroom-story ("The Mutilated Boy"): "I don't know if this is legend or fact – but I haven't let my 5 year old son go in (to a shopping center restroom) alone yet".[22] This leaves no doubt that the scientific and publishing interests of the author draws wide-spread attention to these stories, thereby influencing them to a great extent. This interest leads to an

---

[19]*Ibid.*

[20]Brundvand (op. cit., note 11), p. XIV.

[21]*Ibid.*, p. 83.

[22]*Ibid.*

intense feed-back effect: "I have received batches of newspaper clippings from readers about abduction and mutilation rumours, as well as versions set in missives ranging in style from scrawled postcards to carefully written, detailed letters."[23] The overpowering interest shown in these stories apparently includes all social (or educational) strata. The letters also demonstrate, as the author reveals, the high level of affective participation of the letter-writers and the latent fear of the readers. It is doubtful that the author's englightened attitude or rationalizing interpretations can reassure the reader, to whom the interest alone of researchers means a verification of the stories.

Precisely this emotional effect of urban legends, which is solely psychologically measurable, should be investigated in interdisciplinary cooperation between sociologists, psychologists and cultural anthropologists.

The fact is intriguing that most of the literature about contemporary legends up till now appeared in England and America. Sometimes it is difficult to differenciate among these publications between valid scientific investigations and passing publicistic fancy. The spectrum extends from serious research to anecdotal collections ("An outrageous collection of bunk, nonsense, and fables we believe").[24] The majority contains an enlightening strain that tends a bit to resemble the condescending attitude of German legend collectors and editors of the 19th century, who recorded and published stories of the "ignorant, superstition-bound farmers". The slick lay-out of anthologies such as that from Dale,[25] which groups together merry tales, amusing and anecdotical stories, and even horror-stories under the heading "urban legends", reveals a peculiar phenomenon: the arranging of these stories side by side, their aesthetic and stylistic abbreviation to the essential core and the concurring loss of their communicative coherence with daily reality, makes them appear strangely bloodless. Similar to the European folk-legend collections of the 19th century, they become curiosities for the educated classes, isolated texts that no longer have anything to do with the situative reality of the narrator. The loss of communicative context in these stories is, at the same time, the loss of their cultural identity. Their original narrative foundation, adjusted to the needs of the storyteller and his audience, disappears and the meaning contained in the message can be interpreted at will in any different cognitive interest.

[23]*Ibid.*
[24]P. Dickson and C. Goulden, *There are Aligators in our sewers,* (New York, 1983).
[25]Rodney Dale, *It's true ... it happened to a friend,* (Guildford, 1984).

Alone the fact that the editor of such a collection encourages readers to send in new "urban legends",[26] introduces a reflective, rationalizing element into the continuity of transmission and fundamentally changes the narrative reality. The "Aficionados of the urban legend"[27] castrate popular narrative tradition in this manner, whereas nowadays we could have the opportunity to investigate these phenomena more thoroughly, and with more efficient scientific tools than, for example, the Brothers Grimm.

---

[26]*Ibid.*, p. 95.
[27]*Ibid.*, p. 8.

RELIGIOUS MOTIVATIONS

Reimund Kvideland
(Bergen)

CHRISTIAN MEMORATES IN NORWEGIAN REVIVAL MOVEMENTS

Narrative research has to a large extent been concentrated around a small number of genres and mostly from text analytical perspectives. Although folklorists have for a long time done research on a wide spectrum of traditional narratives, all too often quite a few genres have been considered marginal. If we want to understand the role of the narrative traditions in the past and in contemporary society, we have to relinguish the hierarchical understanding of genres.

According to modern folkloristic theory it is useless to search for universal narrative categories. Storytelling is tied to a specific society, even at a micro level. We should try to find out how stories function in different situations and for various individuals and groups.

First, I want to present a selection of narratives which have been neglected almost entirely by Scandinavian collectors and scholars. For lack of a better term, I will call these stories Christian memorates; they are stories about supranormal events within the context of popular Christianity which have been experienced by the narrator himself. Such stories are found mostly in lay movement and charismatic groups; the are rarely heard in the context of services of the state church.

Second, I want to outline strategies for collecting and analyzing such stories.

I begin with a short presentation of the field and of one informant. In Norway (and elsewhere in Scandinavia), there are many types of stories with themes from the world of religious experience. The most widely spread of these stories fall into the following categories:

a) Stories about miraculous events. Shouts or voices which save people from accidents, are often understood as divine rescues.

In some cases such stories are adaptations of older folk belief. A good example can be found in Anders Gustavsson's material from the Pentecostal movement in Åstol, southern Sweden. An informant relates how his father, a sailor who was returning from the North Sea, woke up hearing a voice which said: "Ludwig, go on deck!" Three times he went on deck, and the third time they were dangerously close to reefs but managed to steer clear. The informant believed that the voice which had spoken to his father was God's voice. However, in form and content this story parallels older stories in which a ship or sea sprite warns of dangers.[1]

Most of the following stories too could be characterized as miracolous, but the stories in this category speak of direct divine intervention in critical situations.

b) Stories about people who escape assault because their assailants see one or several strong men walk with their intended victim. Such stories are common in and beyond Scandinavia, the strong men are believed to be guarding angels.[2] The belief in angels was and still is much more widely disseminated than archive collections indicate. The expression, "guardian angels", for instance, is so generally known even today, that a Bergen newspaper recently (January 1989) used it as a headline to report about a man that had survived three serious accidents. There are many people who tell that they have both heard and seen angels.

c) Stories about salvation experiences form a category of their own, they are primarily encountered in personal testimonies during revival meetings.[3]

Usually the narrator describes himself as sinner, how he resists God's call to conversion and how finally an external event – a death or an accident – breaks down his resistance. He describes the actual conversion and the ensuing conviction of being saved.

His old way of life is seen as in contrast to his new one.

d) Stories about prayer that have been answered form a heterogenous group. New Norwegian material bears less resemblance to the exempla than the material of Bausinger, probably because his material is older and has a different theological background.[4] The younger material at my disposal serves more to prove the existence of God in everyday life than in serious critical situations. Hillerdal followed up his earlier works with a book on prayer hearing. The

---

[1] Anders Gustavsson, "Frikyrklighet och folktro. Konflikt eller anpassning?" *Kattegat-Skagerak projektet Meddelelser* 4 (1984), pp. 81-94.

[2] Arne Sæter, *Når himmelen svarer. En samling vitnesbyrd om bønnhørelse*, (Stavanger, 1957), 61 ff.

[3] See f.inst. Johs. Ludviksen, *Gud i hverdagen*, (Oslo, 1965).

[4] Hermann Bausinger, "Das Gebet in populärer Erbauungsliteratur" in *Triviale Zonen in der religiösen Kunst des 19. Jahrhunderts*, (Frankfurt, 1971), pp. 158-78 (reprinted in Herrmann Bausinger, *Märchen, Phantasie und Wirklichkeit* (Frankfurt, 1987, pp. 133-56).

material treated there was also collected through advertizing in the press.[5] These stories can often be combined with stories about God's guidance.

e) The stories about God's guidance range from simple narratives about someone being "reminded" by God to call upon a certain person to bring food, money or meet other needs, to dramatic stories about following a divinely inspired vocations and literally trusting God to clear all obstacles in one's path. This category also comprises stories about bibliomancy, either by randomly opening the Bible in search for a divine answer, or by picking a card from a pack with printed biblical references.[6]

f) One of the most common categories are narratives about healing, be it through prayer, or other divine intervention. This theme has lead to a rich religious literature. Especially American folklorists have contributed to this kind of research, W. Clements has analyzed the connection between theology and "faith healing narratives" within a pentecostal church.[7] Among Scandinavian folklorists, Bente G. Alver and Torunn Selberg, are currently working with personal narratives about prayer healing as part of an extensive project on alternative medicine.

g) Stories about visions of Jesus are less known outside the congregations than the other categories mentioned here. In 1972 Swedish television invited their viewers to send in stories about inexplainable events. The received material which was of a rather mixed nature, was analyzed by Bengt af Klintberg. For example, a lady, age 65, told a charming story about how she as a six year old saw Jesus in the street of Vadstena.[8]

More sensational, however, was the book "De såg och hörde Jesus" published by Swedish sociologist of religion, Bernt Gustafsson, and theologian, Gunnar Hillerdal,.[9] They collected their material in a rather unorthodox, but effective way, namely by advertizing in the press. To their surprise they got more than 150 letters about visions of Jesus.

---

[5]Gunnar Hillerdal, *Bönhörelse. Utsagor i vår tid*, (Stockholm, 1985).

[6]Karthon Håland, *I frihet og fare. Historien om Marta og Emil Vigdel*, (Stavanger, 1985), passim; Keith Thomas, *Religion and the Decline of Magic*, (London, 1971), p. 118; cf. Hilding Pleijel, "Den lilla Språklådan. Ett särartat gammalt bruk av Bibeln", *Växjö hembygdskalender*, 17 (1988), pp. 37-56, and Arnold Niederer, "Paroles et Textes pour chaque jour". Le tirage au sort de versets biblique, *Ethnologie française*, 17 (1987), pp. 336-41, both with references to the Moravian origin.

[7]William Clements, "Faith healing narratives from North-east Arkansas", *Indiana Folklore*, 9 (1976), pp. 15-39.

[8]Bengt af Klintberg, "Jag såg Jesus i Vadstena. Berättelser om oförklarliga händelser", *Tradisjon*, 3, (1973), pp. 31-50.

[9]Bernt Gustafsson und Gunnar Hillerdal, *De såg och hörde Jesus*, (Stockholm, 1973).

h) Hillerdal supplemented their work with a study of stories about divine revelations in dreams.[10] These stories are not frequent in my material.

i) Some narratives about near-death experiences also acquire a religious dimension.[11]

The list is not complete. It can be prolonged and arranged in several subdivisions, however, it is not my goal to systematize the material, only to indicate the width and the themes of this particular narrative tradition. These stories are largely unknown to people outside the communities where they are alive. Usually, the stories are told as stories about personal experiences or memorates by those who have had such experiences, or by people who are aquainted with them. But they are also told in the third person.

Folklorists have to a large extent regarded this material as non-traditional and therefore very little of it has found its way into the folklore archives. Where else can we find this kind of material? One important source is religious literature, both the edifying and the entertaining.

Martin Scharfe and Hermann Bausinger have used such data for their contributions to a project on popular culture. Scharfe discusses miracles[12] and Bausinger, who derives his material from pietistic children's literature, analyzes stories about prayer, and prayer that have been answered.[13]

In Scandinavia, we have access to an abundance of the same type of source material, found in popular and edifying literature, popular religious novels and children's books. I have used two collections of such stories.[14] Arne Sæter's collection was published by Misjonsselskapets forlag. Det norske misjonsselskapet (The Norwegian Missionary Society) is theologically close to the Norwegian Lutheran state church. In his foreword Sæter stresses that the stories are based in reality. As far as possible they are rendered as they have taken place. Some of the storytellers wished to be anonymous, but their testimonies are as reliable as those of the others, Sæter writes. The second collection has been published by Johs. Ludviksen at Filadelfiaforlaget, the pub-

---

[10]Gunnar Hillerdal, *I drömmen om natten*, (Stockholm, 1982).

[11]Cf. Raymond A. Moody jr., *I dödens gränsland* (Orig. tit.: *Life after Life. The Investigation of a Phenomenon – Survival of Bodily Death*), (Stockholm, 1977), p. 97; Johs. Ludviksen, *Gud i hverdagen* (Oslo, 1965), pp. 62 f.

[12]Martin Scharfe, "Das Wunder in der protestantischen Erbauungsliteratur der zweiten Hälfte des 19. Jahrhunderts", in *Triviale Zonen in der religiösen Kunst des 19. Jahrhunderts*, (Frankfurt, 1971), pp. 102-17.

[13]Bausinger (cf. note 4).

[14]Sæter (cf. note 2) and Ludviksen (cf. note 9).

lishing company of Norway's pentecostal movement. Ludviksen too stresses in his foreword that he recounts either personal experiences or experiences of friends.

Other sources include biographies and autobiographies, which offer the additional advantage, that we can place the narrative material directly in a socio-cultural context. An example is the autobiography of Emil Vigdel compiled by his nephew on the basis of Vigdel's own manuscript.[15]

Emil Vigdel spent most of his life on a farm near Stavanger (southern Norway), where he was born. He made a living delivering milk, but chiefly he was a gardener who sold plants, first for his own account, later as a public employee. Vigdel was a pious man with roots in the evangelical movement. He found it easy to talk to people, had a fine sense of humour and loved to tell stories. During my childhood I often heard him tell stories among friends and to bear witness about his faith. Later on, years elapsed between each time I met him.

In his autobiography, Emil recalls events from his life, things that happened during his childhood and adolescence, incidents from work, war reminiscenses and, most of all, events from his life as a Christian. The book contains stories about God's guidance in choosing an occupation, a wife and generally shaping his future.[16] There is also a story about how he met the devil in the shape of a huge, ugly, black dog,[17] and a story about how he was saved from certain death by a guardian angel. The most dramatic story, however, is how a strong hand lifted him by his neck and from a car seconds before it was smashed by a train.[18] There are also four stories about answered prayers, and two of these will be treated in greater detail:

1. Help while working a stone:
Vigdel was laying a stone wall at the entrance to his home using a lifter. He hoisted a stone nearly two meters long, but no matter how hard he tried, he could not get the stone in place. Everytime he tried, the stone would swerve, it was an impossible task for one person. " – God," he said under his breath, "now you'll have to send a man, or you'll have to come down yourself to give me a hand with this stubborn fogey. If you could just put your little finger on the stone to keep it in place while I lower it". He wasn't sure whether it was right for him to bother God time and again with such trivial matters, but small talk with God came naturally to him – God was always in his thoughts, He was always present, there was no difference for Emil Vigdel between ordinary days and Sundays.

---

[15]Håland (cf. note 6).
[16]Ibid., pp. 11-20.
[17]Ibid., pp. 22f.
[18]Ibid., pp. 39-44.

When Emil got up to stretch his back, he saw a man walking in long strides over the moor towards him. He thought he knew the man. Didn't he work on the neighboring farm? Sure, it was him. What was he doing here, – in the middle of the workday?

– "Is that you, August?" Emil asked, surprised.

– "It is, I'm supposed to get that horse from behind the hill over there."

– "But aren't you walking in the wrong direction?"

– "Yes, I am." August shook his head, confused by his own behaviour, "I must have been walking with my head in the clouds. Suddenly I felt I had to turn and come over here to you, but I don't know why."

– "I do," Emil answered. "I was just talking to God a little, asking him to send someone to give me a hand. You see that stone hanging there, I can't get it into place without help."

With August's help, it took only a couple of minutes to place that stone nicely into the wall."[19]

2) A Piece of Moulding

In the mid-sixties Emil strongly advocated building a youth center. He succeeded building the house through community efforts, individual gifts and a grant. From a water-damaged school he secured unusually beautiful mouldings no longer available commercially.

"Late one night, it was almost midnight, I was installing the last pieces of moulding in the clubhouse when I discovered that I was about a meter and a half moulding short. I looked among skraps of boards and planking, but there was no more moulding. What now? Tear everything down and buy new moulding? No, we could not afford that.

Well, I stopped working and went home. Before I fell asleep that late night, I had my usual talk with God. At the end of my prayers, I added a few words about the missing piece of moulding. I simply asked: "God, can you get me a piece of moulding like that? I don't need much, just one meter and forty centimeters. You were once a carpenter yourself,and know how irritating it is to be just a little bit of material short."

This was exactly what I said.

Next day, we were having lunch when another fellow came in. He nodded at me and said:

– "I found a small length of moulding by the roadside. I threw it into your car, knowing you can make use of almost everything. But it is only a short piece, about one meter and a half."

I must admit, I felt funny, then. I could'nt help myself, but went outside and looked at the moulding. The pattern seemed to be the right one, but it looked too short.

On my way home I stopped by the clubhouse, picked up the piece of moulding, unlocked the door and went straight to the steppladder to check whether the piece fit.

It fitted exactly. God uses a precise yardstick!

As I told you, I have experienced similar things countless of times in my life. And I think many people have such experiences, but not everybody is aware of them.[20]

However, both as historical and as contemporary sources of popular religiosity these sources are not without weaknesses. The stories may be drawn from older

[19]*Ibid*., pp. 24 f.

[20]*Ibid*., pp. 194 f.

literature, perhaps originated within other churches. Fiction and edifying literature are normally produced by authors holding a more or less powerfull position. These authors represent the elite's understanding of what popular relgiosity should be. A recurring theme in older literature for instance, is the statement that the pious poor man is better off than the rich (and perhaps less pious man). Poverty is described as a gift of God. Religious victory and growth are achieved through self-denial. But God can also make use of a rich man in order to help the poor.

As I have shown, Christian memoirs too can serve as important sources. But they too must be used with caution. Attention must be paid to the author's choice of material. What kind of self-image is he trying to give? A correct interpretation requires thorough familiarity with the religious culture to which the writer belongs, the position he holds in the congregation, and so on.

To come up with usable contemporary source material we have to carry out fieldwork both within and outside religious communities. Fieldwork should include interviews, observation and participant observation. It is of utmost importance to elucidate the various functions of narrative types inside and outside of congregations. We need to chart the contexts in which they are used, in the preachers sermon, as memorates in personal testimonies and so on.

Thus far, we can say that the edifying element is always central, and that the narratives ivariably emphasize and support the Christian world view as the only true one. The stories ascertain that God is on "our" side, instead of pointing to the narrator as an exceptional pious Christian. God is the real agent who acts through man. Emphasis on personal qualities is rejected as pharisaical.

In congregations and communities which stress revival and conversion, no one is recognized as a true Christian lest he can tell of his conversion and conviction of being saved. Elaine Lawless has shown how this functions in pentecostal groups in the USA, where the newly converted has to confirm his spiritual baptism through speaking in tongues. Later he is expected to tell about this experience both in his testimony at service and in other situations. The repeated telling of the story serves to confirm the event. These stories provide the pattern for conversion new members are expected to follow. At the same time the stories function as control mechanism keeping the religious experience within certain recognized limits.[21]

---

[21]Elaine J. Lawless, " 'The night I got the Holy Gost...' Holy Ghost narratives and the Pentecostal coversion process", *Western Folklore*, 47 (1988), pp. 1-19.

68

In the evangelical revival movement to which Emil Vigdel belonged, these experiences are accepted, even if not all members can claim to have had such experiences. Outside this millieu it is different, which Emil too is aware of: "When I tell such things, I feel people look at me strangely. Is he quite normal? Doesn't he appear to be slightly overwrought? I do not care much. Those who have experienced similar things, know that God exists and can intervene and help when we ask Him to. For me, God is as real as everything I see and sense around me."[22]

Narrative competance is not seen as valuable in itself – indeed the congregation can take it as a negative factor. His testimony must be genuine, it should come more from the heart than the head. In West-Norwegian revival movements it is decisive that the narrator "has seen the light", that he is virtually saved and freed.

But can these narratives be classified as tradition? Several circumstances point to a positive answer to this question:
1) All the mentioned story types have Biblical parallels either in canonical or apocryphal scriptures. The Guardian Angel of Tobit (Book of Tobit) may serve as an example. Visions of Jesus occurred in the time betwen his death and the ascension. A typical salvation narrative is the account of Saul's conversion. The healing of the sick of palsy in Mark 2,4 is typical for narratives about healings. Torunn Selberg has shown that modern stories about healing are structured in the same way.[23]
2) In some cases these stories are reinterpretations of older folk belief. A good example is found in Anders Gustavsson's material from the Pentecostal movement on Åstol in the South of Sweden.[24]

The warning shouts of an angel have a clear paralell in the spirits of mines.[25]
3) These stories exist both as personal experience narratives and as stories told in the third person (legends).

---

[22] Håland (cf. note 6) p. 90.

[23] Torunn Selberg, *Personal narratives about healing*, Paper read at the 9th Congress of the ISFNR (Budapest, 10-17 June, 1989).

[24] Gustavsson (cf. note 1) p. 88

[25] Ludviksen (cf. note 3), pp. 151-54; Carl-Herman Tillhagen, "Gruvskrock", *Norveg*, 12 (1965), pp. 113-60, 138 f.; Edvard Grimstad, *Etter gamalt. Folkeminne frå Gudbrandsdalen* 3, (Oslo, 1953), (Norsk Folkeminnelags skrifter, 71), p. 10; Jakob Andr. Samuelsen, *Folkeminne fra Modum*, Tillettelagt av Kai Hunstadbräten, (Oslo, 1966) (Norsk Folkeminnelags skrifter, 97), p. 146.

4) Personal experience stories are often moulded in definite form and style, to enable the audience to recognize them and to ask the narrator to tell a particular story.[26]

5) These stories represent the folk religion as an additional element to the official teaching.

Why don't the storytellers tell the Biblical stories just once more? Part of the answer lies in that the Biblical narratives happened several thousand years ago. By using Biblical stories as patterns for personal experiences, we can bridge the breach between then and now. The message of the stories becomes contemporary and thus easier to incorporate into a personal worldview.

The worldview can be of the kind which allows the integration of popular supranormal traditions into a Christian belief system, or which transfers them to Christian values, as Anders Gustavsson has shown it to be the case with regard to South-Swedish Christianity. As far as I can see the Southwest-Norwegian revival movements illustrate the opposite. In this belief system popular supranormal traditions have been completely replaced by Christian notions. God and other heavenly beings have become a natural part of everyday life.

If we want to understand the worldview of such groups within our society, we cannot neglect this part of their narrative tradition.

Contemporary narratives confirm the popular religiosity found in the literary and semi-literary recountals in the same way as memorates confirm popular beliefs encountered in legends. The stories of personal experiences narratives – differ from their literary counterparts in that they are entirely devoid of the dimension of the trivial.[27] The narratives lead us as close to the Holy as possible in modern Scandinavian society, while simultaneously completely integrating the Holy into everyday life. The Holy thus becomes an undisputable part of everyday reality.

Research into folk belief has pointed out that legends provide patterns for the recounting of supranormal experiences. Lawless has shown that stories about experiences themselves form models for conversion stories. There is no reason to assume that this valid only for the type mentioned, it applies to all Christian memorates. Further, it seems reasonable that it also applies to folk belief memorates. This view will complicate source criticism even more because of the necessarily stonger emphasis on social aspects. During AFS's centennial congress

---

[26]Cf. Sandra K. Stahl, "The personal narrative as folklore", *Journal of the Institute of Folklore*, 14 (1977) pp. 9-30; Sandra K. Stahl, "The oral personal narrative in its generic context", *Fabula*, 18 (1977) pp. 18-39.

[27]Bausinger (cf. note 4).

in Boston in 1988 Alan Dundes claimed that all theories on importance in American folklore came from Europe. That American folklore produced new impulses in the seventies, is evident. We can also learn from our American colleagues when it comes to the question of studying subcultures and groupings in our societies. I believe that one of the great challenges in narrative research and folklore as a whole is to complete our genre research by listening to how people express their worldviews through their stories – regardless of genre. A few years ago, when we were discussing singing-activities as a possible new research strategy, Otto Holzapfel said that this would entail a study of narrative tradition as activity. I am convinced that it will be fruitful to proceed with the study of narrative research as socio-cultural activity. The stories about Christian personal experiences are only one example from a field where such an angle of incidence can result in deeper insights into popular religiosity.

Linda Dégh
(Bloomington)

ARE SECTARIAN MIRACLE STORIES CONTEMPORARY AMERICAN FOLK LEGENDS? A PRELIMINARY CONSIDERATION

Over the last twenty years marked by the changing attitudes of folk narrative specialists toward newly sprung materials in the western world, international congresses, like stepping stones, heralded new theories and methods. While we managed to leave behind the confines of the oral tradition of illiterate peasants and primitives, the narrative body of preindustrial cultures as exclusive targets of research, we did not yet succeed in availing ourselves with an adequate amout of material to document the feasibility of our new sophistication. While we experience the never-anticipated multiplication of folklore, particularly folk narratives in the modern industrial world,[1] we still are strong in theorizing on the basis of inadquate materials collected for earlier scholarly purposes. At the same time we are not quite able to identify the social relevance of new storytelling, or take stock of the existing body of stories, and identify their forms, kinds, and categories in terms of a handy taletype catalog or motif index. No researcher believes anymore that traditional folk narratives whither under the influence of technology. We have learned that industrial advancement does not change the basic fragility of human life and does not dispel mental and physical need to respond to social crises, conflicts, anxieties, the sensation of daydreams and nightmares, the excitement of joy over luck, success and adventure, grief over tragedy in the form of narrative. We must realize the validity of what Andrew Lang had noted in his Presidential Address at the 1891 International Folk-Lore Congress: "The materi-

---

[1] For a historic chronology cf. Bausinger (1958 and 1961) as landmarks: Hermann Bausinger, "Strukturen des alltäglichen Erzählens", *Fabula* 1 (1958), pp. 239-54, and *Volkskultur in der technischen Welt* (Stuttgart, 1961).

als of folk-lore," of popular and primitive belief, we can find wherever there are human beings"[2].

Contemporary urban-industrial society creates more subcultures and folk-lore-bearing social groups than ever and develops more and more specific forms of expression. Commercialization, consumer orientation of mass media did not curb the dissemination of folklore as many scholars have predicted. On the contrary, the expert vehicles of communication helped folklore to travel speedier and farther, accomodating and creatively transforming story plots, motifs and episodes for new audiences, for kaleidoscopic reformulations by the receiving folk. Authors in recent years reported a new folklore boom compared to the "down-hill" tendency other folklorists observed when trying to salvage the voice of the past.[3] New narrating communities were discovered with their specific stock of stories – jokes, autbiographical accounts and legends which emerged through alternating vehicles of communication: oral, written, broadcast, print, design, or acting theatrically and ostentatively.[4] Folklorists exploring the current folklore process can be considered as pioneers stepping on new trodden paths. Supported by media technology, social interaction which serves as generator of folklore displays a more expedient and speedier mode of repetition and variation in the modern world then ever before making it difficult if not impossible for the folklorists to catch up with the pace of new development. The folklore process, thus, not only accelerates the production of new forms but also multiplies and inflates traditional forms to satisfy the demand of the insatiable information, indeed, sensation-hungry mass public.

Many ideas have been expressed about how we should try to deal with this material effectively, being insiders as well as outsiders in our own culture. As J. B. Cole so correctly noted: "The objective, systematic recording of familiar, everyday activities in the lives of urban dwellers who may exhibit behavior patterns very similar to those of the anthropologists, may become ... problematic."[5] No doubt, collecting contemporary western urban-industrial folk narratives instead of that of preindustrial settlements of a foreign continent is not easy. It is

[2]Alfred Nutt (ed.), *The International Folklore Congress 1891*. Papers and Transactions, (London, 1892), p. 2.

[3]Dundes (Alan Dundes, "The Devolutionary Premise in Folklore Theory," *Journal of the Folklore Institute* 6 (1969), pp. 5-19) constructed a theory on the devolutionary premise that really never existed, but was provokative enough to argue for the acceptance of new folklore, folklore in the making.

[4]Linda Dégh and Andrew Vázsonyi, "Does the Word 'Dog' Bite? Ostensive Action: A Means of Legend Telling," *Journal of Folklore Research*, 20/1 (1983), pp. 5-34.

[5]Johnetta B. Cole, *Anthropology for the Eighties* (New York, 1982), p. 41.

not enough to act as participant observers in a subcultural group of our own culture. To be effective, we must change our research etiquette and distance ourselves from our own folkloric heritage, the beliefs and general behavioral patterns we share with the group under study.

Among the many narrative genres that enjoy popularity in our society, most attention was given to the joke and the legend. The joke is indeed a modern genre, that stepped out from 19 century newspaper humor pages and traveled with great speed through print and professional humorist's public performance. Nevertheless, oral transmission whose path is impossible to follow from person to person, seems to be more responsible for its incredible spread than jokebooks confined to solitary, or even public reading. While joke cycles erupt in spasms as they comment on significant actual issues and are orally told for entertainment (I believe the printing of joke cycle pamphlets is rather the result of the success of the cycle in oral performance than its initial source), the puzzle of its rumor-like scattering, almost simultaneous emergence in distant cities, even on continents, remains unresolved.

Folklorists are currently discerning the genre they call legend mostly from non-oral sources: newswire, television, radio, the popular press[6] and to a lesser extent from oral telling. While the non-oral records are authentic, much as the retelling of the same story by reporters, writers, actors, artists represent variants and individual creativity, there is a problem with the genuineness of oral versions. Most of what folklorists use was solicited by collectors in the form of tape-recorded interviews, "induced" natural settings, or was "self-collected": written recalls by informants.[7] Except for the careful description of the ritual legend trip[8] and legend telling of American adolescents[9] little is known of spontaneous oral communication of legends or the personality of inspired legend-tellers in modern society. This is the more regrettable because authors speak of "legend telling ses-

[6]Jan Harold Brunvand, "Popular scholarship and the Urband Legend", Papers I. The 8th Congress for the International Society for Folk Narrative Research, eds. Reimung Kvideland and Torunn Selberg, (Bergen, 1984), pp. 89-92.

[7]Typical of student papers filling American folklore manuscript archives.

[8]Cf. Gary Hall, "The Big Tunnel: Legends and Legend-Telling", *Indiana Folklore* 6 (1973), pp. 139-73, and Bill Ellis, "Why Are Verbatim Transcripts of Legends Necessary?" in *Perspectives on Contemporary Legends*, eds. Gillian Bennett, Paul Smith and John D. A. Widdowson, vol. 2 (Sheffield, 1987), pp. 31-60.

[9]Linda Dégh, "The 'Belief Legend' in Modern Society: Form, Function and Relationship to Other Genres," in *American Folk Legend. A Symposium*, ed. Wayland D. Hand (Los Angeles, 1971), pp. 55-68, and Sylvia Ann Grider, "Dormitory Legend-Telling in Progress: Fall 1971-Winter 1973", *Indiana Folklore* 6 (1973), pp. 1-32, and Janet Langlois, " 'Mary Whales, I believe in You'; Myth and Ritual Subdued," *Indiana Folklore* 11 (1978), pp. 5-33.

74

sions" as if that would be most common and face-to-face oral exchange would be the legend's general locus although the natural occurrence of legends is by no means limited to formally planned and arranged occasions. Most of what authors publicize originate from the newsclip service, from correspondents who answer editor's queries requesting information on single legends they have heard about or read, or from student term papers.[10] This would not really matter if authors would not insist on the primacy of oral rendition regulating the legend process without being able (or caring) to furnish convincing documentation. In modern times when folk legends are a part of mass media dominated information exchange we cannot really be particular and rigidly stick to consider only the texts carefully recorded in context.[11] We cannot afford to throw away other variants, rewritten, restylised by newspaper editors, actors, playwrights and others. We need all variants of the same species to understand the full extent of single legends.

A large grab-bag contains the rest of prose narrative materials summarily titled as personal experience stories, roughly classifiable only according to themes or individual biographic accounts.[12] Close scrutiny of these seemingly heterogeneous personal stories may lead to a classification modeled after human career potentials[13]. However, recapturing two recurrent scholarly ideas: "einfache Formen" and "homo narrans" (as proposed over a time-span of sixty years by Wesselski, Anderson, Jolles, Sydow, Ranke, Bausinger and Lehmann), it may still satisfy us to relate these nonfictitious prose forms to the more stabilized fictional Märchen, novella, Schwank and exemplum, and the more fluid nonfictional legend, on the basis of shared episodic contents in order to capture processes of repetition, variation, stabilization and change. Of course, all depends on our interest in these seemingly simple, modest, unassuming, mostly first-person accounts stated as personally experienced. We may be interested in their form and style as narrated texts, degree of traditionality and their place in culture and society. Although such stories were reported by scholars since the 19th century, sociological, or psychological premises concerning the nature of narration. Two di-

---

[10]Ronald L. Baker, *Hoosier Folk Legends*, (Bloomington, 1982); Jan Harold Brunvand, *The Vanishing Hitchhiker. American Urban Legends and their Meanings*, (New York, 1981), and Bengt af Klintberg, *Rattan i Pizzan Folksägner i var tid*, (Stockholm, 1986).

[11]Elizabeth C. Fine, *The Folklore Text. From Performance to Print*, (Bloomington, 1984).

[12]Linda Dégh, " 'When I Was Six We Moved West'. The Theory of Personal Experience Narratives," *New York Folklore* 11 (1985), pp. 99-108.

[13]Linda Dégh, "Beauty, Wealth and Power: Career Choices for Women in Folktales, Fairytales and Modern Media," *Fabula* 29 (1989) 1/2, pp. 43-62.

stinctive characteristics of experience narratives are in the focus of German[14] and American[15] scholars: the "everyday" as opposite to the "personal". The native term used by informants anywhere was always and still is "true story", stressing that the account is a real experience, not invented like a tale but lived through in real life of a particular individual.

Without denying the justification of looking at the everyday ordinaryness or personal uniqueness of experiences stories I would like to argue for their proximity to narratives we identify as legends. Not all but most fit the broader category of legend that includes memorate and fabulate and other subspecies identified on the basis of formal criteria by folklorists. In native terms, as the voice of its bearers, the legend is a story that gives account of a true occurrence that was personally experienced by someone in the real world. There may be other criteria useful for the purpose of breaking up the gigantic artificial category of personal experience stories for a more meaningful reclassification of its materials help us understand better folk narrative categories in our time. Such a classification needs to consider content, form, function, and meaning on the basis of sociocultural, ethnohistorical, situational and intertextual contexts. This demand is not new. Sydney Hartland had stated it almost a century ago: "It is not enough to sort and classify: we must enquire what mean the stories so labouriously gathered, where did they spring, and what relation they bear to one another and to the history of our race."[16]

In this discussion I will examine a set of legends whose legend-status has to be ascertained. They have been viewed both as personal experience stories[17] and as religious legends serving devine confirmation of an organized religion.[18] These legends are emergent from one particular close-knit religious community, the Apostolic Bible Church of Bloomington, a "Oneness" congregation of the Pentecostal faith.[19] The members of the assembly view themselves as children united

[14]Utz Jeggle, "Alltag", in *Grundzüge der Volkskunde* (Darmstadt, 1978), pp. 81-126.

[15]Sandra K. Dolby-Stahl, "A Literary Folkloristic Methodology for the Study of Meaning in Personal Narrative," *Journal of Folklore Research* 22 (1985), pp. 45-76; Literary Folkloristics and the Personal Narrative. (Bloomington and Indianapolis, 1989)

[16]By Sydney Hartland in Alfred Nutt op. cit. p. 16.

[17]André Jolles, *Einfache Formen* (Tübingen, 1965), pp. 23-61, and Max Lüthi, *Das Märchen* (Stuttgart, 71979), pp. 9-11.

[18]Susan D. Rose, "Conversations of Conversions: Interviewing American Evangelical Women," *International Journal of Oral History* 8 (1987), 28-40, and Elain J. Lawless, " 'The Night I got The Holy Ghost...'. Holy Ghost Narratives and the Pentacostal Conversion Process," *Western Folklore* 47 (1988), pp. 1-20.

[19]The "Jesus-only"-concept means that Father, Son and Holy Ghost is one entity for this assembly (cf. Lawless, note 15, p. 3).

by the love of Jesus, in an extended family loosely connected with sister congregations of the same faith. Totally absorbed in practicing religion by their own ideology of serving as instruments of divine order, their miracle stories function as cement binding realms of supernatural eternity and the mortal everyday together. I will present some of these characteristic everyday miracle stories of current significance in order to address the question: do they fit the category of the legend, and if so, is there a need to change the definition I suggested in my earlier writings?

2.

What does the legend mean for its bearers? This is, I believe, the heart of the matter. The legend observed in the field usually entertains an extranormal topic which has three essential qualities. It is of existential importance for people who participate in its presentation, elaboration and discussion, it is surrounded by uncertainty lacking firm knowledge, and it is controversial, invites expression of diverse points of view. In more explicit terms, the legend is a story about an extranormal (supernatural or equivalent) experience attested by situational facts. It happens to average (normal) people within their cultural realms but contradicts accepted norms and values of society at large. Therefore it demands to be communicated while provoking dispute concerning its feasibility. Expression of opinions often also by the presentation of variants is its integral part but negotiation usually does not lead to resolution.

The concerns of the legend are universal. They deal with the most crucial and mysterious questions of the world and human existence; life, death and the hereafter. Contrary to conventional textbook opinions, the legend, in its real, untrimmed form, natural condition, is not simply a coherently shaped untrue story that pretends to pass for true.[20] It is rather the product of conflicting opinions expressed in conversation and manifested in discussions, contradictions, additions, implementations, corrections, approvals and disapprovals during some or all phases of its transmission from inception through elaboration, variation, decline

---

[20] Traditionalists stick to the "presented as truth but in fact untrue"-idea that arches over a long period of scholarly tradition from Friedrich Ranke to Jan Harold Brunvand (Friedrich Ranke, "Grundfragen der Volkssagenforschung" (1925) in *Vergleichende Sagenforschung*, ed. Leander Petzoldt (Darmstadt, 1969), pp. 1-20, and Robert A. Georges, "The General Concept of Legend: Some Assumptions to be Reexamined and Reassessed," *American Folk Legend. A Symbosium*, ed. Wayland D. Hand (Los Angeles, 1971), and Jan Harold Brunvand, *The Mexican Pet. More 'New' Urban Legends and Some Old Favorites*, (New York, 1986).

and revitalization. Anyone who has ever observed naturally emerging legend exchange in a community, and did not limit interest to the bare text, but paid attention to the voices of all participants and contributors can attest to the simple fact, that the legend narrative is incomplete without the narrator's (and his audience's) commentary. Extricating a manifest text from its performance context is as much, or even more, a mistake than having an artist select, at will, one single voice from a polyphonic musical composition and ignoring the rest. But this is not only true of the ethnographically observable oral legend in performance. Variants of legends from historic sources as recorded by historians, writers, artists, scholars or lay observers display similar variability due to the compulsion of their author-reteller-editor to interpret and take a stand for or against the implications of the story.[21] We can likewise observe the same dialectic variability in the legends of our time, as they travel on the wings of mass media, that is, alternate between electronic and oral carriers.

In regard to its dialectic-polyphonic nature, the legend, more than any other folkloric expression isolable for scholarly scrutiny as a genre, must be recorded in full, without editing or arbitrary concentration on one of its component elements to the detriment of all others. But even if a performance at a given occasion happens not to be accompanied by controversy, rebutting comments and everyone seems to be in accord, the well-known opposing opinion, held by the majority, or the opinion-leading minority of society always makes its presence felt. Thus, when the legend-proponent makes his point, he is also arguing against the known contrary opinion. He who racounts a successful delivery from devil possession to a television talkshow host, or he who testifies to a religious community about miraculous intervention of angels in civilian clothing will formulate his story with the anticipation that society at large would find it unacceptable, and that many people would argue against it if they were present.

The eyewitness, reporting the disappearance of the white clad heavenly messenger from his car seat[22] must be prepared for the incredulous smile of doubters. Every statement that counters notions held as rational and authentic, or beliefs that are canonized by elite churches and civil religions[23] and therefore

---

[21] A recent conference on the Pied Piper of Hameln celebrating its assumed anniversary of 700 years fascinatingly demonstrated the dialectics of interpretations of the legend by historic and current scholarship (Norber Humburg, ed., *Geschichte und Geschichten*. Erzählforschertagung in Hameln im Oktober 1984 (Hameln, 1985).

[22] Lydia M. Fish, "Jesus on the Thruway: The Vanishing Hitchhiker Strikes Again," *Indiana Folklore* 9 (1976), pp. 5-14, and Walter Heim, "Moderne 'Strassengeister'," in *Schweizer Volkskunde* 71 (1981), p. 1-5.

[23] John F. Wilson, *Public Religion in American Culture,* (Philadelphia, 1979), pp. 143-68.

are quasi-rational, qualifying as rational, embodies its own built-in dialectics. This is the main identifier of the legend, setting it apart from other folklore genres. In other words, uncertainty and disputability is not only one feature of the legend among others, it is the very essence, raison d'être, goal. The legend demands answers, but not necessarily resolutions, to the most mysterious, critical and least answerable questions of life.

3.

Over the years I have authored and coauthored several essays on the legend with the intention to clarify its main features. Arguing for the disputability factor as crucial, I excluded legend-like narratives that enforce belief and deny the right of disbelief, narratives that express majority opinion and are safeguarded by moral tabus from negation and, what is more, from deviation. These are the so-called religious (Christian-, hagiographic- or Saint's) legends propagated by the Roman Catholic church and the patriotic (heroic) legends dispensed through school education by governments, confirming citizens in civil religiosity. The purpose of reading or telling these stories is a part of religious duty and worship, a culture duliae.[24] But what happens if dissidents sects establish their own belief system in expressive controversy with authoritative canonic legendry?

The legend-dispute as argued before, "resembles strongly the theological polemics of the Reformation and Counter-Reformation because of its topic, methods, passion and unreal atmosphere can be found in every genuine folk legend".[25] This should not come as a surprise. The history of Catholicism is the history of struggle for dominance against deviant religions composed or traditional beliefs, forms of devotion and legends that oppose and challenge the authoritative canon. Personal as well as communal variables of the original Christian belief in western society are composed of learned and inherited elements of religiosity which scatter and reassemble in many ways as the glass shells in a kaleidoscope while none of the traditional elements of homo credens are ever discarded. The degree of dissent is of great variety, from tacit disagreement within the church, Catholic or Protestant, to a complete cutting of ties and seeking new affiliations. Group exodus can result from learning about visions and miracles by individuals aspiring sainthood but rejected by church authorities, or from the attraction to charismatic personalities – evangelists, prophets, gurus –,

[24]Dégh-Vázsonyi (op. cit. note 4), pp. 2-11.
[25]*Ibid.*, p. 6.

touched, by God. Testimonies in narrative form surrounded both through the ages and are repeated again and again today, attracting millions of pilgrims. As *Die Welt* (January 16, 1989) reports, pilgrimage is in high fashion and young wanderers make up the majority. The model – miracle of accredited saints – is followed even by unauthorized contemporary saint's legends, appearing almost weekly in the popular press, to carbon copy accuracy. Examples are the bouncing of the sun and color change of the rosary while children converse with the Virgin Mary in Medjugornie, Yugoslavia, "to challenge Lourdes, Fatima and Guadalupe for Roman Catholic Marian devotion" (*Time*, July 7, 1986) and a similar vision was experienced at the St. John Neumann church during the Feast of the Assumption in Lubbock, Texas, in 1988 (*The Herald-Times* of Bloomington Aug. 16, 1988). Tears are shed by the altar image of the Madonna in a Chicago church, (*Expressions* 3/1, 1987), and by the likeness of St. Nicholas in Tarpon Springs, Florida (*National Enquirer,* Oct., 1975). Vision of saints occur in a tree in Eisenberg, Austria ("authentic" pilgrim reports are presented in a pamphlet by Josef Maller, Wien, 1972), in a picture window in the Bronx, New York (*The Courier-Journal*, Louisville, Kentucky, 1971 November 22) on a tortilla in Lake Arthur, New Mexico (*Newsweek*, Aug. 14, 1978). The oral spread and media popularization of the modern exempla mirabilis signals critical opposition with canonical religion.

In the past, individuals were less eager to move from church to church in search for a satisfaying doctrine than nowadays as elite churches accomodate to secular culture, and their grip on the supernatural weakens. As W. S. Bainbridge reports, "Existing conservative denominations and new sects will expand to fill the gap. Originally finding their social base in disadvantaged groups, they can grow into the mainstream of the society..."[26] Increase of membership in fundamentalist churches is fenomenal in our days. Even within the same denomination, congregations enjoy great autonomy in their style of service, worship, preaching and other ritual practices. In my own modest sample sixty-two of one hundred Pentecostals have canceled their membership of the church in which they were raised, and for fourty among them this was not the first church of choice.

---

[26]William Sims Bainbridge, "Is Belief in the Supernatural Inevitable?", *Free Inquiry* 8/2 (1988), pp. 21-26.

4.

The Pentecostal church whose one assembly I studied, is the fastest growing among the fundamental churches and has been considered the third large force in Christendom, next to Catholicism and Protestantism.[27] In adition to its main spiritual appeal I see its attraction to the individual in that it opposes everything characteristic of the modern urban technological lifestyle in mass society. It gives a sense of belonging and security to the lonely individual craving for a warm, loving, family-style support group with old fashioned homeliness and lack of sophistication. Fulfillment to achieve happiness; rebirth into a heaven-bound brotherhood can be attained only by total submission, humility, hard work and soul searching. Purification, spiritual catharsis is achieved by dedication to Jesus, that is rewarded by the grant of the Holy Spirit (speaking in tongues) and deliverance from sin by baptism. During a mentally and physically gruelling emotional exercise to alter consciousness, individuals kneeling at the altar with raised arms are assisted by the congregation through constant encouragement, and performance of the koreography of the expected endowment. By imitating the process by singing, clapping, shouting to the dictum of the music, relatives and friends moan, cry and collapse with the candidate and burst into speaking in tongues until the goal is achieved and baptism: deliverance from sin by total immersion is administered. If the person who seeks the Holy Spirit does not succeed, there is always hope for next time. Individuals see themselves as "nothing", empty vehicles through whom the Lord communicates his messages to the world. It is through chosen individuals that he manifests his miracles as testimonies of his love of mankind. People are trained in mental excitation, to consciously seek alteration of their state of consciousness and states in which wakefulness and dreaming by glossolalia or kinetic behavior is the highest level of achievment manifesting union with the supernatural. What a difference to the almost inhumane stuffyness and depersonalized blandness of elite congregations with a learned theologian on the top of the hierarchy.

There is a great deal of informality in that haven for lower middle class co-religionists who call each others brothers and sisters and take turn in performing community functions, be they ritual, cermonial, artistic, organizational, promotional, charitable, entertaining, clerical, domestic or janitorial. Everyone's talent is utilized in the activities: arts, crafts, construction, acting, singing, music making. The total membership together participates in the creation of the sacred

---

[27]Felicitas D. Goodman, *How About Demons?*, (Bloomington, 1988).

space for worship, to accomodate Jesus and his messengers (angels) whose presence is often alluded to on the premises of the church.[28] Membership in the congregation is individual and voluntary without social pressure because unlike in high churches, participation is selfless, and does not help status elevation or professional gain. From the time of their birth, children are participants in all church activities thus conditioned by the unrestrained loud outbursts, music, preaching and unnatural behavior. But when they grow up it is their decision to stay or quit. Likewise, not necessarily both marriage partners, siblings and parents share membership as family unit.

Total involvement is characteristic: life centers around the main goal: conveying the messages of Jesus, propagating his miraculous deeds and living a life that secures eternal bliss in heaven when the time will come. Therefore, constant ideological fixation is necessary around the clock. Religion is the way of life and is divided into two parts: in and around the church, and outside of the church.

Normally, there are three evening services from seven-thirty to ten-ten thirty in the Apostolic Bible Church of Bloomington, Indiana, a congregation of a membership of two hundred men and women. Almost all work outside of their household. The majority – sixty-five per cent of the attendants are women many of whom work only part time and do office-apartment or private house cleaning, work as kitchen help, nurse's aid, saleslady or clerical employee. Informants in general, contradicted Lawless' observation that women "largely surpassed male participation in the service"[29] and stated that the reason for their greater visibility for the outsider is that their jobs allow them more freedom for practicing religion than the more responsible ones men hold as farmers, factory workers, electricians, truckers, rapairmen, salesmen and shop owners. Nevertheless, separation of gender-roles in whorship is explicitly stated by both men and women following the guidelines of the Bible.[30]

The service conducted by the preacher, Brother Coffman is a loosely structured complex which usually consists of the sermon, testifying, praying and speaking in tongues with interpretation. But this is not necessarily so. Depending on individual needs, the emotional conditions of the membership, triggered by unforseeable coincidences, the sermon may be omitted for spontaneous testifica-

[28]See text sample nr. 4.

[29]Elaine J. Lawless, *Handmaidens of the Lord. Pentecostal Women Preachers and Traditional Religion*, (Philadelphia, 1988), pp. 152-56; *Ibid.*: God's Peculiar People. Women's Voices and Folk Tradition in a Pentacostal Church (Lexington, 1988).

[30]Goodman (Felicitas D. Goodman, *Speaking in Tongues. A Cross-Cultural Study of Glossolalia* (Chicago, 1972), p. 10) notes that in their trance state women tend to be more glossolalic, men more kinetic.

tion of miracles, "running around the church in the Spirit and worshipping", crying, screaming, praying, moaning, dancing, speaking in tongues and interpreting the Lord's words.

Between services, there are prayer meetings twice or three times a week. The "prayer-line" is set for individual and communal praying for a purpose: a concentrated, intensive, deep supplication for a miracle: to heal someone sick or in trouble, to fulfill a fervently desired wish, to ask for guidance, consolation and interpretation of the unfathomable.

In addition to regular services and prayer meetings is the culminating ritual performance: the revival, led by a respected evangelist from another assembly. "Being in revival" means daily services for a week to a month, or even more, highlighted by the initiation of new recipients of the Holy Spirit, tongues, tongues interpretation and baptism of the novices. Revival season is a special time of complete devotion in which experiencing an altered state of consciousness, falling in and out of trance, is expected to come forth as a result of the grace of the Holy Spirit. The visiting preacher brings new testimonies and evidences he experienced elsewhere in order to enhance the revival. He acts as contact to other assemblies whose members eventually also visit in order to spread the news of miracles personally encountered, and help to make them happen again.

The experience of church performances during service is essential for the membership therefore tape recording is routinely done. Church members collect tapes for keeps and borrow cassettes from each other for copying. Particularly successful testimonies, sermons, tongues and interpretations are replayed by individuals while they do their daily chores, concentrating on particularly poingnant, prophetic passages. They rethink, reinterpret the texts while they are alone and converse with Jesus whose presence they feel. The exposure is so intensive and so customary that there is no feeling of mysticism or awe but rather a peculiar kind of domesticity in their encounter with divinity. People are cheerful and smiling while reproducing their conversation with "the Lord" in a very ordinary, everyday language. They thank Jesus for deliverance from a bad headache, a flu, or express gratitude for the successful sale of an old car as recounted to a friend who dropped in or just phoned. Narratives – mostly conversion and miracle testimony accounts – declare liberation from accepted norms of religiosity, challenge, and invite debate on two fronts: adherents of mainstream religions and unaffected or dissenting family members. The stories, repeated by intensive solitary rethinking or social retelling at a variety of occasions within and without the congregation reaching the larger community of Pentecostals are legends in the best sense of the word.

5.

The primary context of these legend narratives is religion. Religion for Pentecostals is the way of living focused on heaven. A joyous expectation and a constant excitement for being possessed by the Spirit of God, they experience divine miracles as daily events. The miracle of being in touch with Jesus all the time, talking to him informally at any hour, is regarded as evidence that they made the right choice turning away from the frivolities of earthy life. The promise of eternal happiness in Heaven has its price: no one knows the time of being called, so a constant readyness must be maintained without indulgence in earthly pleasures. Pentecostals are righteous and conservative in their judgements, intolerant of deviation, while they show love and tolerance toward the irreligious, rebellious, even scandalous lifestyles of their children in which drugs, alkohol, extramarital pregnancy, lack of motivation, are quite common features. The tolerance is in accord with their humility and piety: prayer will do miracles and in good time bring the erring children back to church and endow them with the Holy Spirit. "You do your best to stay alive" a woman told to a gravely ill young man, "I will take care of the rest". She organized a prayer-line to coerce Jesus to healing him with the hope that experienced miracle will bring the black sheep back to church and impress others sharing his wasteful lifestyle. The same woman felt an urge to leave the service at a point and enter a solitary room of the church building where Jesus had predicted as an answer to her fervent supplication, that her son, a rock musician will come back to her from California. The same evening he called to tell her that he will return in two weeks.

There are plenty of opportunities for legend telling, both formal and informal. During regular services and revivals, people are asked to come forward and testify about a miracle they themselves or someone else experienced, when "Jesus touched them". The testimony is accompanied by spontaneous formulaic responses ("hallelujah", "thank you Jesus", "amen", "praise the Lord", "I love you, Jesus") and often precipitates other testimonies and unpredictable emotional outbursts and tongues. Similar legends are often included in the sermon of the preacher for illustration, enhancement and indeed, entertainment. The manner of telling is remarkably informal and personal, full of autobiographical detail and admission of human weaknesses that the audience gratefully acknowledges with a chuckle. The preacher, like in traditional Christian religions uses a part of the legends as exempla, to elaborate on his chosen biblical theme and another part for presenting himself as simple, unassuming human being trying hard to deserve the grace of the Lord. Apart from public narration, legends may emanate from solitary prayer. The supplicant's conversation with God may result in the decoding of a secret message or in finding the key to a problem so that when returning from the prayer room he will be ready to tell his legend.

Everyday miracle stories do not need specific occasions to be told, they may be a part of any gathering where people converse; whoever feels the sensation of "being touched" and the urge to tell, picks up the telephone or walks to the neighbor who is of the same mind. The individual, burdened by the new knowledge needs to tell it and to hear the reaction of others and discuss its feasibility. Although coreligionists basically agree, there are always nuances of disagreement in story formulation and in the interpretation of the experience. Generally accepted theses always gain confirmation by new illustrations.

The congregation in itself is the perfect resounding board for miracle legends which strengthens the individual's self-confidence. Yet, both the legend proponent and the supporters are aware of the fact that in the eyes of eilite church membership and the general secular public they are sharers of a marginal religion. The low esteem of the sect puts membership on the defense. They are aware and try to downplay the fact that the noisy Pentecostal ritual is a target of mockery, and they accept with pride the nickname "holy rollers" or "Jesus junkies", arguing with the authority of the Bible as their source. "We worship the Lord loud, with noise", "we sing and dance in the Spirit", "we are crazy in the Lord", "we shout". Therefore legends not only confirm the belief of the membership but fight the doubting outside world, specifically in the defense against non-fundamentalist Christian prestige churches as much as against the general irreligious demeanor of the modern world as individual church members experience them in daily encounter.

Pentecostals are simple people and know very little of the outside world, particularly about other great religions, Catholicism, Islam or Buddhism. Their information is limited to sources that can be obtained by interpersonal contacts within the small world in which they live: family, neighbours, co-workers and coreligionists, hence legend dialectic manifest in testimonies to bring back, convert and save the erring deviants on their own turf. Nevertheless modest in education, verbal enculturation, mental conditioning, training in meditation, fasting and other disciplinary exercises give Pentecostals remarkable self awareness and assurance evident in their eloquence in argumentation. Appealing to emotions, not reason, narrators just like preachers manipulate and enrapture their audiences effectively by using subjective, not objective facts.

Are these miracle legends controversial? Are they amenable to debatability? Do they challenge and motivate, do they incite opposition? Yes, they do. Although they stand firm on the soil of the religious subculture, the experience that demands to be communicated is controversial by its very existence as supernatural encounter of each single individual. "O Lord, you are using me!" exclaimed a young woman, trembling with fear, as she unconsciously was driven to the altar to testify about her own healing, in order to assist in the healing of a blind girl. The legend is a constant reminder of the presence of miracles, the credibility of the incredulous. The ambiguity is built in but differs in degrees if addressed to the sectarian, the hesitant, the skeptic and the unbeliever. These stories are arguments for acceptability of the sect addressed to the mainstream. More importantly and more directly, they target the unfaithful who were raised as Pentecostals but abandoned the faith and are caught in the conflict between two worlds: orthodoxy and freedom of choice. The group of legends generated by prayer on regaining erring souls appear in cycles, marking episodes of visons, precognition, prophecy and miracles.

The miracle legends of the Pentecostal assembly in Bloomington constitute miracles of conversion, healing, and divine intervention in everyday affairs. They are simple, modest and rooted in the lives of smalltown people from the "Bible-belt" of the American midwest. A modest sample below will illustrate the tone, and the style of this peculiar stock of legends: a new addition to complicate the thorny problem of finding a definition and creating an order for this elusive genre. All texts I am presenting here, are lifted from their natural conversational and ritual contexts in which legends thrive. They are relatively short although some in my collection are long, extend to thirty minutes or more, and are linked up as a response to someone else's legend. Some were told in instalments because there was temporal distance between the miracle experience and its outcome and impact on those involved.

1.

(Told by L. S. 41, mother of two, wife of a plant foreman and occasional housecleaner: She told this as testimony in church at the next service, and then, to me, in 1985 and again in 1986.)

... I forgot to change my batteries and they were dead. Anyway, I took the cassette recorder to church, Tuesday night, to tape this evangelist, Brother Clifton. I called Suzy, I said: "Suzy, my batteries are dead." And she is the kind of lady who lays hands and does miracles ... Okay, I had dead batteries Sunday night already. And I talked to Suzy, I said: "Suzy, I had forgotten my batteries today, help me to pray for, that the Lord revive these batteries." But anyway, as we were singing, I see some red light on it ... And as she starts singing, I just turned it on and waited to the preacher to get up there and ... I just set it on my lap and I said: "Lord, in the Bible days, in the valley of dry bones you resurrected those dry bones. You resurrected those dry bones, you put life back in those dry bones, so you put back life in those batteries." And as the evangelist gets up. Brother Clifton comes to the podium, and he gets up, and he starts for the podium, Suzy says: "Oh, Leatha, look." And those batteries, the red light flashed on, and Linda, they lived. And they were dead Sunday. I don't feel it was my prayer that did that. And I told Brother Clifton after the service. I sad, "Brother Clifton, I don't think it was my prayer." And they were dead Sunday, I mean, they were dead. I feel like it was the Holy Ghost that whenever he got up and went to the podium, resurrected those dead batteries. I was amazed. And it was played, the next night, three hours on dead batteries ... even four hours ... (she continued here with a miraculous healing story)

2a

(from the sermon of Brother Don Dick at a revival service, 1985 October.)

This boy could not sleep at all. He had a guitar and his father said: "Where did you get this guitar? And the boy said, "well, I got it in a pawnshop." And he said: "And where did the pawnshop get it?" He said: "I don't know but I will find out," he said. He found out, and took it back, and found out, the pawnshop got it from a rock musical group. This particular musical group was known for dedicating their instruemnts to the devil. They had services, just like ... this building, I am sure, has been dedicated to God (Hallelujah, praise the Lord). This musical group dedicated its instruments to the worship of the devil and they had a big time (oooh Jesus!). And this guitar the boy had, had been dedicated to the devil. And that's the reason that he could not sleep at night, that there was an evil presence in the room. And the boy said: "Pastor, what should I do?" And the Pastor said, "Well, I read it to you from the Bible," he said. "The graven image of ungodly presence should be burned with fire. It is an abomination, that the Lord, thy Lord commands, in thine house shall be burned. Because it is a cursed thing. So that you utterly detest it and utterly destroy it." Said the boy, "So, pastor, that's what I shall do?" The Pastor said: "I think so. Abhor it because it is a cursed thing." So the boy went home and got the guitar and broke it up in little pieces and took it out into the backyard. Poured gasoline on it and set it on fire. Then, some time later, he came back to the pastor, some days later and said: "I just want to tell you, Sir, before there was a strange, but weird and ugly spirit in my room, and now there is a strange but very wonderful spirit." He said that everything was just fine. "Thank, you," he said. (Praise the Lord! Thank your Jesus! Amen!)

2b

(in continuation) You mean to say that evil spirits inhabit in all? This pastor in the United Pentecost Church told me this very story. He said "yes, you absolutely can use my name if you want to because every word of it is true."

One night my teenage boy was gone from home. He was spendin' the night with some friends and he was said he was backslidin' and he said he was in with those very things I am talking about. And he said: "My wife and I was retiring for the night, we just got ready to go to bed." And he said: "We heard this loud noise at the other end of the house. It was so loud that it was frightening. I knew," he said, "I knew, I have to go see about it because something was down there." He said, "I was going all way down the hallway. When I got down there, I opened the door to our teenage son's bedroom. And when I did, something came out of the bedroom door, ran across my feet and went straight down the hall and out the front door." He said: "Right down on the floor. It was evil. It was wicked" he said, "it had just a bad spirit, it had just a bad spirit about it," he said. "I went right on him, I turned the light on, and walked into the room. And when the door closed right inside of the door, there was one of these hideous, demonic looking pictures, from one of those groups." He said: "Yes, you can tell, I know that evil spiritism is associated with all of that kind of stuff. You can read about it on one of those books in the Christian bookstore. (Praise the Lord.)

2c

One of the famous pastors, his son got involved in this. Went out and bought a rock musical record. It had a demonic looking pictur on the front. The boy took it home, and laid the album cover up against the stero, put the record on, and laid down and began to listen to it. The boy was having an absolutely excruciating earache. He could not even go to school because of them and they could not find out what was wrong. Medical examination turned out nothing at all. A preacher friend came by, and they started talking about it and he said that "This boy's dad sounds to me like it may be the activity of an evil spirit." And the boy's dad said: "Do you think so?" They went upstairs where the boy was and he was laying on the bed, and just wallowing in pain, of this excruciating pain. He started talking to him. They saw this album over there and came to find out when the boy first brought the album home and laid the cover against the stereo and was laying there listening to it. He said himself that "the evil picture in front of the album literally came right off the album, moved right across, and came over right, stood over me while I was laying on the bed." He said: "The thing just stood there and started laughing at me, and" he said, "the pain was so excruciating in my ear," he said, "it never left since." "So," he said, "That's what it was." And they destroyed those records that the boy had and then, that dad and that preacher took authority over and commanded that evil spirit to leave. The power of the thing was broken immediately, the boy's earache went with it when the evil spirit went, and he was never troubled with it again ... (Amen).

88

3

(Told by evangelist Bob Utterback from Linton, Indiana, at a visit to his former home church in Bloomington in 1985 December. He is a retited electricain.)

I remember one time, I was at the city of Newcastle. I was preaching for a revival at that time. I was driving the company truck. That company truck broke down and I had two dollars in my pocket. I remember that I made it to the Chevrolet garage, it was a Chevrolet truck, and they said it will take about thirty-five to forty dollars to fix the truck. On a Friday night, the shops were closing down pretty fast, it was Friday evening. I had to be at a certain place in Greencastle and I called the company in Terre Haute for the work order. They said, no problem, just have it charged to the company. I turned around to the man and I said: "Could I have some credit here?" "Well," he said, "yeah, but your company just bought two new trucks and that exhausted the credit line and the company is now in the process of ... I forgot now what they called it ... they could not do it without the meeting of the board, and the board is meeting in four months. O my, that's a terrible thing. And I remember walking out on the sidewalk in front of the Chevrolet building. I look up to Heaven, and said: "Lord, – you won't believe this, – I need forty dollars." I remember, I looked down and the Lord spoke to me. And he said: "The next car you see to slow down and stop, ask the man a loan of forty dollars." (laughter). Praise the Lord. (laughter). I said: "Well, Jesus, come on, let's see if somebody was jumping fast ... then I would ask. I would, in Jesus' name. And allright, I tell you something. I obeyed. I stepped up to an oversized van that slowed down at the curb. I said: "Excuse me, mister," and I presented my name, and I said to him: "the Lord said you loan me forty dollars." He said: "O, he said that?" (laughter). I sad, "Yes, he did." He said: "Oh." And he loaned me forty dollars." (Praise the Lord). Amen.

4

(told by Bob Utterback at a revival in 1987)

"What my eyes have seen, what my ears have heard, what my heart has felt ..." (Praise the Lord).
We had three men coming to the Linton Pentecostal church one morning, a beautiful morning it was. If I remember right, it was a cold day and it was very sharp wind a-blowing. And I don't know what the temperature was, but it was quite cold. I rememb-er we had a hard time, in fact, we could not bring up the building to temparature, and the wind was blowing so hard and so strong. There were three men who came in. They stood in the back row of the church, and as we taught Sunday School, we was teaching about the innovations of Elijah and Elisha, and the subject came up from the Bible, something about different things that happened in those days. I remember the names, one that came back later, about twelve years later. I will tell about him a little later on. But he seemed to be the spokesman of the three, and he told us just exactly how they done in those days as like he knew. And I can't tell you all the details, but I remember that he told us how they done some of their cooking, just that we know he had been there. I remember that after church, the men, and if I remember right, they had no overcoats, they had a suit on. Two men got up immediately and left the building well

into the parking lot and stood there for a good thirty minutes. Stood up there in the parking lot with just their suits on them and the temparature was terrible. It was bitter cold that morning. This one man stood behind and he told us a lot of things. And he talked with us. In fact, he played on everything he could get his hands on in that church. And he did not ... I'm afraid, I don't mean to insult nobody, but he did not play as he has trouble playing.

My wife became worried about the meatloaf that was in the oven at home. And he brought that up, and said: "don't worry about your meat, it's allright. And it will not be burned." I said: "What are you doing down here?" He said: "We are down here ... helping the winter warm. Cut some wood." I said: "Can winter warm itself up?" "No, she needs help. And we want to help her. Amen." That makes lot of sense. You know, those Holy Ghost-filled people that boast to be filled with the Holy Ghost? They would not go across town to cut wood to people. Would not even ... oh, shouldn't I say it? (Say it!). I might as well say it: they would not even cross the town to go to church (that's right). Amen.

My wife said something about cooking. But she said: "I wish I knew to cook better." He said: "What do you want to cook?" he said, and told her exactly how to cook. Praise the Lord. She went home and did as he said. She did not burn anything (laughter). Praise the Lord.

During this thirty minute talk there was something that was not quite normal. I began to press him to come home with me. He said "no, but I will be back to see you some day." And he said: "Some day I will go home with you. There will be three, at least three different times."

One night I rose in my bed and I walked through the house about three o'clock in the morning. And I felt the presence of this individual (ghost?), and I turned to look and I expected to see him standing there. But he was not. I remember, and I am going to tell you a little bit about him later on, how he painted the building in legend we are worshipping.

But when we were trying to acquire a loan, we was a new church, everyone was trying us, we were strangers in town. We have been in all the banks, and the banks said no, and the only way to do it was to put up my property, and that was proper. I was trying to own the church under trustees, under guardians. This is how it had to be done. And suddenly, one night, this same man came into our building. He walked up to me and my wife after church. He said to my wife, he said to her: "On ... you go in and you ask them for a 21,500 dollars and you don't even have to fill an application, it would be ready for you." And he turned, and walked through the door, and we never seen him again.

My wife went to the place, went in there. She said: "I am here to borrow some money." The man said: "How much do you want?" "21,500 dollars." He wrote on a little piece of scrap paper that he had on his desk. He said: "How you gonna pay the money back?" He looked back at her. They grinned at each other. "O yes, the same way as you painted the house. Allright. I can't see a problem, why we can't loan you the money." And we borrowed the 21,500 dollars.

Now, you may laugh at that, and you can snicker me the wire, but to me, I feel this was done working in a supernatural way. Praise the Lord. (Praise the Lord). A lot of people don't know these things (right). And you would not know if I hadn't told you (right). Praise the Lord. I said, you would not know (Thank you Jesus). Amen.

Sabine Wienker-Piepho
(Freiburg)

"LIEBER GOTT, SEI SO FROMM, LASS UNS GUT NACH HAUSE KOMM!"[1] MEDIEVAL TRADITIONS AND MODERN STORYTELLING IN MOTORWAY-CHURCH MANUSCRIPTS

In his satire on the "Small world" of academia, a cult book among "conferees"[2], David Lodge describes the strange inscriptions in the chapel at London's Heathrow Airport:

> At the bottom of the stairs there was a small vestibule with a table displaying devotional literature ... on the wall was a small green baize noticeboard on which visitors to the chapel had pinned various prayers and petitions written on scraps of paper: 'May our son have a safe journey and return home soon', 'God save the Russian orthodox Church', 'Lord, look with favour on thy servants Mark and Marianne, as they got to sow Thy seed in the mission fields' 'Lord, please let me get my luggage back (lost in Nairobi)'[3]

Although these examples may be fictional and the last one in particular be satirically exaggerated or simply invented; they appear on the same level as the entries in the books in German motorway-churches. There are seven such churches (as of 1989) of either catholic or protestant or both confessions, and in almost everyone there is an empty album on a chain for visitors to write in[4].

---

[1]"Dear God, be so pious, lead us safely home" (The "pious-God" nonsens is – in German – underlined by the grammatically incorrect ending of the phrase).

[2]"Conferees", according to Lodge (cf. note 3), are those pilgrims of the international scientific jet set, who go on "pilgrimages" like their ancestors in Chaucer's Canterbury Tales, and his satiric novel incipits with an ironic paraphrase of Chaucer's famous "prologue".

[3]David Logde, *Small World. An Academic Romance* (Harmondsworth, 1984).

[4]For this information the following are thanked: Gesellschaft für Nebenbetriebe der Bundesautobahnen mbH (Bonn). – The seven motorway-churches and -chapels are (Sept. 1989): 1. Dammer Berge (At the AI Düsseldorf-Bremen, both confessions), 2. Roxel (AI Düsseldorf-Bremen, catholic), 3. Nievenheim (A57 Köln-Düsseldorf, catholic), 4. Maria-Schutz-der-Reisenden, Adelsried (A8 München-Stuttgart, catholic), 5. St. Christophorus, Baden-Baden (A5 Baden-Baden – Basel, catholic), 6. Geismühle (A57 Köln-Krefeld, ev.-luther.), 7. Exter (A2 Herford-Bad Oeynhausen, ev.

These books measure circa 35 by 40cm and have about 600 pages each, sufficient for approximately one year's use. Each new year (or when they are completed) the priests replace these books. The old ones are kept in an archive. There is no curatorial obligation to provide such writing materials. The priests, however, have to include the petitions of the past week in their Sunday intercessjons.[5]

"Dear God, be so pious and lead us home safely", dated 16 Nov. 1988 and signed with the initials "E.Y.H." only, is written in the album of the Chapel of Mary, Protector of Travellers, on the A8 from Munich to Stuttgart, near the Adelsried junction. This (Catholic) church, the oldest of the seven (founded in 1958), is looked after by a priest from Augsburg who reads three masses there every Sunday and on Holy Days. This citation may be considered as entirely typical in its content and structure, and it reveals the basic sentiments of many of the drivers who stop here: *expressions of gratitude* and *requests* for help are the commonest forms, which recur as stereotypes so often that they deserve to be called the dominant *topoi* of these motorway-church manuscripts, thus representing the popular religiosity of motorists. The direct context is clearly reflected in most of the petitions and thanks, as it is in the example cited: the driving, the journey, the destination and, accordingly, the associated need for protection is the focus of the texts, many of which, though occasionally written in an emphatically profane tone and with a certain humorous bravura into "God's guestbook" still betray a tendency to seek meaning in a vague, supernatural, "still-divine" power: "Dear God, thank you that there was so much dough today" and "Thank you for the lovely day, o Lord, yours Inga" (11.7.88 Adelsried) or "Dear God, thank you for this day and your guidance" (9.20.88 Adelsried), "Let my son get better, K." and "Dear God, let me get home in time without traffic jams before my rich aunt dies!".

If there is no such book for petitions ("Fürbitten" or "Anliegen"-book), the clientele helps itself by improvising with institutional scraps of paper: in Roxel, for example, people have seized the postcards sold here, written down their problems and finally heaped them on the altar into a big pile, which the priest does not remove.[6] Such initiatives demonstrate a very interesting general need for blank paper in sacred places; recently Martin Scharfe noticed and described an analogue scriptural mourning behaviour, when Olof Palme was murdered in

---

luther.). An "Auto*fahrer*"-church in Windach/Ammersee (Bavaria) does not lie directly on a motorway and may therefore officially not be called "Autobahnkirche".

[5] Personal interview with Pfarrer F. Schmerbeck (Baden-Baden) in Sandweier, Dec. 88.

[6] Cf. Gereon Vogler, *Besinnung am Rande der Autobahnkirchen und -kapellen in der Bundesrepublik Deutschland unter besonderer Berücksichtigung der Religiosität von Distanzierten*, Bestandsaufnahmen, Analysen, Anfragen, Perspektiven. Diplomarbeit (Bonn, 1985), pp. 57 ff.

1986.[7] This need seems to be so urgent that even criminals once have betrayed themselves by written entries: German newspapers reported in 1988 on a case, were the police could gain control over the escaping route of a wanted murderer by means of motorway-manuscripts.

Although *continuity* seems to have become something like *gesunkenes Wissenschaftsgut* by now, some questions, which narrative research and any folkloristic analysis should ask of these notes and books must deal with the possible relations to past forms of storytelling or storywriting into books or of other documentations of popular religious expression. From what does this need for *"promulgation"* derive (the term used e.g. by Kriss-Rettenbeck and others, for the act of exposing oneself "sue sponte" and publicly in writing or in pictures, an impetus which is – in its broadest sense – characteristic of *votives*)[8]? Are the drivers who stop at these churches and write these entries unconsciously the modern successors of former gifted storytellers or of the pilgrims of earlier times who documented their gratitude, their religious devotion and their commitment as exempla mirabilis in *miracle books* whether by writing themselves or by commissioning a scribe to do so?[9]

Analogies may be supported, firstly, by points of detail: In view of the textual heterogenity of the entries, the motorway manuscripts cannot be classified as one unified stylistic type: on the one hand we find brief, uneducated visitor's comments, mere protocolls actually. But on the other hand there are longer, narrative, nearly epic and often very picturesque entries, which betray a developed storytelling talent of the motorized homo narrans. Rhymes are also popular, and mostly, like the prose entries, beginning with the opening incipit-formula "Dear God...!": "Lieber Gott, auf der Hinfahrt hatten wir den Segen Dein', die Rückfahrt laß auch behütet sein" (Dear God, we had your blessing on the way here, may You also protect us on the way back). One entry consists of a transcription of the entire 23rd Psalm, in which the not very expert writer has evidently aimed at calligraphic perfection. On the 29th of october in 1988, an ambitious visitor in Baden-Baden filled in the complete song "Jubilate Deo, Alleluja", including the

---

[7]Martin Scharfe, "Todengedenken. Zur Historizität von Brauchtraditionen. Das Beispiel Olaf Palme 1986", *Ethnologia Scandinavia* 19 (1989), pp. 142-53.

[8]Lenz Kriss-Rettenbeck, *Ex Voto. Zwischen Bild und Abbild im christlichen Votivbrauchtum* (Zürich/Freiburg, 1972), p. 276 and pp. 303 ff.; cf. also Martin Scharfe, *Evangelische Andachsbilder. Studien zur Intention und Funktion des Bildes in der Frömmigkeitsgeschichte* (Stuttgart, 1968), pp. 219 ff.

[9]In a recent dissertation promoted by Niederer in Zürich on the "Miracle of Eisenberg" the "applied myth" is also interpreted in the sense of these modern, promulgative miracle reports (cf. Doris Groscurth, "Das Wunder von Eisenberg. Europäische Wallfahrten zu modernen Marienerscheinungs- und Wunderorten", Diss. phil. Fak. (Zürich, 1988), pp. 133 ff.).

music. Occasionally *pictures* replace the written word: a painted church with an open portal and the sophisticated caption "You need only find the door", or a car with a cross hovering above, or the thousands of inevitable hearts crossed with arrows – all these inscriptions amount to "votive paintings on a debased level".[10] The majority of these manifestations of religious popular graphology are, therefore, not only private images of a certain "relationship to the transcendent"[11] but also – as a sort of "edificatory literature" – devotional encouragements for *following users*, readers of these messages. This represents another traditional feature of the genre: miracle-books, too, always show a certain concern for transmission to future readers ("heilbringende Schau"). In motorway-books there are also repeated entries by the same person, usually making a votire offering by a particular promise or oath to the superior power represented here. It is done in the classical "do-ut-des"-manner:

> Dear God! I promise to go to church once a week
> if my wife and my child come back to me, Hans.

Most of the entries, including those by repeated visitors are *anonymous*. In contrast to the home parish church with its communication between the priest and individual members of the congregation, the highway church guarantees absolute discreeteness. This form of a "touristic care of souls", therefore, does not enable the pastor to lead personal dialogues with the modern pilgrims. Selfevidently, it also prevents the folklorist from gathering information by participating observation. Fears concerning the keeping of secrets spoken in confessionals, or the fear of mockery by non-believers or neighbours of, possibly, another confession, are anulled here.

There must be a certain interrelation between anonymity and authenticity in written devotionals which has – as far as I can see – not been investigated as an important factor in source criticisme yet. Anonymity here seems to increase reliability: people really trust into the discreeteness and seem to confess their individual truths frankly and without fear. This anonymity is also a traditional characteristic of the old libelli miraculorum: Theopold cites an entry in the (18th-century) miracle book of Grafrath, which concludes: "Name and origin carefully

---

[10]Rudolf Kriss: "Neuerwachen des Wallfahrtsgedankens," in Wallfahrt und Volkstum, *Forschungen zur Volkskunde* 16-17 (Münster, 1934), p. 201 f. (quoted in Karl-Sigismund Kramer, "Typologie und Entwicklungsbstimmungen nachmittelalterlicher Wallfahrten", *Rheinisches Jahrbuch für Volkskunde* 1 (1960), pp. 195-211).

[11]Lenz Kriss-Rettenbeck, *Das Votivbild* (München, 1961), passim (and cf. note 8, p. 47).

kept secret"[12]. Since the Enlightenment, he comments, anonymous entries had become fashionable; members of the upper classes in particular preferred not to reveal their identities. In our times as well as then, this was meant as a protection against ridicule. Anonymity, however, does have its other side: those who are "putting up at God's inn" (headline in the German magazine "Bild") often neglect any clothing etiquette, and in summer many motorists pray in bathing suits, a trend, one may also observe in other churches that are attractive for tourists. Above all, *theft* is a daily occurrence; this detail may suggest another parallel with traditional religious customs: former miracle books were also fixed on chains, because they were believed to have had medical healing properties, and the chains prevented them from being stolen and let for money, or sold to "confused and grieving persons", who put the book for "four nights under the head", as early entries from the Pürtner miracle book (1664-65) prove.[13] However, the motive for stealing these books today, will presumably remain unknown. – There are further analogies in the use of *hieratic formula*, such as "V.G.F.A." (votum feci, gratiam accepi – restricted obviously to catholic visitors –) or "ex voto" (I have committed myself). This has by now become less common, but is still not unusual. In general one cannot distinguish between catholic or protestant inscriptions.

Anonymity, the soliloquial, secret character of the inscriptive act (which comes, in this respect very close to Donald Ward's concept of "idionarrating"[14]), makes it difficult to reach conclusions about the context, the sociology and the cultural milieu of the writers, even after the profound investigations of Vogler (1985) and Rams (1980), dealing with the theological implications of the institution of "Autobahn-Kirchen".[15] Vogeler, especially, gives rich statistical material, based on his own empirical explorations. In the end, however, there is not any reliable information on *"performance"*, which will – as with Ward's "idionarrating" – complicate source-criticism to a great deal. Any analysis of these inscriptors as a group therefore will remain speculative and incomplete. The simple fact that almost every text is written by an unpractised hand and in a rather unpolished

---

[12]Wilhelm Theopold: *Mirakel. Heilung zwischen Wissenschaft und Glauben* (München, 1983), p. 64. – Cf. also Kramer (note 10), p. 209 f.

[13]Theopold (note 11), p. 54 f. (= reprint of one page with entries from 1664-65).

[14]Donald Ward, "Storytelling in Contemporary Societies. Idionarrating and social change," in this *ScriptOralia*-edition (1990).

[15]Vogler (cf. note 6) and Maria Rams, "Die Autobahnkirche St. Christophorus zu Baden-Baden. Realisierung neuer Aspekte einer Patoraltheologie oder Kunst am Bau auf dem Sektor der Theologie?" Versuch einer Analyse unter liturgischen, pastoraltheologischen und künstlerischen Gesichtspunkten, Dipl. Arbeit (Masch.)., (Freiburg, 1980).

style proves little. The general observation made with reference to *graffiti* (which are also *anonymous*), of a need to set down in writing a simple experience of the world in order to leave an immortal trace of one's existence, fits poorly here.[16]

Highway pilgrims cannot simply be lumped together with the tourists who deface every pyramid or wall with their exhibitionistic "Kilroy was here". Rather the assertion is valid that the motorway-church manuscripts are definitely no *"scrap books"* ("Sudelbücher"); indeed, blasphemeous or ironic remarks are practically never to be found in the latterday miracle books, nor, on the other hand, elaborate entries that strongly suggest a reflective or meditative spirituality and closeness to God. Some seem to express an immature insecurity concerning the act of writing as such: "Holy sheepshit, why all this?" (Adelsried 11.8.88) while others betray a sense of superiority over those who do not perform such acts:

> Wo der Herr nicht mehr regiert,
> rasch der Pöbel dominiert,
> und den Staat ins Elend führt!
> (Where the Lord no longer rules, the plebs are soon on top and the state is ruined).

In general, one may speak of a non-classifiable conglomerate of stereotype whishes, clichés, ambivalent feelings of guilt and naïve emotionality ("Dear Lord, please protect all participants of the ladies' gymnastics excursion", Baden-Baden 11.16.88). Very often simply signatures appear. Some pages, therefore, are degraded into mere records of presence. This is why Baden-Baden offers two different kinds of books: one "namebook" and another "petitionbook" – a differentiation which is often neglected by the motorized homo credens. Once again one may find both: complete adresses including post codes and phone numbers (even academic titles are not withheld from God!), and anonymous laconic comments.

Harmening describes reports of miracles ("Mirakel-Topoi") also as *"answers to prayers"*[17], and the modern motorway-texts which consist of personal experience stories (memorates) of prayer hearings correspond to their foregoers also in this particular aspect: "Dear God, thank you! Please keep on answering my prayers" (Adelsried 11.88). Unfortunately, more detailed information is seldom given. In general one searches in vain for precise statements, for

---

[16]Ernst Abel und Barbara E. Buckley, "The Handwriting on the Wall. Toward a Sociology and Psychology of Graffiti," in *Contributions in Sociology* (Westport and London, 1977), p. 15-29.

[17]Cf. Dieter Harmening, "Das Mirakelbuch der 'Crescentischen Gutthaten' ", *Zeitschrift für Volkskunde* 61 (1965), p. 15-29.

excessive reports of miraculous healing or conversion for example, such as still crop up in popular pilgrimage notes in remote chapels in the countryside, where visitors seem to have much more leisure time than motorists, but they do exist even here; gratitude for help, blessings, and acts of grace are expressed in a rather generalized fashion in motorway churches. Most common are entries of a somewhat worldly character. These reveal deeply felt irritations, which are perhaps nowhere so directly and plainly expressed in other written forms (except, maybe, in the most intimate private diaries): "Dear God, help me to cancel the investigations against me at the law court in Constance, and enable me to pay back all my debts" (Baden-Baden 11.15.88, name withheld), or: "Dear Lord, help my mother to get her driver's licence" (Baden-Baden 11.19.88). Personal crises, especially problems in personal relationships, helplessness in the face of material difficulties, and dull, diffuse anxieties concerning general political and ecological threats are revealed in entries such as: "Protect us from catastrophes like in the Rhine and at Chernobyl", "Help my love for Ilse", "Dear Roumania, help Transylvania" or "Bless Franz Joseph Strauß and Bavaria". Short formulas like these, but also longer "mini-autobiographies" of the most private kind for the Lord's orientation do, however, loose their profane connotation, when one reflects the situation in which they were written: in sacred rooms with a direct address to God.

Undoubtedly, the impetus which drives people to put down their unfathomable fears in written letters and to relate their intimate sorrows and anxieties in a sort of "correspondance with heaven"[18] is connected with another traditional, at present perhaps more or less latent belief in the *magic of the written word:* a kind of rune sorcery, intended to function *apotropaically* and to protect the writers from the concrete dangers of the motorway. Therefore, any written entry certainly has also a cathartic function as a "crisis-solving mechanism", as Hauschild puts it.[19] In this sense every cultural determined action inhibits such "letting-of-steam" functions ("valve"-functions). A special *superstitious* component of the Baden-Baden Autobahn-church refers to a fashionable mystic trend; Religion and superstition amalgamate here in a very peculiar way, although many of the visitors do not realize the fact: The architecture of this modern *pyramid* attracts all those newagers, who believe in earth rays. They maintain that in the very

[18]Cf. Herbert Nikisch, "Schreiben und Glauben. Anliegenbücher als Beispiel moderner Volksreligiosität", (MS)Paper, Congress "Volksfrömmigkeit" (Graz, Mai 1989), forthcoming in 1990; – This quote refers to Walter Heim, "Briefe zum Himmel. Die Grabbriefe an Mutter Theresia Scherer in Ingenboht," *Schriften der Schweizerischen Gesellschaft für Volkskunde* 40 (Basel, 1961).
[19]Thomas Hauschild: "Protestantische Pilger und katholische Körperschaften. Süditalienethnographie zwischen Imagination und Realität," *Zeitschrift für Volkskunde* 82 (1986), p. 43.

98

centre of every pyramid people may gain new energy, and that even blunt razor-blades, placed in these centres, will become sharp again by secret healing forces.[20] However, when asked, the priest of this church, which has 2000 to 3000 visitors daily (!), knew nothing of this coalition of religion and superstition or of any other especially *esoteric* attraction of his church.

As a certain "religiosity of crises" in times of catastrophes, such as the Second World War, a *renaissance* of votive custom (which had been thought already extinct) can be observed, as Kriss-Rettenbeck has pointed out.[21] Accordingly, it becomes apparent that, as German motorways become more and more chaotic and dangerous, an *increasing need for transcendental protection* against accidents and death in traffic is felt. No one is lonelier than the driver who, after long hours of enervating, exhausting driving through jams and total blockings, stops at one of these "petrol stations for the soul" (Rams) in order to rest for a while. Sometimes, when the motorway traffic comes to a complete standstill, there is much time to ponder over life and death. Not seldom then horrific scenes on the wayside, as a "memento mori", remind the driver of the other world. Senseless deaths in pile-ups, today's holocaust turn motorways into "routes de passage" and it is this new, this quasi "initiated" point of view which is reflected in the church manuscripts: "Give peace to those who died because of fog and speeding, and forgive those who caused this horror", or: "Prevent me from driving recklessly myself" (both Baden-Baden, 11.88). Such a specific religious state of mind also finds its complementary parallel expression in "aids to prayer", printed in several languages, that may be bought for 10 pence in Baden-Baden:

"Holy Mary, protector of the travellers! During my visit to the motorway church I found your picture. In your life you travelled too (e.g. to Egypt), so you know all the dangers of the road, because you experienced them yourself. Therefore I turn, full of confidence, to you: First help me to be thankful for all the good things that I have lived to see until now, things that I've unfortunately mostly taken for granted. Teach me to be thankful, that I may always become happier. But also help me to pray: let me reach my journeys end without any trouble, without being involved in an accident, without causing danger to anyone and let me experience security and protection wherever I drive and let me give that the others, too. Virgin Mary, protect me against myself whenever I would like to drive recklessly. Let me foresee the danger and let me be

[20]As an introduction cf. Max Toth, *Pyramid Prophecies* (New York, 1979). According to an official opinion poll of the German Institute of Demoscopy *Allensbach* from May 1990, Superstition in Germany has increased (10 % versus 1976!) and still keeps increasing (cf. *Badische Zeitung* May 16th 1990). Enquiries may be addressed to: Institute for Pyramidology, 31 Station Rd., Harpenden/Hertfordshire AL 54 XB).
[21]Kriss-Rettenbeck (cf. note 11), p. 20.

someone who protects others on the road. I will let you guide all my journeys, also the last one. So I am sure you will lead me to God, where all the roads ends. Amen."

Many entries, e.g. the "not-driving-recklessly" formula in the foregoing paradigma, have obviously been inspired by this prescribed prayer formulas.

Inscriptions of this sort have existed since classical times.[22] Miracle books (the oldest of which, the "Buch der Maria-im-Elende" from the Harz mountains, is said to have been written in 1420) therefore already have their own history (habent sua fata libelli) when they appear in the Middle Ages. But defining the phenomenon as a *genre* seems to be a highly problematic procedure. Assion has proposed a remedy for the terminological confusion: literary criticism and folklore use the term "miracle" not only as in the wonders that happen in fairy tales and hagiographical narratives (both vitae and post mortem legends), but also as a general synonym for anything "remarkable, unusual, surprising".[23] In this most general sense motorway manuscripts also correspond to profane *storytelling traditions*, mostly *legends*, for example,[24] which – although not being told in the 3rd person as their foregoers – claim to be absolutely true in spite of impossible happenings and supernatural wonders. Sometimes our modern sources contain "faith-healing-narratives" (as Kvideland calls them in this volume), "belief accounts" in the form of continuous stories: a visitor who came weekly to Adelsried in January 1989, thus gave a regular report of the Bible-like unbelievable palsy-healing (cf. Mark. 2,4) of a certain "little Sebastian". This is told as a personal experience story in the first person, as is the majority in my material.

Another function of these books preserves traditional features, too: Miracle books served also as means of advertising for particular sacred places. The more numerous, spectacular and impressive were the proofs of the holy shrine's potency assembled in this medium (which, from the 16th century on existed not only in manuscripts but also in print editions), the greater was the holy place's prestige.[25] In an essay on the contemporary pilgrimage to his famous chapel, R. Bauer, pilgrimage-administrator in Altötting (Bavaria), stated bluntly in 1971: "Propaganda is essential to a place of pilgrimage".[26] Even the restless tourist of

---

[22]Peter Assion, "Die Mirakel der Hl. Katharina von Alexandrien. Untersuchungen und Texte zur Entstehung und Nachwirkung mittelalterlicher Wunderliteratur", Diss. (Heidelberg, 1969), pp. 5-16.

[23]Assion (cf. note), p. 12.

[24]The inner relationship miracles: exempla and miracles: legends is analyzed e.g. in Harmening (cf. note 17), pp. 21 ff.

[25]Cf. Harmening (note 17), p. 18.

[26]Frank Baer, *Votivtafelgeschichten* (Rosenheim, 1976), p. 8.

100

today seeks shelter in a group identity, and some entries, therefore, testify to a
certain search for "corporative",[27] for collective identity, which might emerge
within such a large number of fellow-believers.

The morphology of such text compilations will not alter with the situative
context in which believers and non believers live, but so will the content. Cultural
change, therefore, will not alter stable elements like the essential, somehow *cultic*
character of the act of writing into motorway books, at least as long as the procedure today is legitimated by the same religious institutions as hundreds of years
before. In these perspectives, contemporary motorway-church inscriptions can be
interpreted as survivals and modern equivalents to traditional continuities which
deserve close attention from investigators of both popular religion and "narrative
theology" (a term cited by Bausinger[28]) and of modern religious storytelling
which paradoxically seems to proliferate more and more in our technical world.
Beyond this, the textual phenomenon which is on one hand partially described by
Harmening as "Breite Erzählfreudigkeit des ergriffenen Gemüts" (eager telling
of stories by those deeply affected by their experiences) and might on the other
be characterized as "small talk with God", has not been at all investigated yet as
far as this important kind of source is concerned. It certainly belongs not only
marginally to the wide field of religious narrative research.

---

[27]Harmening (cf. note 17), p. 19.
[28]Hermann Bausinger, Art. "Erzählforschung" in *Enzyklopädie des Märchens* 4 (1984), Sp. 345
(Quoting: Harald Weinrich, "Narrative Theologie", in *Concilium*, Intern. Zs. f. Theologie 9
(1973), pp. 329-343.

NEW GENRES

Bengt Holbek
(Copenhagen)

THE FAMILY ANECDOTE: EVENT AND NARRATIVE

The term "family anecdote" is intended to describe accounts of events that have taken place within living memory and within one's own family circle. The definition is not to be taken in a categorical and dogmatic sense; what I want to do is mainly to indicate a target area.

Family anecdotes – in this sense – are not traditional. They are not handed down from generation to generation for the simple reason that they are closely associated with people we know from personal experience. They do not have to have a punch line or even a rounded narrative structure. Mostly, they depict a situation in which somebody said or did something characteristic, interesting, stupid, or amusing. If the family anecdote develops intrinsic narrative qualities, if it is carried on to new generations or outside the family circle because it can stand by itself, it has a good chance of becoming tradition; but by the same token, it passes beyond the circle that I want to discuss here.

If the family anecdote is not tradition, some purist may argue that it isn't folklore. I will concede the point. It is not even folklore in the very broad sense given to that word in Dundes' definition, according to which "folk" can refer to any *group of people whatsoever* who share at least one common factor and "lore" refers to a long list of items, all of which share at least the quality of being transmitted within the "folk". The family anecdote is thus hardly folklore in the accepted sense. Nevertheless, it is something that is told.

Everybody knows family anecdotes from personal experience: what Auntie Olga said when I was born; what my father said the first time I came home drunk; how my sister and I set fire to the shed when we were playing at cooking; and so on. Family anecdotes are found in the countless memoires that are printed nowadays, not to speak of the interviews and "life stories" steadily produced by folklorists who can no longer find any traditional folklore and still want to do fieldwork. I am interested in family anecdotes for two reasons: in the first place, I am interested in the question as to why we select certain events as memorable and not others; this is mostly a psychological kind of question. In the second place, I am interested in the manner of presentation; in this respect at least, there is some kinship to folklore. I am thinking of memorates and a certain category of wellerisms. Naturally, there are relations to other established folklore genres as well, mostly to anecdotes in a broader sense. I shall take the material to be discussed from personal experience, not only because it is easy for me to get hold of, but also because I think I can interpret it with some degree of certainty. Interpretation is always difficult, but it helps a lot if one is close to the material to be interpreted.

The number of experiences accumulated in a middle-aged brain is vast beyond count. We experience things every single minute of every day and night, year in and year out. Most of them we forget so utterly that they cannot possibly be recalled. The overwhelming majority of experiences are so similar to others that they leave no trace in our memory, and I think we should be grateful for that. How many times have I taken a cup of coffee or said hello to someone I knew? The question cannot be answered and I am not interested in an answer. But there are things I remember, most of all from my childhood and early youth. This is well known: nearly all memoires are most detailed and most vivid for the first fifteen to twenty-five years. After that time, they are as a rule more cursory, more summary. Part of the explanation is undoubtedly that when we grow up, many experiences are new; later on, there are more repetitions. But I think there is more to it. Now I am venturing into the field of psychology without any licence to do so, but I shall stick closely to my own observations in order to minimize the dangers of amateurism. Let me give you an example:

I have three older brothers and some younger brothers and sisters as well. When I was small, my parents bought mugs for each of the four brothers. The oldest got a green one, the next a blue one, the third a red one, and mine was yellow. Since then, I have always felt that those four colours were the only ones that counted; they were organized in a hierarchy in which yellow was my colour; it was the lowest, but nevertheless, I could at least claim a place in the hierarchy. When my younger sisters and brothers grew up, they also got their own mugs, but there were repetitions of the four canonical colours, fortunately, however, with a different shape of the mugs. When recalling this insignificant detail, I also recall that I experienced the world as static. I was aware that I was growing, but apart from that, everything was and should always remain exactly as it was. This, I felt, was right. Deviations from the established pattern were experienced as threats to this secure sphere, and naturally I resented them. Thus, I resented my younger sisters and brothers getting mugs of their own. As a matter of fact, this conservative streak remained in me throughout my childhood. Everything was judged by the standards I first defined as right and all deviations were inferior: other people didn't make the right kind of food or their speech was wrong, or their behaviour, or their religion. This innate conservatism is of course part of the pattern we call ethnocentrism. I think all children are conservative.

We had a sandbox and in order to avoid territorial wars, my father meticulously divided it into four equal parts. Then my sister graduated to sandbox status and he drew a circle in the middle, taking a part of each of the original lots. I still remember with great shame how I reacted the first time this attack on my territorial integrity took place. I repeatedly struck out the new borderline and reclaimed the lost land, but everytime it was taken again by the invader, strongly supported by my father and my older brothers. I made a terrible nuisance of myself, not least because I realized very well that the claim was well founded, both because of the theory and because of the force mustered against me. Finally I was kicked out for the day and the following day I bowed to the inevitable; but I bore a grudge against my innocent sister for years.

Why do I still remember this, fifty years later? It must be because of the strong emotions involved. I felt that my position as the forth of the quartet, low as it was, was threatened by an intruder. And if I think of other episodes of my childhood, I can in many cases still remember my feelings on those occasions.

The sandbox episode does not become a family anecdote, at least it does not become part of my repertoire. I am still ashamed of it. On the other hand I have nothing against reminiscing about episodes in which other family members made fools of themselves. In some of those cases, I could feel superior, a pleasant feeling I do not mind remembering. I believe this feeling of smugness gives rise to a lot of family anecdotes. Thus, I recall that my father was passing through the kitchen one day when he discoverd that the coffee pot was boiling. In those times, fathers did not make coffee. He shouted instead: "The coffee's boiling!" My sister then shouted from upstairs: "Pour cold water into the spout!" Now the Danish word for "spout" can also be used as a slang word for "nose". My father had a prominent nose and he was a bit sensitive about it. He got furious, thinking that she was impertinent, and forgot all about the boiling coffee. There is a Danish expression "to pour cold water into the blood", meaning to calm down. But a fourteen year old girl does not say that sort of thing to her father, especially when substituting "snout" for "blood" – which is what he heard. Since that time, we always advised each other to pour cold water into the spout when tempers got too high. It took a long time for my father to live it down.

He had quite a repertoire of family anecdotes about his clashes with his own father, a stern gentleman of the old school, born in the 1860's and still a terror to his family in his old age when I knew him. He was a wine merchant, married an Italian lady and lived for many years with his family in France, Spain, and Portugal. French was the only language permitted at dinner table. He had the habit of complaining about the salad: it hadn't been washed properly, he maintained, and every day they heard his invariable "du sable!" upon which the maid had to take the salad out and bring it back properly washed. My father said that he got so far as to complain of the sand even before he had tasted the salad and one day, my father himself said "du sable!" just as the maid came in. My grandfather rose half out of his chair with a furious shout: "Tu te moques?" – "Are you mocking me?" – and of course there was no answer to that. But he did not complain about the sand after that.

It is customary in Denmark to eat a goose for Christmas, at least if you are well off and the family is large. One Christmas evening, my grandmother was not satisfied with the goose, it had not been properly done, and she went on complaining about it until my grandfather took the goose and threw it out the window. The maid of course fetched it and cleaned it, and when she served it the second time, she pretended that it was another goose. There were no more complaints.

Grandfather was the undisputed master of his own house and he had firm ideas about everything. Every Sunday afternoon, he took his two sons for a walk. This was after they had returned to Denmark, some years before the first World War. He hated cars. Whenever a car came along, he stood with his back to the road until it had passed, and he ordered the boys to do the same thing. They would have liked to peek, cars were new at the time, but that was not permitted. My father described these Sunday afternoon walks several times. He hated them. The boys were dressed up in sailor's suits, complete with caps, as was customary among the bourgeoisie at the time, and the boys felt that they looked ridiculous. My father, being the older, walked on his father's left side, half a step behind him, and his brother walked on his right side, a full step behind. Then they conversed, i.e., their father talked and they had better answer "Yes" and "No" at the right places. One day they walked in a park where they met the King of Denmark. My grandfather greeted him most courteously, but the two boys took off their caps with a gesture they thought was smart. Unfortunately, their father had noticed it. As soon as the King was out of earshot, he began training them in the noble art of greeting kings, 18th century style. They were sent off, ordered to turn about, march up to him and greet him properly, and then again, and again, and again. The orders were given in a very loud and furious voice and after a while, there was a crowd of spectators, many friends and acquaintances between them, watching two red-faced boys greeting their father over and over with their ridiculous sailor's caps. – I have often wondered why my father told us that anecdote. Probably he felt that it was his father who made a fool of himself, but ostensibly, the point was that we ought to be grateful that we were not subjected to such humiliations.

A final one: when they were somewhat older, my father planned a picnic together with his brother and and they wanted some wine. Then they planned a ruse: the sister, who was the oldest of them, went to her father and asked for two bottles of wine for the picnic. It was granted. Then my father went and it was granted again, although irritably. Finally my uncle made the same request and was told that it was all right and he was not to be bothered any more. So they made off with *six* bottles of wine, got good and drunk and made a scandal. Naturally, all three of them claimed wide-eyed innocence. How were they to know what the wine would do to them?

There are many more anecdotes of this kind, but four examples will have to do. They all depict the character of my grandfather and the young people's reactions. Thinking back on these anecdotes, I believe that my father tried to define his own position between the roles of father and son. On the one hand, he had seven sons and three daughters to manage, and we were an unruly lot. He had to be strict and sometimes not a little despotic. He was also the managing director of a factory with a couple of hundred employees, which means that he was used to making decisions and to seeing that they were carried out. On the other hand, he also remembered very well what it was like to be the son of a true *pater familias* of the old school, a patriarch who brooked no contradiction. At the age of 23, my father was told, with a box on the ear added for emphasis, that he was to *obey* a given order; his father even used the word *lystre* which is otherwise used about dogs and other animals.

He could not, of course, maintain discipline in his family in that manner. Times had changed and besides, my mother would not tolerate it. She was willing to support his authority, but within reasonable limits. I think that the anecdotes he told us served the purpose of demonstrating that we really had very little to complain about. They also created a feeling of intimacy, as Sandra Stahl (1985) points out: by telling these anecdotes, my father made us party to his rebellion against his own father.

It is impossible now to check the veracity of these anecdotes. All the members of that generation are long dead. But my father would often quote the

Italian proverb: *Si non e vero, e ben trovato*. If it isn't true, it's well invented. I believe that some of those stories were invented, or they were at least adapted. And this brings me to the second point I wanted to make: the true storyteller wants to create a pleasing effect. My father had no access to traditional tales. In his social class traditional folktales were not accepted. What does a storyteller do if he has no traditional body of material to draw upon? He draws upon his own experience. We may put it this way: my father turned his childhood into stories, or into episodes of an epic. This epic had only two main characters, father and son; subordinate characters appeared from time to time, but all were subjected to the main theme, the son's epic struggle with his father.

If the family anecdotes are regarded in this way, it appears that they are after all related to the traditional folklore we are all familiar with. It is even possible to apply some of the analytical tools otherwise reserved for traditional narratives.

Last year I had occasion to study Olrik's Epic Laws once more – not the brief exposition which appeared in German in 1909 and in English in 1965, in Alan Dundes' *The Study of Folklore*, but the fuller discussion in Olrik's book *Principles of Research in Oral Narrative*, which was published in 1921 and is soon to appear in an English version. I found that Olrik's observations could be applied to the family anecdotes:

In the first place, Olrik speaks of the *clarity* of the narrative. The Danish word is *overskuelighed*, it means something that is easily grasped; *clarity* does not quite hit the mark, but one has to make allowances in a translation. Oral narratives are always vastly simplified as compared to real life, but simplified so as to emphasize the points the storyteller wants to make. And this characterizes the family anecdote very well.

Next, there is the *Law of Two*. Only two characters at a time are permitted to interact. Sometimes one of them is doubled according to the *Law of Twins*, they then appear as weaker individually than single characters. In the anecdote of the meeting with the King the father is contrasted with two sons and in the anecdote of the wine for the picnic, the father is even contrasted with three characters, the sister and two brothers, but they act in concert and thus the Law of Two is upheld.

The *Law of Schematizing* says that the characters are given only the individual features necessary to the telling of the narrative. In this case, we are dealing with known individuals, but nevertheless, this law, too, is operative inasmuch as only those traits are singled out which are necessary for the telling. If I had known my grandfather only through my father's ancedotes, my impression of him would have been very onesided indeed.

The law of *Plot Constraint* says that the only individual features that count are those which are expressed in action. This is also true of the anecdotes I have told you. They leave little room for reflection or introspection.

The next law is difficult to express in English. Olrik says that the events of the narrative form a clear image in the minds of storyteller and listeners. It may be called the law of *Graphic Expression*, or of *Palpability*. The narrative culminates, according to Olrik, in *tableaux* like the scenes we know from Medieval illuminations of manuscripts, or fresco paintings in churches: the hero confronting the dragon, the fox preaching to the geese, the saint being tormented, etc. Oral narratives possess this quality, they appear to the mind as a succession of vivid images; and this is certainly true of the family anecdotes.

The *Law of Contrasts* says that when two characters interact on stage, they represent the greatest possible contrast with regard to individual features and very often also with regard to what they do. Also this law may be observed in the anecdotes I have quoted.

There are further laws, but they need not concern us here, since they deal with full-blown narratives. The family anecdotes are not really narratives, at least not the ones I know about; they concentrate on a single scene and a single event.

I do not quite know what conclusion to draw from this little analysis. It is obvious to me that the anecdotes my father used to tell us about his own childhood were not haphazard recollections, but carefully selected events, which may have been more or less substantially improved in the telling. It is quite certain that he had not been schooled in traditional storytelling. Nevertheless, he organized his material precisely according to the Epic Laws defined by Olrik on the basis of the investigation of thousands of traditional narratives. Does this mean that the Epic Laws describe a *cultural tradition* which the storyteller picks up unconsciously, or does it mean that they describe *constant characteristics of the human mind*, patterns one falls into because they are the only possible ones? This might be worth discussing.

I shall not try to formulate an answer. For the time being, it suffices to observe that when my father wanted to tell us anecdotes about his childhood, he told them in the manner of traditional tales.

Instead, I want to bridge the gap between the family anecdotes and the more conventional categories of folklore. In this, I can draw upon the experience of others. Many folklorists have for instance studied the phenomenon von Sydow termed *memorate*, the personal recollection of uncanny or supernatural events, or rather, the telling about them. There are uncountable numbers of memorates on record in the folklore archives and they have been subjected to numerous studies. Memorates are of course a construct, a genre which exists only on the scholar's desk. In real life, they form part of the broad and endless stream of what Hermann Bausinger (in *Enzyklopädie des Märchens*) terms "alltägliches Erzählen", everyday narratives, many of which belong to the subcategory which Sandra Stahl (1985) terms "personal narratives". The family anecdotes I am concerned with are a sub-subcategory, and they have attracted little attention so far.

Some of the observations I have made on the family anecdotes seem to be valid for everyday narratives in general. We find the principles of narrative organization described by Olrik as Epic Laws everywhere. And what is more: these little anecdotes often seem to contain the germs of what could easily develop into fullblown tales. To mention but one example: the story of how my father connived with his sister and brother to swindle six bottles of wine from their father is based on one of the best known of all traditional patterns, the confrontation of the little, but smart, character with the big, but dumb one. There is a glee to this sort of anecdote which hardly needs explaining. If we search through a collection of memorates, we find that they are often formed in a pattern that might, we feel, develop into legends if the association with specific people and places was forgotten. Thus, there are the stories about death omens. A certain omen is seen or heard or felt and soon afterwards, a member of the family dies. This sort of thing can easily develop into a regular narrative which will go on even when the persons in question are forgotten. There is nothing new in this observation; I merely want to point out that such everyday narratives as the family anecdotes possess some of the characteristics of traditional tales already at the outset.

The same is true of the relation between everyday narratives and wellerisms. Somebody made a remark which was remembered, like my sister's "Pour cold water into the spout", and it was repeated with a reference to the situation. There is for instance a fine collection of wellerisms by a Swedish dialectologist who was interested in the form and therefore recorded numerous wellerisms which were hardly traditional, or not yet traditional, since they referred to people who still lived or were still remembered (Wide 1957). I think that there is a constant flow of material from the sphere of everyday narrative to that of traditional narrative. The serial numbers are filed off, as one American writer put it, that is, the associations to individuals and their characteristics are eliminated and instead, that which is typical and generally interesting is emphasized. This process may be described in terms of Olrik's Epic Laws, some of which I have referred to above. It seems that they are operative already at the outset, when family anecdotes and similar narrative material are first told in the circle of family and friends, but they go on: the characters opposing one another are more strongly contrasted, they become types rather than individuals; the narrative is arranged so as to be pointed towards a climax, a cutting remark or whatever it may be; one may find repetitions according to the Law of Three etc. I have found illustrative material in Evald Tang Kristensen's collection of anecdotes about clergymen and church service, but it would be easy to find instances elsewhere as well.

The anecdotes discussed here seem to have one thing in common from a psychological point of view: they deal with the problem of identity. I have tried to call to mind the feelings associated with the anecdotes I tell about other members of my family and those they tell about me. As far as I can make out, the situations they deal with are ones in which our mutual relations are defined, or re-defined. In the painful sandbox episode, I distinctly recall feeling threatened. In the case where my sister told my father to pour cold water into the spout, there is the feeling of glee: my father, the undisputed authority of the house, made a mistake, he was made to look ridiculous. It is the same with the anecdotes he told us about his own clashes with his own father: when they swindled him out of six bottles of wine, they outsmarted him and thus put him down. When my father imitated the complaint about the sand in the salad, he was impertinent; he daringly asserted himself by hitting at his father's weak spot. When he told us about the punishment for greeting the King insolently, we could still feel an echo of his outrage at being disciplined in such a humiliating way.

If family anecdotes are to become part of tradition, this very personal feeling is of course insufficient. The individuals have to turn into types. And that is what we find in traditional anecdotes like the ones about clergymen I referred to. Instead of *my* confrontation with *our* vicar, which I remember because I bested him by means of some clever remark, the anecdote that will become folklore will feature *a* clergyman and *a* clever parishioner, and the clever remark will become the point of the anecdote. The parishioner will so to speak assert his identity on behalf of all parishioners.

Family anecdotes may not be folklore, but they are among the sources of folklore.

112

Bibliography

Bausinger, Hermann, "Alltägliches Erzählen," *Enzyklopädie des Märchens* I (1977), p. 323-30

Dolby-Stahl, Sandra K., "A Literary Folkloristic Methodology for the Study of Meaning in Personal Narrative," *Journal of Folklore Research* 22 (1985), p. 45-69

Dundes, Alan, *The Study of Folklore*. (Englewood Cliffs, N.J., 1965)

Kristensen, Evald Tang, *Vore Fædres Kirketjeneste* (Århus, 1899)

Olrik, Axel, "Epische Gesetze der Volksdichtung," *Zeitschrift für deutsches Altertum* 51 (1909) p. 1-12

Olrik, Axel, *Nogle grundsætninger for sagnforskning* (Copenhagen, 1921)

Vide, Sten-Bertil, *Ordspråk, ordstäv och talesätt från sydvästra Småland* (Lund, 1957)

Bengt af Klintberg
(Stockholm)

DO THE LEGENDS OF TODAY AND YESTERDAY BELONG TO THE SAME GENRE?

The Discovery of a Contemporary Legend Tradition

Among the narrative genres in European oral tradition no genre except the folktale has attracted more scholarly interest than the legend. The amount of legend texts collected is considerably higher than the number of folktale texts, since legend tradition has been part of a common heritage in a way that the folktale never was. These legends have above all been collected in traditional rural societies. In recent years, however, a rich tradition of legends, set in a modern urban environment, has been discovered by folklorists all over the Western world. The first scholarly studies were published in the early 1940's.[1] But it was not until the late 60's, when Linda Dégh and her students started to explore legend narration at university campuses and in other urban environments in the USA, that the present folkloristic interest was seriously awakened. Since then progress has been rapid. The most conspicuous contribution so far has been the three books by Jan Harold Brunvand, starting with "The Vanishing Hitchhiker".[2] Since 1982 seminars for scholars interested in contemporary legend have been arranged in Sheffield every summer. While preparing this paper, I have had

---

[1] Marie Bonaparte, "The Myth of the Corpse in the Car," *American Imago*, 2 (1941), 105-126; Richard K. Beardsley, Rosalie Hankey, "The Vanishing Hitchhiker," *California Folklore Quarterly*, I (1942), 303-335; Beardsley and Hankey, "A History of the Vanishing Hitchhiker," *California Folklore Quarterly*, 2 (1943), 13-25.

[2] Jan Harold Brunvand, *The Vanishing Hitchhiker. American Urban Legends and Their Meanings* (New York-London, 1981), *The Choking Doberman and Other "New" Urban Legends* (New York-London 1984), *The Mexican Pct. More "New" Urban Legends and Some Old Favorites* (New York-London 1986).

114

access to Vol: I and II of the seminar reports "Perspectives on Contemporary Legend".[3]

Genre-theoretical Divergencies

Neither Linda Dégh nor Jan Harold Brunvand have expressed any doubt about the generic affiliation of the contemporary legend: it belongs to the same genre as the traditional legend. Linda Dégh states: "The newly discovered narratives cutting across cultural borders and greatly assisted in their spread by mass media, are not really new in form, function, or meaning. Their originality is, in fact, an optical illusion; it reflects an adjustment to a modern environment and does not touch upon essentials below the surface."[4] Brunvand also emphasizes that the contemporary (or urban) legend belongs to the same genre as the traditional folk legend: "As with any folk legends, urban legends gain credibility from specific details of time and place or from references to source authorities."[5] As opposed to the traditional legend in which events generally are dated several generations ago, the modern legend is set in a recent past: "In the world of modern urban legends there is usually no geographical or generational gap between teller and event."[6] Several legend scholars who have participated in the Sheffield seminars have also stressed that the "modern" and "urban" character of the contemporary legend is a surface phenomenon; what we deal with is in many cases an old legend tradition which has been adapted to modern Western society (see expecially Noel Williams' informative article[7]). The same opinion is expressed by Ulrika Wolf-Knuts in a recently published critical examination of the discussion around the genre terminology of the contemporary legend, a study that has been very useful in the preparation of this paper.[8]

---

[3]Paul Smith, ed., *Perspectives on Contemporary Legend. Proceedings of the Conference on contemporary Legend, Sheffield, July 1982* (Sheffield 1984); Gillian Bennett, Paul Smith, J. D. A. Widdowson, eds, *Perspectives on Contemporary Legend*, 2 (Sheffield 1987).

[4]Linda Dégh, "The 'Belief Legend' in Modern Society," in Wayland D. Hand, ed., *American Folk Legend. A Symposium*, (Berkeley-Los Angeles-London, 1971), 55-68, p. 57.

[5]Brunvand, *The Vanishing Hitchhiker*, p. 3.

[6]*Ibid.*, p. 4.

[7]Noel Williams, "Problems in Defining Contemporary Legends," in Paul Smith, ed., *Perspectives on Contemporary Legend*, (Sheffield, 1984), 216-228.

[8]Ulrika Wolf-Knuts, "Modern Urban Legends Seen as Migratory Legends," *Arv* 1987 (printed 1988), 167-179.

Other folklorists have offered another opinion, namely that the contemporary legend differs from the traditional legend to such a degree, that one must call in question whether they belong to the same narrative genre. The views which have been expressed may be divided into two groups, the first saying that contemporary legend much more than traditional legend stands in a close relationship to personal experience stories, the other expressing the view that it has a closer relationship than traditional legend to older and newer humorous genres such as *schwank* and joke. Wilhelm F. H. Nicolaisen and Gillian Bennett are representative of the first position. They have found that a structural scheme for personal experience stories, presented by the linguist William Labov, can also be applied to contemporary legends.[9] Nicolaisen has suggested that folklorists could liberate themselves from a fruitless terminological discussion by abandoning "legend" as a term for those contemporary narratives which until now have been given this name. As a tentative term, while waiting for a more distinct term to be invented, he has suggested "legend-like experience stories".[10]

Nicolaisen and Bennett have also pointed to the close connection between *schwänke* and tall tales and contemporary legend.[11] David Buchan has, without questioning the generic term legend, noticed the great similarities on motif level between modern legends and older *schwänke*, trickster tales and exempla. He has also emphasized the black, violent humour of the narratives.[12] Observations of the background of modern legends in old *schwänke* have also been made by Maja Boskovic-Stulli.[13] In his interesting article on the structure of contemporary legends Daniel Barnes has demonstrated that they often have an elliptic form, where parts of the plot are left to the imagination of the listener. In this they resemble other genres containing a surprise element, such as jokes and riddles.[14]

These divergent viewpoints motivate the question: do the legends of today belong to the same genre as the legends of yesterday? Before answering the question I would like to go back to two earlier occasions, when folk narrative

---

[9]Wilhelm F. H. Nicolaisen, "Perspectives on Contemporary Legend," *Fabula* 26, 1985 (printed 1986), 213-218, p. 215; Nicolaisen, "The Linguistic Structure of Legends," in Gillian Bennett, Paul Smith, J. D. A. Widdowson, eds., *Perspectives on Contemporary Legend* 2, (Sheffield, 1987), 61-76, p. 64; Gillian Bennett, "What's 'Modern' about the Modern Legend?" *Fabula* 26, 1985 (printed 1986), 219-229, pp. 223 ff.

[10]Nicolaisen "Perspectives on Contemporary Legend", p. 218.

[11]*Ibid.*, Bennett (cf. note 8), p. 222.

[12]David Buchan, "Nåtidssagn i dagens Storbritannia," *Tradisjon* 11 (1981), 17-30, p. 27.

[13]Maja Boskovic-Stulli, "Zeitungen, Fernsehen, mündliches Erzählen in der Stadt Zagreb," *Fabula* 20 (1979), 8-17, p. 14.

[14]Daniel Barnes, "Interpreting Urban Legends," *Arv* 49, 1984 (printed 1986), 67-78.

scholars discussed problems which may serve as a background to the present issue. The first occasion was a series of meetings in the first half of the 1960's, devoted to the plans for a European legend catalogue. One of the publications from this period is the report of a "Tagung der Sagenkommission" in Budapest in 1963. The second occasion was the renewal of folkloristic genre theory which took place in the years around 1970.

Tagung der Sagenkommission

The purpose of the meetings of the legend commission, to create a European legend catalogue, was in a way more practical than theoretical, and the commission had no difficulties in coming to an agreement as to the contents of legends: they were about supernatural beings, witchcraft and other beliefs and about historical events and persons. Concerning the form, however, two different views were expressed. One, which had earlier been presented primarily by German scholars, was that legend was such a formless genre, that there was no real use in putting forward a formal definition. In Budapest this view was defended chiefly by Lauri Simonsuuri, who had published a catalogue of the types and motifs in Finnish mythical legend tradition, based on all of the collected material regardless of form. The other position was that it is in fact possible to discern at least three formal categories in the material which had until then been labeled legends. One consists of narratives with a fixed plot, circulating in oral tradition, another of narratives describing the real experiences of the narrator or a person he knows, and the third of non-epic statements about beliefs. This view was represented by Oldrich Sirovatka and Carl-Herman Tillhagen. The latter described a genre terminology, which has since then been accepted by most Nordic folkloristis and which has been formulated most clearly by Lauri Honko.[15] According to this terminology, the term legend ought to be reserved for the first of the three categories: narratives with a fixed plot, circulating in oral tradition. The second category could be called memorate, and the third belief or belief account. The legends could be further divided, according to their distribution, into migratory legends and local legends. Only the migratory legends have a plot interesting

---

[15]Lauri Honko, "Memorates and the Study of Folk Beliefs," *Journal of the Folklore Institute* 1 (1964), 5-19.

enough to be detached from its original context and transmitted to other persons and places, and only they should be registred in a European legend catalogue.

Renewal of Genre Theory

As early as in the 19th century a common thought was that the products of folk literature, when studied in a diachronic perspective, might change from one genre to another. The Brothers Grimm maintained, as is well known, that some of the folktales and legends which they published could be transformations of ancient Teutonic myths. Tylor and his contemporaries considered certain children's games and nursery rhymes to be survivals of past religious rites and incantations. However, the genre concept as such was for a long time rather unproblematic. It seems as if many folklorists agreed with C. W. von Sydow in his view of the genres as being natural, a kind of species within oral tradition, comparable to the species of plant or animal life. Von Sydow himself was inspired by an almost Linnéan explorative urge when he identified and named genres within folk tradition, genres which had earlier had no scientific appellation.[16] A modernization of folkloristic genre theory took place in the years around 1970, thanks to contributions by Lauri Honko, Roger Abrahams, Dan Ben-Amos and others. A representative selection of articles has been published by Dan Ben-Amos in 1974 under the title "Folklore Genres",[17] and they were supplemented by papers in a section at the ISFNR congress in Helsinki in 1974, called "Genre Theory in Folkloristics".[18]

Most important in the genre concept which has since then been generally accepted is that a genre is conceived as a matrix, a set of rules and conventions for how to perform a certain folkloric creation. Genres are, in the words of Ben-Amos, cultural, cognitive categories, together forming the grammar of folklore. A person who has learnt the specific rules and formulae of a certain genre just needs to learn the plot to be able to enact it in accordance with the proper matrix. In a discussion of the genre concept it is furthermore necessary to pay full attention to the difference between scientific and ethnic genres. The former are analytical categories, defined by folklorists, which aim at being transcultural.

[16]Bengt af Klintberg, "Skall vi bekålla våra genresystem?" in Gun Herranen, ed., *Folkloristikens aktuella paradigm* (Åbo, 1981), 75-95, p. 80 f.

[17]Dan Ben Amos, ed., *Folklore Genres* (Austin, 1974).

[18]Folk Narrative Research. Some Papers Presented at the VI Congress of the International Society for Folk Narrative Research. *Studia Fennica* 20 (1976).

They are intended to be ideal-typical, which means that they are created by the scholar on the basis of characteristic, frequent traits in the material. Ethnic genres are those culture-specific concepts used by people in a certain region in order to name and classify their own tradition. Scientific and ethnic genres have been created with quite different purposes: the scientific genres should preferably not overlap each other, and the genre terms should be objective, while ethnic genre terms are sometimes used synonymously and contain evaluations.

The Belief Aspect

Older definitions of the legend often emphasize that legends are narratives, to which people give credence; they are believed to be true. In their important article "Legend and Belief", Linda Dégh and Andrew Vázsonyi rightly criticize such definitions.[19] They are based on the assumption that all individuals in a society share the same beliefs, which is not the case. On the contrary, there is good reason to suppose that a variety of attitudes as to the trustworthiness of legends can be found in all societies. Every society has believers as well as sceptics. The definition therefore must focus not upon the reaction of the listener but on the form: legends contain stylistic features aiming at giving credibility to the content.

My own view is that the belief aspect has a fundamental importance when we discuss legend as a genre. Every folklorist who has studied contemporary legends can testify as to the strong reactions expressed by people who learn that a narrative they have judged as true is in fact a migratory legend. Many will defend its trustworthiness vehemently or make reinterpretations favourable to their belief attitude. This strong reaction is caused not only by their anxiety of appearing prejudiced and naïve. The contents of legends are not neutral information or mere entertainment; they touch upon cognitive areas which are filled with deep emotions and evaluations. A person who is forced to alter his view of the truth of a legend may have to alter his entire world view.

Gillian Bennett has claimed that these emotional pressures do not occur in connection with traditional legends, only in contemporary legends.[20] My experiences have been different. While recording traditional legends in the Swedish

---

[19] Linda Dégh, Andrew Vázsonyi, "Legend and Belief," *Genre* 4 (1971), 281-304 (reprinted in Ben-Amos, cf. note 16, 1974).
[20] Bennett (cf. note 8), p. 229.

countryside, I have several times found them to be perceived as absolutely true. A farmer in the province of Blekinge told me that his grandfather had once been sent to fetch water in a well. The surface of the water was convered with round yellow leaves, which he swept away before he filled his bucket, but one leaf was washed into the bucket. When he came into the house it had been changed into a gold coin. I recognized the legend – it has been told along the Swedish and Finnish Baltic coasts – and I cautiously mentioned that I had heard this in another parish. – Oh, so the story of grandpa's gold coin has travelled that far, was the answer.

It is possible that scholars who maintain that traditional legends are no longer conceived as trustworthy information have been influenced by the popular use of the word "legend" or, with other words, by "legend" as an ethnic genre in Western societies. There one finds a widespread association between "legend" and "old". This connection may be explained by the way in which legends have been collected, and it demands some further comments.

The Popular Notion of the High Age of Legends

Many folklorists working with contemporary legends have certainly had the experience that non-folklorists have difficulties in accepting the word "legend" (Sage, sagn etc.) for this contemporary narrative tradition. In his review of my collection of Swedish legends of our time, "Råttan i pizzan" (= The Rat in the Pizza)[21] a leading Swedish historian wrote that he accepts my definition of the stories as legends "under tacit protest". To him, some were too humourous, others too macabre and frightening to correspond with his concept of a legend. When the book was translated to Norwegian and Danish, the subtitle was changed from "folksägner i vår tid" (= folk legends in our time) to "moderne vandrehistorier" (= modern wandering stories) and "hverdagens vandrehistorier" (= wandering stories of everyday life). Since humourous and horrifying motifs are by no means missing in older legends, the quality that explains the objections to the term legend among non-folklorists must be that contemporary legends do not give the impression of being old.

One reason for this is to be found in the way legends have been collected. In many countries collection has been dictated by antiquarian interests: the value

[21]Bengt af Klintberg, *Råttan i pizzan. Folksägner i vår tid* (Stockholm 1986).

120

of the legends lies in the historical information they have preserved. When, for example, the systematic collection of legends was first carried out in the 17th century in Denmark and Sweden, it was above all legends attached to ancient monuments which were recorded. During the Romantic age a general consensus as to the topics of legends was established: they were about historical events and beliefs about the supernatural in peasant society. If we compare the legends which were collected in Scandinavia in the 1840's and 1940's, we will find a striking resemblance. The field collectors have asked for and received the same wellknown legend complexes. Traces of the radical changes in Western society during that century – industrialization, emigration, political struggle – are extremely sparse.

If we examine the popular or ethnic genre term for legends (Sagen, sagn) in Europe, we will find that they have not been called legends until they were old. Characteristic of a new legend is that it has no ethnic genre denomination at all or at most a neutral appellation such as story or tale. In records of court trials from past centuries one finds several wellknown migratory legends, but they are never classified as legends. These early legend variants, like legends noted by clergymen on visitations, travellers and authors of diaries, often have the same freshness and authenticity as the modern, urban legends that are documented today.

It is instructive in one more respect to confront the popular opinion of what characterizes a legend. A common reaction upon different contemporary narratives, told as true, is that they are "negative", while the treasure of old, traditional legends has a "positive" content. The reason for this is that many contemporary legends reflext prejudices, fears and aggressions against alien elements in one's environment. The old legends, on the other hand, are conceived as positive because they are said to strengthen people's local identity and stimulate their imagination. The reason for these quite contrary attitudes is that the old legend tradition which has survived is the result of a selective process. Many legends reflecting fear and suspicion lost their socio-psychological function when the fears turned out to be unfounded. It is very likely that the contemporary legends which have now been discovered by folklorists will go through the same process of filtration.

The Relationship of Contemporary Legends to Personal Experience Stories and 'Schwänke'

After this background, sketchy as it may be, we can more easily comment upon the genre-theoretical divergencies with which we began. The first question was whether contemporary legends are closer related to personal experience stories than are traditional legends, and if this connection is so strong that a new genre term is required for the contemporary legend. My opinion is that this is an old and wellknown problem within legend research, which has now been brought to the fore again by Nicolaisen and Bennett. Legend scholars have for a long time been aware of the similarity as regards contents and structure between legends and personal experience stories. Some have preferred to see them as two subcategories within the legend concept, others such as Honko have reserved the legend term for narratives with a wider circulation than personal experience stories, which have been kept separate under the genre denomination memorates. Regardless which genre terminology one prefers to use, it cannot be denied that the division made is a division into two scientific, analytic categories. It is only the scholar who knows that one narrative in a repertoire might have an international spread as a legend, while another narrative goes back to a real experience, interpreted in accordance with tradition. The storyteller has no possibility of adopting a macroperspective; for him or her both narratives are classified as belonging to the same category. What is two scientific genres also can be seen as one ethnic genre. The Norwegian folklorist Otto Blehr has argued against the distinction legend-memorate, pointing out that it does not exist among storytellers. Instead he has suggested "folketrofortelling" (folk belief story) as a composite term.[22] The distinction between scientific and ethnic genres makes this controversy unnecessary. All three terms are justified: a folklorist who intends to analyse which narratives might be traced back to real experiences and which ones belong entirely to a narrative tradition needs both "legend" and "memorate". He who analyses narratives from the perspective of the narrators can do with one genre term, and this term could very well be the term used by the narrator himself, the ethnic genre. If we apply this position to Nicolaisen's suggestion, we have to accept that both "legend" and "personal experience story" are needed as long as we have a wider, comparative perspective. If we adopt a perspective focused on performance, the ethnic term of the narrator would be better than "legend-like experience stories".

---

[22]Otto Blehr, *Folketro-og sagnforskning* (Bergen-Oslo Tromsö, 1974).

122

The second issue concerned the striking humourous element in contemporary legends. Does this humour justify defining contemporary legends as belonging to another genre than traditional legends? Here we can establish first that the shift of a narrative type from one genre to another is a wellknown process. That some older *schwänke* appear as contemporary legends is no more remarkable than, for instance, that the same trickster episodes may appear in fictitious as well as realistic genres. Secondly, we can observe that the humour of the contemporary legend is of a special kind. It is often a grotesque and macabre humour, closely connected with fear, and its effect depends to a high degree on identification: the listener is told that this really happened, it could just as well have happened to him. This connection to every-day life distinguishes humourous contemporary legends from jokes and tall tales, which are more (jokes) or less (tall tales) obviously fictitious.

It is moreover a misconception to believe that the humourous element should be less in traditional legends. If we take examples from Scandinavian legend tradition, we find many legends about confrontations with erotic supernatural beings in nature, legends which are at the same time dramatic and which display a grotesque humour. A popular legend about a household spirit on a farm says that he leaves the farm when he is rewarded with new clothes – he does not want to make his new clothes dirty by working. A person tries to fly to the witches' sabbath, but he misreads the flying formula and has to rush up and down the chimney all night. A man meets a giant who cries because he is so small, compared to the other giants. Treasure-diggers experience grotesque comical visions, which make them break the taboo of silence, etc.[23]

The humourous element in contemporary legends thus does not require any other genre appellation than legend, as long as the narratives are performed in accordance with the specific matrix of legend. Having stated this, I would however like to emphasize that I think Daniel Barnes' observations about the structural influence from jokes on contemporary legends are quite right. There is no doubt that elliptic structures and suprising endings are more frequent in contemporary legends than in traditional ones. A historical explanation for this is that legends have always been influenced by other dominant genres. For example the northern Scandinavian mountain pasture culture had a rich tradition of shepherd songs, many of which have been integrated into the legends of the region. The joke is a dominant genre in contemporary urban societies, and it has probably influenced more genres than the legend.

---

[23]Bengt af Klintberg, *Svenska folksägner* (Stockholm 1972).

Conclusion

Like many other legend scholars I see no reason to conceive contemporary legend as a separate from traditional legend. Unlike Bill Nicolaisen I believe that it is worthwhile to tie the study of contemporary legend to that of traditional legend and the legend terminology elaborated for it. Present legend material makes it possible to point at neglected areas in earlier collections, and the old material reminds us that some parts of contemporary legend tradition are insufficiently documented. In the old tradition, legends about supernatural beings, witchcraft and historic events are over-represented, while legends reflecting change and innovations in peasant society are under-represented. It is likely that the recent legend material has an over-representation of sensational, macabre and humourous narratives, while narratives about the supernatural might be under-represented.

A comparison between legends of today and yesterday may as well make us discover that many modern legend complexes have their functional equivalents in older tradition. Many of the legends about UFOs, for example, have their close counterparts in old legends about encounters with the spirits of nature. In both cases the "other people" reflect certain aspects of people's own society. The old legends about the magical practices of people from foreign countries have the same function as today's legends about immigrants maintaining their primitive habits in modern flats, that is, to give contour to one's own normality by describing offences against norms. If we conceive legend as a scientific, ideal-typical genre, then it is my opinion that old and new legends belong to the same genre, which has continuously changed concurrently with changes in society, but which has not been documented continuously – quite the contrary. A historical perspective will help us to see which of the modern legends merely seem to be new and which are really new.

JOKE-LORE

FOLK-LORE

Lutz Röhrich
(Freiburg)

JOKE AND MODERN SOCIETY

In modern industrialized society the joke seems to be the most important and most vivid genre of folk narrative, and perhaps the only one, which is not in danger of extinction. Almost every year new series of jokes appear which, like fashions, flourish for a while, then fade away and can no longer be regarded as contemporary. Most new joke fashions are international, the process of generation is becoming shorter and shorter and the fashionwaves follow each other faster and faster. Wellknown joke cycles of the last decades include surrealistic jokes, moron jokes, cruel jokes, Polack jokes (parallels to Frisian, Aarhusian etc. jokes), Lahian humour, animal jokes such as horse-and-dog-jokes, shaggy-dog-stories, elephant-and-bunny-jokes, wide-mouth-frog-jokes, chicken-jokes or dead-cat-jokes.

People reacted spontaneously with ad-hoc-jokes to current political or technical events. There were space-jokes in reaction to the landing on the moon and space travel. The second Council of the Vatican was accompanied by a great number of Council-jokes (namely priest-and-nun-jokes, celibate-jokes or Trinity-jokes).

> Priests may get married now, but only
> after they turn 80 and get
> their parents' permission!

The election of a Polish pope caused Polish-pope-jokes to pop up:

> What do you call holy water now? – Eau de Pologne!

Even his joy of travelling found its expression in popular mockery:

> What is the difference between God and the pope? –
> God is everywhere, the pope *has been* everywhere.

Even the highly sacred loses its aura of taboo through the comic element and the same is valid for worldly power and the powerful. Peculiarly (and, of course, not just accidentially) catastrophies rather than the positive trends in politics, encourage people to react with jokes. Not even the saddest event is spared from being joked about. Examples are Challenger-jokes, Chernobyl-jokes, Ethiopia-jokes, terrorist-jokes ("When the Red had seized power in Bonn ...") or even Biafra-jokes:

> What is the world's shortest book? –
> The Biafra cookbook!

The violation of taboos related to destruction, death and sickness, nourishes the development of jokes. A great number of jokes, therefore, deals with the sick, addicted, handicapped, mad, stutterers, deaf, smokers and those who are sick with leprocy or AIDS:

> What does A.I.D.S. mean? Ab in the Sarg! (into the coffin with you!)

> What comes after AIDS? After Eights!

> Kriegst Du AIDS beim Zungenkuß, ist es mit der Liebe Schluß
> (If you get AIDS by French kissing this will be the end of love)

It still remains an open question, where this obvious joy of the sickness-phobia originates from.

Another contemporary phenomenon is the mockery and the critique of older narrative genres which still take into account the miraculous and the supernational. Parodistic retelling of well-known, traditional folktales, expecially legend- and fairytale-jokes (Pied Piper of Hamelin, vampires, comical variants of stories of mermaids or nymphs with a fishtail) appear again and again. The best known fairytales are most appropriate for ironic parodies or cartoons: Snow White, Little Red Riding-Hood or the Frog Prince. The surge of Frog-Prince-jokes, some people have maintained, coincided with the marriage of Prince Charles and Lady Diana. In fact, a special synchronicity has been noticed in the USA. This event was among the greatest media-reports of the second half of this century. Infinitely often, too, the fairytale of the Three Wishes has been transformed, mostly within a new historio-political context:

> When Sleeping Beauty was born the three good fairies came with their gifts. The first one said: "She shall become a Nazi", the second: "She shall become a very smart girl", and the third added: "She shall become an honest girl!" Then the black evil fairy who was not invited rushed in. She could not but restrict the gifts: "All three wishes shall

never be fulfilled together. At the most, two at once. If she becomes smart and a Nazi she can't be honest. If she becomes honest and a Nazi she can't be smart. If she becomes smart and honest she can't be a Nazi".

The jokes always make fun of the optimism of the fairytale. They doubt the perfect fulfilment of wishes and the happy ending. There is psychological reflexion and a certain fractioning of the naive fairytale action. The rediscovery of the fairytale by modern pedagoges ("The Uses of Enchantment") created a new wave of fairytale literature on a popular scientific level, and sometimes the fairytale turns from a harmless tale for infants into an aggressive erotic tale:

> Little Red Riding-Hood was walking through the woods on her way to visit her grandmother, when suddenly a wolf jumped out from behind the tree. "Ah-ha!" the wolf said, "Now I've got you. And I'm going to eat you!" – "Eat! Eat! Eat!" Little Red Riding-Hood said angrily. – "Damn it! Doesn't anybody fuck anymore?"

Fairytale-jokes, however, maintain the staff and, very often, even the narrative structure of the tale, but they revise it. They betray a disillusioning, blasphemic scepticism against the romantic idea of true love, and represent a massive critique of a time which doesn't believe in wonders.

In spite of being a narrative which stimulates laughter, the joke has very serious backgrounds. It concerns general social problems and is, therefore, to be evaluated as an indicator of culture and social structure. Alterations of this very structure, of the technical world, of morals and political systems immediately appear in the joke. Dead-baby-jokes, for example, surely have something to do with the growing popularity of the pill and the legalization of abortion. Something similar is happening recently concerning the discussions about gene-manipulations. Mainly, technology has provided new possibilities for the joke: train, car, plane, radio and TV always offer the latest themes for caricaturists. TV-jokes signalize the dominance of TV-entertainment, computer-jokes the inhumanities made possible by data storage. Computer-jokes also disclose the feat of dehumanization of work and of communication. Robot-jokes, finally, have their origin in peoples' fear of loosing their jobs to automatisation. Many modern jokes deal with human beings who are treated just like machines or technical tools.

> Two retired gentlemen watch some autoparts being replaced in a garage. One says: "They ought to know how to do that with us people, too!" and the other responds: "I would be content with another bumper!" (The German word "Stoßstange" clearly refers to the "penis").

Consequently, the motorized society has brought forth car-jokes and driver-jokes. They deal with accidents, drunk driving, troubles with the police, speeding and other traffic crimes, with the special social prestige of some cars, with stolen cars, or with women who cannot drive or their stupid helplessness in accidents. Jokes also have something to do with the commercialization of our industrial society and, therefore, entire series of jokes have been thrown on the market. One example is "Put the Tiger into the Tank". The supply of picture-jokes in which the actors emerge from the TV and carry their problems out into the real world of the audience is inexhaustable. This functions as a signal for the lack of human interrelation in a society, which spends almost all its leisure time in front of the television.

With an incredible speed, jokes adapt to new political constellations: there is not one death of a prominent politician which does not lead to a new joke fashion, as, for example, Breschnev-jokes, Franco-jokes, etc. There is an international type with the structure: "Three statesmen are sitting in a plane ...". Such jokes have been known for some time. The punch-line can differ, the characters may even be interchangeable, the plot, however, will always end with someone's jumping out of the plane. Basically, this is a joke dealing with a method of how to get rid of politicans, which is nothing but an established right in a democracy. The remarkable fact, however, seems to be the method: one can only get rid of them by letting them drop out of a plane. Good jokes never take a threatening situation seriously and neither does the joke narrator. Thus, political jokes, for example, serve as indicators, as barometers for general trends. They depend on the amount of freedom and inner peace of a country and have, therefore, a valve function. A society which is politically suppressed will always produce political jokes. Brecht's dictum, therefore, is still valid: "One cannot live in a country without humour, but it is even worse in a country that *needs* humour!" Political jokes, however, do not only deal with politicians. There are also those jokes which diagnose the inner state of a society. The German anti-Turk-jokes are certainly not only documents of innate xenophobia or unexterminable racism. Rather they have their specific significance within the momentary state of the West German society, and emerge from high unemployment and, simultaneously, very liberal laws for political asylum. There is a hidden longing for more employment and more housing places for the fellow countrymen behind most of the Turk-jokes, which are all generally very brutal and savagely cruel. There are especially prejudices against guest-labourers, who are said to exploit the country economically without paying taxes or without even actually working. Recently, expatriate- or asylant-jokes pursue the same direction. Not seldom, narrators of such jokes are unemployed themselves or worried about losing their occupations. Of course, however, jokes of this sort are also thoughtlessly transmitted by people who do not know what they are doing and who often regret their laughing afterwards because there are so many tactless and instinctless jokes. You can probably do something for the appeasement of a country by not transferring jokes to others. One should, on the other hand, not overestimate jokes, for they will "never be eaten as hot as they were cooked". They serve as *verbal* rather than as *real* reactions to tensions and aggressions. Jokes mock everything deviating from one's own norms, e.g. jokes about minorities, sick, mad or handicapped people. One will always look for and finally find scapegoats in the lowest and weakest social spheres. The one who is least protected usually attracts the aggressions of others. In content and structure these jokes correspond to the Italian- or Polack-jokes in the USA.

Jokes, therefore, are not timeless. Thus, if jokes are correlated with social change one should ask, which of the former joke-categories have shrunken or vanished completely. Today one cannot find "casino"- or "Minna"-jokes (generalizing name for maid servants) because there are no more servants and no more influential, monoculed, arrogant and stupid Prussian officers around. These jokes were current at the turn of the century. Other examples: the nuptial night-jokes or jokes about unmarried couples in hotels! All these well known excitements of past decades are no more ridiculous in times of moral change and growing sexual freedom. The "old maid" and her male pendant the "old bachelor" no longer produce excited laughter in societies where the forms of partnership have changed, where marriages without license and the cohabiting of young people belong to the daily routine, where the titel "Ms." does not differentiate between married and unmarried women. This basic change in intersexual relationships is clearly reflected in jokes. It seems to be one of the consequences of the women's lib movement that one speaks less of "gentlemen jokes" (which were normally told only among men) but rather of "anti-feminist-jokes" which men should not tell at all. For centuries the woman was, as evil stepmother, old maid, maid servant, secretary, whore or sexsymbol, the focus of masculine jokes. As a "wife" she has to be old, ugly, gossipy or jealous, a punishment for her husband, in any case:

What do cafeteria-food and wives have in common? –
You stir around in both lustlessly!

Male joke narrators do not even restrain from killing their wives in fantasy:

"I would like to have arsenic" says the man to the druggist. "Do you have a prescription?" he asks. "No, but I have a photo of my wife!"

In jokes misogynic attitudes like this prove to be stable despite all social transformation and of emancipations. Ecspecially emancipated women are the victims of mockery:

> What is the difference between a wife and a working-woman?
> The wife is an unemployed sex-animal and the working-woman is a nonsexual work-animal.

> Former men are called eunuchs, former women feminists.

But there are also tendencies against men in jokes. The hostile image then refers to the authoritarian patriach as a relict of a pre-emancipated epoch. The cunning and the notorious fraudulence of women has long been common f.e. in proverbs ("Xantippe"). Timeless, also, are the stereotypic anti-heroes of the jokes: henpecked husbands, cuckolds, drunkards, liars, awkward fellows and fools. Well known are jokes about men seeking shelter from emancipated women in "houses for men". Jokes of this sort underline the fact that they are results of a patriarchal culture. Even when men are stupid and weak loosers – as this very often happens in sex-jokes about impotence – mostly men are the narrators. Secretly or in public they identify with the winners, however, clearly sharing great subconscious fear of belonging to the looser group themselves. Jokes about "house-husbands" are not so much antimasculine, but rather should be taken as warnings for other men not to give up their traditional privileges. In this respect, there is hardly any development to be seen since the merry tales of the Middle Ages.

Jokes can even be called psychograms of society when they don't name their protagonists and instead transpose the action into a ficticious world of animals. Animal jokes are almost examples of a translation into another realm and, thus, permit people to talk easily about taboo themes:

> After a long summer break on the alpine meadows two cows meet again in the stable. One cow is happy and relaxed while the other is showing a sad, dissatisfied face. They begin to chat about their summer experiences. Says the happy cow: "I had a splendid summer. There was a young bull on the next paddock who pleased me very much!" "Oh", says the young cow, "my summer was boring and tedious. We had a stupid ox in the neighbourhood, who was always talking about his operation!"

If people chat about fellow-beings by changing them into animals they become careless. This is what makes the topic so interesting for a sociological point of view. "Chicken"-jokes recently became very popular, especially by the caricaturist Peter Gaymann. Here, too, human behaviour can be deciphered from the animal joke: when a cock wants to find out which of the hens had betrayed him by laying a square egg, or, when hens, united for their five o'clock tea chat about their past partnerships and sigh: "All cocks are pigs" one quickly recognizes the human parallels.

Not seldom fables also gain new functions today by becoming mere jokes, e.g. in the stories on "mouse and elephant" or on "cat and mouse". The humour lies in a "morality" which is completely unexpected and shows surprising consequences:

> A mouse escapes from a cat. On a meadow there is a cow, who accidently lets a cowpie fall right upon the mouse unless one can only see the tip of the mouse's tail. The cat sees this tip, draws out the mouse, cleans her victim in the gras and devours it. What is the moral?
> 1) not everyone, who shits upon you, is generally against you,
> 2) not everyone, who draws you out of the shit is your friend,
> 3) if you are already in shit, pull at least your tail!

As the joke serves as an indicator of the society which produces and laughs about it, it could also be characteristic for the individual narrator: "Tell me what you laugh about and I will tell you who you are" is already common in ancient rhetorics. It reappears, modified, with Freud and psychoanalysis. The favourite joke of a patient could be the key for his therapy, because it often betrays his innermost problems. Autobiographical components of a joke should, however, in any case be kept under the doctor's oath of silence. The individual repertory reveals in a mostly painful way the personal interests, the intellectual milieu, the problems and the sublimations of the narrator, which the doctor should keep private. Many people, therefore, never tell their favourite joke and, indeed, nobody can be forced to tell disadvantageous stories of his own. But this provides problems not only for psychologists. Even folklorists have to care about the vital transfer of jokes. We should not only stress the relation narrator/listener but also the general context! A folklorist has to ask not only about the motivation of this or that joke and the "text", but also about the people behind it and *their* motivations; what are the conscious or unconscious elements that force someone to create, to memorize, to suppress or to retell a joke? One quickly hits upon the narrator's personality structure here. With all their inclination for the absurd jokes mostly grasp the characters of the people, for jokes offer models for identification. Therefore, many people maintain to have invented a joke, even if it can be documented in history. And finally, there are the "true stories" which equal jokes. Contemporary folklore research on oral history f.e., should include the autobiographical aspects of jokes, too. Countless are people, though, who need jokes to master difficult or tragic events. According to the motto: "Laughter is the best medicine" some people take jokes as help and compensation for mourning.

I got a letter on my book on jokes. A man wrote: "After an air raid upon Freiburg when I stood watching the ruins of my house the remark 'That could have been worse' came up to my mind and I could not help to associate a joke:

> A man used to repeat "this could have been worse", especially among his compagnions in the inn. Once his friends, being sick of his stereotype repetition, determined to invent a story, which would clearly fobid this answer. "Have you already heard", they shouted one night, "yesterday Miller came home one hour earlier than usual, and met Weber in the bedroom with his wife. He shot Weber, his wife and himself. All three are dead!" "That could have been worse!" "Why, if all are dead?" "If Miller came home earlier the night before, I myself would be a corpse now ...!"

Laughter often functions as a valve in situations of crises. Boccacio, for example, let his novellas be told in a circle of young ladies and gentlemen who escaped to the countryside from the plague in Florence, who, therefore, would have had enough reason to be scared and depressed. But none of the hundred novellas name the plague. There are only joyful themes which cause laughter and forgetting. Jokes, thus, are strongly intertwined with the narrator's biography and the concrete situative context. The best proof is a lamed young man who works on a collection of jokes in order to entertain other patients. By doing so he attracted not only visitors but managers a repertory that helps him to cope with his own sickness. His favourite joke was the following:

> Three handicapped people make a pilgrimage to Lourdes, a blind man, a man with only one arm and a lame man. The blind jumps into the water and can see again, the ampute jumps into the water and gets back his other arm, and the lame dives with his wheel chair. When he comes out his wheel chair has got four new tyres!

Humour, one wants to conclude here, belongs only to those who are also capable of self irony. Thus, Sigmund Freud, when he was 70, called humour the "triumph over the ego".

The favourite joke of a woman who was several times betrayed by her husband, than deserted and finally even tricked out of her money (she is forced now to work as a waitress) is also typical:

> Three women died and come to St. Peter, who asks them how often they betrayed their husbands. "Five times" says the first. She gets a yello habit, and is sent into the left corner of heaven. "Three times" says the second, gets a blue dress and is shown into the right corner of heaven. "Never" says the third wife. She gets a white dress and wonderful pair of wings. And when asking: "Am I an angel now?" she receives the answer: "No, just a stupid goose!"

The autobiographical parallels are obvious. She herself was a "stupid goose" who lost everything because of her decency. But by telling this joke she somehow puts herself above the situation and is able to laugh about herself. If a man had told this joke one could probably have noticed a certain anti-feminist connotation. If a woman tells it, however, it reveals much of her experience and her genuine humour.

> A situation at the market. A husband and his wife ponder over the problem to buy reduced but somewhat spoiled fruit. The peasant who begins to enjoy his pretty female customer, says: "Even a beauty may have a tiny fault!" and then he tells his own favourite joke: "A woman goes to the doctor who makes her undress herself and then flatters her much. Back at home the wife reports this to her jealous husband: "And then he admired my pretty bosom, and then he said my waist was built perfectly!" Says the man: "And he didn't comment on your ass-hole, did he?" Answers his wife: "No, we didn't talk about you!"

Seen from the context this joke is ambiguous and has a double meaning: It is not only the jealous husband who is ridiculous, but also the male listener. The teller's strategy aims at the beautiful wife of his listener and he operates with the devaluation of the rival. This sanktionable action is no taboo because of the fictious character of the joke. The success or the failure of a joke depends on the concern of the listener and his ability to pass over it discretely.

The joke depends on its situative context; told in one place with much laughter it could effect slight smiles only in another, and deep concern, anger and disgust in a third. But context-studies and careful investigations or repertories have not been written yet.

The joke encompasses all sides of life, private and intimate ones as well as public, professional, religious and political ones. It is determined socially as well as culturally and individually. Neither the lowest nor the most elevated themes are spared out. Nothing is too holy, nothing is too secret; everything can be seen through the joke and, therefore, be laughed about. Although the joke causes laugther its background may be serious, no matter if it concerns religion, politics or sex.

As far as the social and the individual components of a joke are concerned, there is much to do – in spite of many hopeful starting efforts so far. There is almost no study on the historical change of the jokes during the last decade or even this century. The main question would be: which needs do new joke-waves fulfil? There are not enough investigations on innovation, dissemination and reception of jokes. There is also lack of analysis concerning topics, tendencies and techniques of jokes as well as of their bearers, on productive, transmissive and com-

136

municative forms. There are also no monographies and no investigations on repertories which could represent as a solid basis for studies of narrator's personalities, investigations which imply the historio-geographic backgrounds, the preferences and the intentions of the listeners, too. Last but not least there is a crucial lack of investigations on the vernacular of joke analyzis (aggression, transfer, deviation from and control of norms, valve function, transpositions into other fields and levels, omission, reducement etc.) which could be elaborated only interdisciplinatorily. All in all: it's a broad field for future folkloristic studies.

Bibliography

Apte, Mahadev, L., *Humour and Laughter. An Anthropological Approach* (Ithaca and London, 1985)

Burns, Thomas A. and Inger H. Burns, *Doing the Wash. An Expressive Culture and Personality Study of a Joke and Its Tellers* (Norwood/Pa., 1975)

Dundes, Alan, *Cracking Jokes: Studies of Sick Humor Cycles and Stereotypes* (Berkeley/Cal., 1987)

Grotjahn, Martin, *Beyond Laughter. Humor and the Subconscious* (N.Y., 1957) Dt. Ausg: *Vom Sinn des Lachens* (München, 1974)

Hirsch, Eike Christian, *Der Witzableiter, oder Schule des Gelächters* (Hamburg, 1985)

Huffzky, Karin, *Wer muß hier lachen? Das Frauenbild im Männerwitz* (Darmstadt, 1979)

Inge, M. Thomas, Ed., *Studies in American Humor* (San Marcos/Tex., 1985), Studies in American Humor 1 ff. (1982 ff.)

Klintberg, Bengt af, "Biafravitsar", in *Tradisjon* 2 (1972), 61-72

Legman, Gershon, *Rationale of the Dirty Joke. An Analysis of Sexual Humor* (N.Y., 1968), Dt. Ausg.: *Der unanständige Witz, Theorie und Praxis* (Hamburg, 1970)

Marfurt, Bernhard, *Textsorte Witz. Möglichkeiten einer sprachwissenschaftlichen Textsorten-Bestimmung* (= Linguistische Arbeiten 52), (Tübingen, 1977)

Moser-Rath, Elfriede, "Frauenfeindliche Tendenzen im Witz", in *Zs. f. Vkde.* 74 (1978), 40-57

Nierenberg, Jess, " 'Ich möchte das Geschwür loswerden'. Türkenhaß in Witzen der BRD", in *Fabula* 25 (1984), 229-240

Oring, Elliot, Ed., "Humor and the Individual", in *Western Folklore* 43 (1984)

Oring, Elliot, *The Jokes of Sigmund Freud. A Study in Humor and Jewish Identy* (Philadelphia/Pa., 1984)

Preisendanz, Wolfgang u. Rainer Warning, *Das Komische* (= Poetik und Hermeneutik VII), (München, 1976)

Röhrich, Lutz, *Der Witz. Figuren – Formen – Funktionen* (Stuttgart, 1977, München, [2]1980)

Röhrich, Lutz, *Tierwitze und was dahinter steckt* (Freiburg, 1977)

Werner, Angelika, "Zur Sozialpsychologie des Behindertenwitzes. Der Körperbehinderte als Witzfigur" (Mskpt.), (Reutlingen, 1978)

Zwerling, Israel, "The Favorite Joke in Diagnostic and Therapeutic Interviewing", in *Psychoanalytic Quarterly* 24 (1955), 104-113

Pack Carnes
(Lake Forest)

THE DYNAMICS OF THE JOKE AS
A CONVERSATIONAL GENRE

The Joke is generally studied outside of its context: as a distinct utterance, or as a member of a set such as a class of jokes (e.g., pseudo-riddles, or "shaggy-dog" jokes) or a joke "cluster", united by theme or by character (e.g., Rumanian Political jokes, Jewish jokes, or "Graf Bobby" jokes and the like).[1] Jokes are found in a number of environments: in sermons, speeches, professional reportage, and – increasingly important for Joke tellers – the printed joke collection. However, the joke is rarely studied in what is most likely its most common context, within a conversation, and as a distinct element within that matrix. The joke is found there among other conversational types: anecdotes, memorates, legends, rumor, as well as a host of interstitial materials. This paper will deal with the joke as a specific genre, although of differing types, in one environment: the "ecology" of conversation.

This context contains a number of forms: information bearing forms such as personal narratives, some legends, rumor, as well as non-informational materials or "pathic" communication forms that are used for various social strategies such as greeting, asking about family members, about summer vacations, etc., all generally done for the sake of the form. These are naturally highly formulaic ("How have you been," "Give my best to your wife," etc.), and are used essentially to elicit a friendly response. Jokes fall into that category. They are non-information-bearing in virtually all cases (save for the very special case of a joke being used rehtorically; a situation that is quite rare in conversation), and the telling of a joke is very much a socially strategic performance.

---

[1] Content seems to be in fact the most common etic and emic classification scheme as well as the focal point of most studies of jokes from Freud on. These studies often effectively remove the true context (that is, the conversational metrix in which they are found), causing various sorts of distortions, not the least of which is the assumption that the jokes found among certain groups have the same effect across that society.

138

This analysis is based upon a rapidly expanding series of recorded conversations, ones that contain a significant number of jokes. These tapes, now 43 in number, were collected by me and by two colleagues, as well as six students all over North America, from 1973 to the present.[2] Of the 43 tapes used in this discussion, 30 were all male (though with one or two females entering into the conversation, but not participating, at a later time in three cases), seven were all-female, and the remaining four were mixed groups from the start.

The joke functions quite differently than other forms as a result of its conversational context.[3] It reacts to its context in specific ways and it, in turn, affects the conversational matrix, at times radically. The joke responds to a number of factors: the composition of the conversational group (sex, age, status features, for example, although this seems to be of less importance as might have initially been thought), the size,[4] relationship of the teller to the other members of the group,[5] and other factors not yet analysed or identified.

---

[2] The recordings were made in eleven American and two Canadian cities, from California to Vermont, and from Montreal to Tucson, Arizona, fairly evenly spread out over the past sixteen years. There are some 30 more that have not yet been analyzed, although some of these have been used in previous studies. The recordings were made without the participants' knowledge by a hidden recording machines. Each participant, however, in each case from which material is used here, was told of the recording immediately afterwards and was asked if she or he would like to have the type destroyed or erased. Each participant was told what the tapes would be used for, and was given the chance to decide whether or not his or her material should be used. All the participants enthusiastically gave their permission for the use of the tapes.

[3] Discussions that approach the specifics of jokes in conversation are rare, but include especially: Harvey Sacks, "An Analysis of the Course of a Joke's Telling in Conversation," in *Explorations in the Ethnography of Speaking*, ed. Richard Bauman and Joel Scherzer (London, 1974), 337-353; Mahadev Apte, *Humor and Laughter: An Anthropological Approach* (Ithaca, 1985); Regina Bendix, "Playing the Joker: Personal Biography and Attitudes in the Study of Joke Performance," *Folklore Forum* 17:2 (1984), 209-219. See also the short description of conversational strategy in Victoria Reifler Bricker, "Some Zinacanteco Joking Strategies," in *Speech Play: Research and Resources for Studying Linguistic Creativity*, ed. Barbara Kirschenblatt-Gimblett (= University of Pennsylvania Monographs in Folklore and Folklife, no 7; Philadelphia, 1976), 51-62. A detailed description of a single joke, although from an entirely different orientation and with different goals is found in Thomas A. Burns, "A Joke and its Teller," 6 vols. (Dissertation: Indiana University, 1972), and Thomas A Burns with I. H. Burns: *Doing the Wash: An Expressive Culture and Personality Study of a Joke and its Tellers* (= Norwood Folklore Originals, no 2; Norwood, 1975), and Thomas A. Burns, "Doing the Wash: Cycle Two," *Western Folklore* 43:1 (1984), 59-70. None of these, however, have results anything like those below.

[4] To my knowledge, this very important factor has not yet been studied. The mechanics of the joke are clearly strongly influenced by the size of the group available to hear it. Just as there seems to be a "critical mass" in conversations, that is, when a group becomes too large for effective communication across the group, satellite conversations begin, breaking up the conversational group into smaller units. The joke often reunites these groups, but not always successfully.

[5] Close knit groups, with members who know each other well seem to be more likely to tell *specific types* of jokes: for example, those with explicit sexual content, racial jokes, and other categories. Jokes are apparently also selected for (or against) as a function of the immediate constitution of the

The joke within a conversational environment can be approached from a number of directions, and in this preliminary study, five are suggested. These deal with the joke in its conversational matrix: 1) as text, 2) from the idea of context, 3) with a consideration of its texture or its performance featues, 4) focusing upon the reception of the text within its immediate environment, and finally, 5) from the point of view of its structure. There is a great deal of overlap in this division, but each brings us closer to the problems of the dynamics of conversational genres as a whole and to those of the joke in particular.

Text. This cover label can be sub-divided into text studied from the point of view of its content, as well as studying the text from the angle of its variants and version. Text also equals text and "sub-text", or "parallel-text", a concept that is at the very heart of the mechanism of the joke, but which would take us too far a field in this limited study.[6] Texts can be approached from the point of view of its membership in the set of all versions of that text. Each version does not represent a different text so much as a different element of the open-ended set that is the true definition of that text.[7] In any given conversational condition, any version – even a truncated punchline of a known joke – is a member of that set. Each functions as a more or less unique text, as the constituents of a conversational group are, on the one hand, unlikely to have heard a version of the joke before (or it would not be told), or it is recalled or mentioned after being "triggered" by the mechanisms of joke "chaining" in conversational context. In these latter forms, the truncated punchline is all that is mentioned, recalling more or less the full narrative, usually with the same sort of laugh response from the other members of the conversational environment. Text, then, is a complex quality, and this quality involves a self-correcting mechanism against the repetition of a joke in an identical context.[8] Often a repeat is possible if the exact composition of the group is not the same, on another occasion.

---

group. Jokes known to have told in close knit groups may be retold in a group containing new members, even just a few new members.

[6]The idea of a parallel text, actually a parallel *Gestalt* of the narrative, is the primary mechanism of the joke. The narration of a joke text creates at least two "parallel texts," which are reunited only at the punchline. One of the fundamental aspects of a "good" joke, is that the parallel narration be instantly understood at the juncture of the two and that the parallel narration be kept completely hidden until then.

[7]This point is made more clearly for other genres in Pack Carnes, "The Proverb and the Fable: Intertexts and Reception," forthcoming in *Proverbium*; and in the introduction to Pack Carnes, *Proverbia in Fabula: Essays on the Relationship of the Proverb and the Fable* (Ber, 1988), 11-14.

[8]There is one fascinating exception to this. During two of the seven tapes of female conversations a particularly dominant narrator was asked to repeat a joke told earlier to the group. No new members had arrived. In one of the joke sessions a particularly fine joke teller was asked to repeat a joke yet *again*, for the third time. Each telling was met with nearly hysterical laughter. There is

140

The text is also variable with regard to characters, especially among the ethnic joke. This is common enough among any number of narrative types and is clearly a commonplace among orally transmitted genres, but there is a subtle difference with jokes. There is in fact a sort of "generic" ethnic joke, with a sort of "plug in" slot for virtually any ethnic group.[9] Contextual considerations often force such changes, using jokes to meet a "target of opportunity", or to make (or to continue) a point about a certain group. And, it must be said again, as the joke is essentially a noninformational form, stereotypes are used as much for instant characterization within any given text as anything else. One example will suffice:

- If an X and Y jump off a tall building, who will hit the pavement first?
- who cares?

Significantly, this joke also has a large number of alternative answers: if a black and a chicano are the chosen ethnic target, the black would hit first because the Chicano stops at the seventy-fifth, the fortieth and the thirteenth floors to spray paint graffiti on the wall. If the two are a "Pollack" (or Italian or Irish, or an "Aggie," a student from Texas A & M University, etc.) and a black, then the black would hit first, because the Polack gets lost, and so on. The exact stereotype is not generally chosen for a specific group any more than being chosen because it fits the ethnic "slot."

The text also is functional. That is, the placing of a joke into the conversational matrix will condition or sensitize that medium by eliciting similar jokes with the same characters, the same stereotype (or with in fact *any* feature of that joke) in a process I call "chaining". Textual studies involving content analysis – even of clusters of joke texts with the same central character or stereotype – are difficult to effect in conversational studies, but there are possibilities here, and I will return to this point later.

Texture or performance features. Performance characteristics are generally of great importance in conversational studies, and are virtually always neglected in content studies. These features are especially important in the telling of jokes, perhaps more so than with any other conversational genres. The performance

---

no other incident similar to this one in any of the male tapes, although there are incidents of a particularly successful joke being repeated for the benefit of people who joined the conversation later.

[9] Studies of the joke from the point of view of content without context very often overlook this very important aspect of joke telling. What is told in one context as an ethnic joke with Italian stereotypes can and very often is repeated the next time with other ethnic groups as the target. Clearly judgments about the "meaning" of jokes depending upon content alone need to be reconsidered when such variation is found.

features range from those needed by a good teller (timing, skill in disguising the "parallel text" until the punchline, etc.) to those that a nondominant joke teller uses, often a disclaimer or humble-formula such as "I can't tell jokes", "I never remember jokes," "I heard this joke from my brother," and the like.[10] The jokes told or attempted by such narrators are often incomplete and are (surprisingly often) finished by a more experienced or more dominant teller. Many performance features are significantly different than those found in other conversational genres in type as well. The use of dialect, for example, is unlikely to appear in general conversation, but might well be found in jokes. In such cases even a language stereotype is acceptable, even essential.[11] A number of the performance features of a successful joke narration are shared with other similar narrative forms, such as historical anecdote, or personal narratives, but jokes do seem to have rather special performance requirements. A receptive conversational matrix tends to draw these out. The performance characteristics are important not only for the enjoyment of the narration, but also for gaining the floor and for cloture of the "performance". Opening formulae need to be delivered properly for communication to be effective. Since the joke is essentially an non-information-bearing genre (although there are didactic and rhetorical reasons for telling jokes in other contexts,[12] this is generally not the case within a conversational matrix) other means have to be employed to gain and maintain the floor. There are successful strategies for establishing the right to tell a joke: not only the opening formulae, but occasionally a special sort of persistence. There is one such extraordinary case on the tapes, which although very specific, still is illustrative of the strategies necessary to be successful in joke telling. At the end of a chain of Italian jokes, a good joke teller began with:

How do you know there is an Pollack at a cockfight?
– someone enters a duck.

There is no indication that this is a three-part joke, and his joke triggered another right away, from another joke-teller:

Why do Italians wear hats?
– so they know which end to wipe.

---

[10]On the use of disclaimers in joke telling, see Carol Edwards, "Stop me if You've Heard this one: Narrative Disclaimers as Breakthrough into Performance," *Fabula* 35 (1984), 214-228.

[11]For the concept of language stereotyping in narration see Pack Carnes, " 'Then Say Shibboleth': Language Stereotypes in International 'Neck-Legends'," *Midwestern Folklore* 15:1 (1989), 15-24.

[12]See Anton C. Zijderveld, "Jokes and their Relation to Social Reality," *Social Research: An International Quarterly* 35 (1968), 286-311.

The original narrator is so concerned about gaining the floor that he interrupts the laughter and has to repeat the opening question:

> There's more: How do you know that there's an Italian at the Cockfight – the fight with the duck. OK, How do you tell that there's a pollack at the cockfight, there's a duck entered, OK? Now: How do you know there's an Italian at the cockfight? – someone *bets* on the duck.

He then keeps talking this time, to retain the floor:

> Wait, wait, there's another: How do you know that the Mafia is at the cockfight? – the duck wins.

Context. The context in which jokes are told both conditions the jokes being told (that is, the text) and is in turn conditioned by those jokes in that the telling of a particular text will initiate one of the most significant features of the dynamics of jokes, the phenomenon of chaining. The immediate constituents of the context determine to a large extent the timing of jokes told, the type of jokes told, both in content and in structure. But the jokes told or other materials that have previously appeared in the conservation strongly condition the jokes told from that point on. This is one of the most important considerations of jokes seen in context. The context is *itself* the primary triggering device for the continuation of jokes from the dominant and sub-dominant narrators. There is naturally a possibility that a joke might be told because of a point to be made later on, or as a rhetorical device to introduce or to drive home or illustrate some point of view. Although this use is perhaps more likely to occur in a monologue rather than in conversations, there are two recorded instances in my data of a conversation approaching a monologue with a single dominant narrator. But in nearly all other cases of jokes told after the beginning of a conversation, something in that conversation precipitated the telling, usually another joke of the same type.

Reception. Virtually all the points made about the content and its context can be approached from the point of view of the hearer as well, and with some important consequences that very much affect the conversation's future. The understanding of a joke by the immediate conversation members, and understanding the joke on a level that elicits a response is clearly either a stimulus or a deterrence to future joke telling. The consequences of visible positive reception can encourage or discourage an otherwise non-dominant teller to attempt a joke. And the reception of the joke will clearly affect his participation in further attempts during the same session. The immediate reception of a joke is not only important for itself, but also conditions future joke participation. Jokes are notoriously polyvalent. Jokes are very often not understood completely or not understood in precisely the way the narrator intended. A participant who does not understand the joke is unlikely to contribute further jokes on the same chain, and will often in fact interrupt it by asking for an explanation of the joke.[13] Performance features obviously mediate the possibilities of recognition of the proper "field" (the parallel field) united at the punchline, guiding the receptor to the proper conclusion. The receptor needs to be aware of the alternative field possibilities, and the joke teller must choose the text well, using only those jokes for which his context is a legitimate target. The reception of the joke "positively," that is, with the appropriate laugh response, depends upon preknowledge of the alternative field possibilities. One of the very understudied aspects of jokes in context is the feeling of belonging that arises from having understood a joke told with exceptations that the target receptor is aware of the pre-requisite materials that allow just that. The reception of the joke causes both the enjoyable result and the subliminal message that the receptor is in harmony with the joke teller. The reception of the joke thus acts upon the conversation, almost always making it enjoyable and difficult to terminate, indeed conditions further joke participation – until the supply of jokes runs out.

The conditioning and prompting of further jokes occurs in a variety of ways: which include inhibiting or restraining further attempts in a subdominant narrator, and perhaps paradoxically reinforcing the attempt of a dominant narrator, who might redouble his efforts to "get one off," to a non-responsive "ingroup".

There are a number of other considerations involved in the reception of the joke in context. These include function (whether didactically intended, didactically received, the response of an "outgroup" member to the content of a specific stereotype, the contrary response of "ingroup" members.[14] Although it appears that the first narrator of a class of ethnic stereotypical joke might well take that into consideration (occasional tentative openings are heard: "This is a terrible joke," and the like), it seems just as certain that once the subject is broached, no restrictions at all are placed upon succeeding elements in the "chain." The responses to the first joke might well condition the observed "respectability" of

---

[13]This happened in a large number of cases. I do not think that it is at all the case that ethnic jokes are all received the same way as a number of studies assume. In any given joke-telling session, some ethnic jokes often do not "mean" anything at all – except of course a laugh.

[14]See especially, Howard J. Ehrlich, "Observations on Ethnic and Intergroup Humor," *Ethnicity* 6 (1979), 383-398; and Stanley Brandes, "Jewish-American Dialect Jokes and Jewish-American Identity," *Jewish Social Studies* 45:3-4 (1983), 233-240, for excellent discussion of the effect of ingroup humor in the USA. A Welsh example is investigated in Nicholas Gadfield, et al., "Dynamics of Humor in Ethnic Group Relations," *Ethnicity* 6 (1979), 372-382.

144

such jokes, although as we have seen, content is only one of the triggers for joke chaining. My sample is not large enough to make any firm statements about the receptor's response to stereotypes, but other research has suggested that there are differences in "ingroup" and "outgroup" responses (see note 14). Further research is needed to understand how this reception conditions the telling of further jokes in a direct chain.

The chain involved is a specialized unit within a joke's conversational matrix. The boundaries around the joke telling also condition their reception. Unlike many other types of conversational forms, the joke draws in a tight boundary around itself, and all satellite conversations cease or are caused to be stopped by members of the conversation. The joke is given every chance to be heard once the opening formulae are offered and received. This opens another series of possibilities within the joke's reception field. The joke might begin a series of jokes on the same or a similar topic. Ethnic jokes might trigger another ethnic joke, with the same stereotype as the first, or it might evince a totally different stereotype, but still an ethnic joke. Or a joke might be elicited within the group by the structure of the first joke (pseudo-riddles seem to act as an invitation to other jokes of the same format, rather than staying within the ethnic stereotype established by the first joke). Thus: a pseudo-riddle joke about a "Pollack," is just as likely to bring forth another joke similar in structure, rather than another joke specifically on a "Pollack."[15] The connections that trigger joke motifs are often deeply submerged in the conversational past. Virtually anything or aspect of any joke (or conceivably anything in the conversational stream) can trigger another joke.

Structure: At least one structural element is important to the joke as a conversational genre: the boundaries.[16] The joke shares with a number of forms the idea of the introduction formula. Just as "Once upon a time," signals a Märchen,

---

[15]Of great interest is the "fashion" demonstrated by these. During the midseventies joke-sessions demonstrated that the telling of one of the "in fashion" types: the "pollack" jokes, for example, would elicit a number of similar Pollack jokes, and a "light-bulb" joke would trigger a series of "light-bulb" jokes. But when the joke motifs available at the moment dried out, a "pollack" joke often elicited another ethnic joke or a "light-bulb" or an "elephant joke". It is important to recognize – and here again, the context study alone can demonstrate this phenomenon – that after the supply of "light-bulb" jokes was exhausted, there was in every case, a shift to another type of joke of the same structure. Later on in the session, another light-bulb joke shows up, and is offered even though an entirely different variety is in progress.

[16]Obviously many other structural considerations are important for various reasons. One comes to mind as very worthy of continued study: some jokes have their structure altered by having already been heard by most of the people present, and, when triggered, are not repeated, but referred to only in truncated form, generally just the punchline. The effect of this, when referring to a very successful joke is often as strong as at the first telling.

jokes have culturally specific opening lines. In American joke sessions, these is often a variant of "Did you hear the one about ..." The joke's uniform use of stereotypical characterizations allow a narrator to begin with an opening line such as "A Puerto Rican and an Italian walked into a bar ..." or "A New Yorker was driving down the street ..." and have all the members of the conversation immediately recognize that they are hearing a joke.

This opening formula is very important, and has an interesting effect on the other members of the conversation. It generally stops everyone from talking and even often stops satellite conversations betwen two or more members somewhat removed from the narrator. This phenomenon is very effective. Most other conversational forms (such as anecdotes, legends),[17] the very special opening silences what we might call a critical mass of listeners. Even those who had heard the joke before will generally not violate these boundaries. The "membrane" enclosed in narrative is unlike any other modern conversational genre in this regard. The other end of the joke is also marked as a definite line, the punchline with its desired response: laughter.

The text, incidentally, functions within the matrix both to trigger new jokes and to cause "echoes" in many cases. These echoes are found in a surprisingly large number of cases. At the end of the joke, with the punchline and the laughter (often over the laughter) other members of the conversation will offer, one or more alternative punchlines to the joke just heard, introduced with formulae such as: "The way I heard it was ...," or "I heard it with a New Yorker ..." There are even jokes about these "echoes" satirizing in "meta-jokes", the telling of jokes by different groups or individuals.

In these five areas, I have wanted to demonstrate that *in situ* studies require a different set of parameters and effect different sets of results. Viewed from these points of view, the joke takes on dimensions that are closer to its actual form and effect. We see that jokes are quite often fragments, sometimes only punchlines, instead of the reconstituted forms found in most studies. We see that the choice of a particular joke is as likely to depend upon a key or phrase or even the structure of the joke-type than upon the content of that joke.

I do not wish to claim that non-contextual studies of the jokes are of limited value. I have published some of them myself; but a study of jokes in their natural

---

[17]The pseudo-riddle has the same effect of course. The question form is unmistakably a joke, and not a true riddle. However, as the pseudo riddle is not meant to be answered (unlike the true riddle), there are many awkward moments in the telling. Part of this is reception. Very often the pause between the first line of the pseudo-riddle and the punchline answer is misjudged by the narrator, or the narrator waits an uncomfortable length of time until some one says "I don't know." or "I give up."

environments puts a significantly different light on the form, showing it to be a dynamic, ever-changing form. Within the ecology of the conversational stream, jokes are found embedded like special cells, changed by the matrix and radically altering the immediate conversational environment and the future course and direction of that stream.

Ulf Palmenfelt
(Stockholm)

STEREOTYPICAL CHARACTERS IN EROTIC JOKES

Every week several hundreds of jokes and anecdotes are sent to Swedish magazines by readers. A small number of these are published, often together with the sender's name. The publication of these jokes can be seen as an ongoing process performed on a public arena by a small group of specialists conducted by a powerful stage director, the editor of the magazine's comic section, and with the readers as a silent audience.

For this investigation I have examined almost 2.000 jokes sent by readers to one so called gentlemeen's magazine during one month, March of 1983, and I have read the comic sections of four "gentlemen's magazines" from the last ten years. In this paper I will confine my interest to the jokes with erotic content, and by this I mean jokes concerning the relations between the sexes.

The four major Swedish gentlemen's magazines sell between 40.000 and 75.000 weekly copies each (1988). All of them have a recurrent comic section to which readers are invited to contribute. They also publish richly illustrated feature stories (often about sensational, shocking or entertaining matters), pictures of unusually beautiful cars and motorcycles, pictures of nude girls and – after 1981 – pornographic pictures. All of them have a section where readers write about their sexual experiences – and a subject of folk discussion in Sweden is whether these stories are made up by the editors to fool the readers or vice versa.

When you read the comic sections of these magazines you soon start to recognize the names of certain contributors. About 30 or 40 persons participate with one or several stories almost each week in almost all four magazines. A glance into other types of magazines that also carry a comic section – family, women's, trade unionist and daily newspapers – shows that the very same names reappear in them. There exists a small group of story writing specialists that supply different kinds of weekly magazines and daily newspapers with material for their comic sections. On the other hand, in my material a few persons can be found who

148

wrote very long and very private letters with very few jokes in them that never were published.

This social aspect of the letter-writing is often encouraged by the editors of the comic sections. These appear with their photographs – sometimes in several places in the same page. In their accompanying columns they tell about their children, their pet animals, and their everyday life. The obvious goal is to create a picture of a completely normal fellow human being that leads an ordinary life and who can be trusted to receive your private letters and your – sometimes – obscene stories with tolerance and understanding. Of course it goes without saying that an editor who wants to receive erotic jokes cannot expose an attitude of moral condemnation. Instead bad language, racism and cruelty in the readers' stories are silently excluded from publication. Stories that touch upon the taboo limits may be published under the head-line "This Week's Worst One" together with a picture of the editor where his face is supposed to express utter disgust.

Other means of stressing the importance of the social contact are that the editors mention contributors by name, quote telephone calls from readers, and urge readers to contribute to their pages. Like many other public persons the editors like to emphasize their own popularity. One of them once wrote about how he intervened to protect a lady who was attacked by a drunken man in an underground train in Stockholm. The drunken man looked at the editor with a glassy look for quite a while, then he said: "Did you ever hear the one about the guy that was impotent?"[1]

The editors use three kinds of arguments to encourage readers to contribute to their pages. The first one suggests that there exists some kind of in-group solidarity between the contributors to the comic sections. The editor may invite the reader to "join the company"[2] or he may scorn the reader for laughing at other person's stories and not returning some stories of his own.[3] Since the contributors' names and domiciles are published together with the stories, writing to the magazines also offers an obvious opportunity of seeing one's own name in print, which may tempt the reader's vanity. In a letter to me one of the contributors wrote that he never told a joke orally, but that his workmates often told him stories since they knew he "contributed to different magazines with stories and so on."[4]

---

[1]Fib Aktuellt 12 (1979), p. 68.
[2]Stopp Fib Aktuellt 41 (1985), p. 28.
[3]Stopp Fib Aktuellt 43 (1984), p. 78.
[4]Ernst Holmgren, Letter from April 2nd (1988).

The second argument used by the editors is trying to arouse the instinct for competition in the readers. The comic section of a magazine can be seen as a synthetic scenario for a story telling session where different tellers appear on the stage inspired by the topics already heard and influenced by the linguistical style already used. Of course the smoothness in the performance, the individual subordination in favour of the total impression, and the overall harmony in this synthetical story telling session would be impossible without the skilful stage direction of the editor who tries to be invisible but whose intervening measures include even the smallest details.

It would be wrong, however, to describe the contributors as inactive pawns in the game passively moved around by a resolute director. Without their industrous fieldwork in collecting stories from oral and written sources and without their energy and creativity in writing down these stories there would be no comic pages in the magazines. Rather I would suggest the image of an ongoing collective process where everybody involved influences the others and is influenced by them.

For instance a common linguistic code has been developed. Stories can be introduced by different formulaic expressions: "And then we have the one about ..." which suggests that this story has been preceded by several others. Or "It certainly aroused big excitement when ..." which is a very literary opening formula supposed to create curiosity about what is coming, but impossible to use when the story is told orally. Some stories are told in the form of a dialogue:

– Do you want to come along to the discoteque?
– No, I always get pregnant there.[5]

Others are told as a monologue:

I didn't know what happiness was until I married Mona, and then it was too late.[6]

Some are told in a conversational manner using the first person singular like a stand up comedian chatting with his audience:

Did you hear about the young bride who gave her husband a dozen of oysters and afterwards was disappointed that only seven of them had worked?[7]

---

[5]Fib Aktuellt 46 1/2 (1978), p. 77.
[6]Aktuell Rapport 39 (1983), p. 55.
[7]Stopp Fib Aktuellt 9 (1984), p. 70.

The characters in the stories are given stylized designations consisting of an adjective and a name usually beginning by the same letter. Naturally it is impossible to translate these denominations but to give you an idea about how they may sound I have made up some examples in English: Willing Wilma, Busty Betty, Silly Susan, Tipsy Tim, Bragging Burt.

The element of competition was further emphasized in one of the magazines, which for a couple of years published a "top twenty ranking list"[8], where story-tellers could challenge each other by sending in a story which the challenged person had to beat by returning an even funnier one. The editor was the judge who chose the winner of the "match". A similar idea was the basis of a program in Swedish radio, where listeners were supposed to telephone to the program and tell a joke which the program makers "exchanged" for another one, if they liked it.

The third argument is economic. Some magazines pay a small amount of money, the equivalent of about 4 USD, for each published story. A series of six or seven published stories may be awarded 15 USD.

In this continuous reciprocal performance different moral and ethic standards and sets of values are demonstrated through the stories. In the erotic jokes these are expressed partly in the form of stereotypical characters, partly in the form of stereotyped opinions. By stereotype I mean the belief that the members of a group possess certain external and internal qualities because they are members of this group.[9]

The male stereotypical characters can be seen as incarnations of men's dreams about what kind of man they would like to be, while the female stereotypical characters impersonate both men's wishes for attractive and sexually willing women and their disappointments with real women who were not like the ones in the stories.

First I will mention three male stereotypical characters: the count, the Finn, and the traveling salesman.

The count is elderly, aristocratic and always sexually alert, even if sometimes he wants more than he actually manages to perform.

---

[8]Veckans Stopp (1981-1982).

[9]Magne Velure, "Rykten och vitsar om invandrargrupper," in Nils Arvid Bringéus and G. Rosander, eds., *Kulturell kommunikation* (Lund), p. 145; – cf. also Magne Velure, "Djävla utlänning! Rykte og vitsar om innvandrarar i Sverige," *Tradisjon* 13 (1983), pp. 3-21.

> The 80-year-old count called for his servant and said: "Today I'm in the mood for sex, James. Go up to the countess for me, will you?"[10]

Thanks to his noble position the count is able to disregard social decorum: he is a glad anarchist satisfying all his primary needs and leaving all the dull everyday problems to his servants. In the stories the count stereotype represents the longing for free, uncomplicated, irresponsible sexuality, but also the hope for a vital old age.

The Finn is perceived as standing on a lower level of civilizisation than the Swedes. He has an animal force which makes him sexually powerful, immune to alcohol, and a fierce knife fighter, but he also has the courage to ignore regulations coming from government and authorities. In the stories two different attitudes can be found: one of repudiation combined with gratefulness that "we" have advanced higher along the ladder of development; the other one of admiration and envy of the untamed powerfulness of our Eastern neighbours.

> When the workmates asked the Finn why he always sat on the toilet, he answered that the doctor had warned him against lifting heavy objects.[11]

In the erotic stories the Finn stereotype represents the dream of brutal, animal sexuality undisturbed by psychic problems and by modern society's demands.

In *The travelling salesman* stories it is always night and the main person is always away from home, in a hotel or in a farmhouse where there lives a young and beautiful -- and willing -- daughter.

> Once a travelling salesman received a telegram from his wife reading "Don't forget you are married". He answered immediately: "Sorry. Got the telegram too late."[12]

The travelling salesman stereotype represents the dream of leaving the dull everyday life, the possibility of experiencing an erotic adventure in a foreign but stimulating surrounding, but it also contains the presumption that a woman alone in a strange hotel feels the same longing for night company as a man does. As a married man you can dream of being in the lucky position of the travelling salesman, but he is also a dangerous person, for it may be your wife he is seducing the next time. In the stories, the doctor, who may see your wife naked, and the postman, who comes to your house when your wife is alone at home, may be as dangerous as the travelling salesman.

---

[10]Fib Aktuellt 12 (1982), p. 77.

[11]Fib Aktuellt 49 (1978), p. 78.

[12]Lektyr 38 (1984), p. 96.

152

Among the female stereotypical characters I am going to mention the nun, the secretary and the unfaithful wife. The nun is a grown-up woman that is sexually unexperienced like a child and totally ignorant of the appearance and functions of a man's body. She may mistake his sexual organ for a trumpet you are supposed to blow or for a machine that produces soap as you pull it. To a man with a regular sexual life the nuns' chastity is hard to understand. In the stories it is explained in three ways: either the nuns are old bores that deny every form of pleasure, or they are so starving for sexual satisfaction that it is dangerous for any man to approach a convent, or they satisfy themselves with candles and other oblong objects:

> The abbess told the nuns: "Today we will have bananas for dessert." The nuns shouted for joy until she added: "Mashed bananas."[13]

The nun stereotype serves as a model of thought for mens' fantasies about how a woman without sexual life reacts.

The secretary is young and beautiful, easy to seduce and so stupid that you need not fear to be made responsible for any undesirable consequences. She is the one that lies down on her back during the fire-drill because she thought it was an office party. Many famous actresses have pulled on her blond wig to play her part on the white screen. She is the late sister of the seductive Eve of the Garden of Eden and of Alexander's young fiancée who rode naked on the back of her boy-friend's teacher, the old Aristotle. Maybe this stereotype was created during the Middle Ages as an inverted counterpart of the frail and bloodless noble lady of the ballads. In the stories of today the secretary stereotype represents mens' dreams of the attractive ever-willing girl that never needs to be persuaded, but the frightening reverse side of the coin is that her nymphomaniac desire may be too demanding for the poor man's capacity.

The wife of the erotic stories is uninterested in having sex with her husband but he is convinced that she betrays him as soon as he turns his back to her.

> A farmer's daughter was seduced by a travelling salesman. The furious farmer shot at the salesman with his gun and yelled after him: "You have taken advantage of my daughter!" The salesman, still running, yelled back: "Yes, and your wife too! She is the one that loaded the gun with blanks!"[14]

Not only does the wife deny her husband the sexual pleasures of marriage, she denies him all other pleasures too. Marriage in the erotic stories is a prison

---

[13]*Ibid.*
[14]Fib-Aktuellt 46 (1987).

to the husbands and their wives are the gaolers. A man who feels that his wife denies him satisfaction of his sexual needs may dream of replacing her with a more willing woman. Therefore the erotic stories have an abundance of unfaithful husbands acting out this dream. The wife stereotype visualizes the disappointment felt by sexually unsatisfied husbands, but also their fear that the wives' lack of interest is a proof that she satisfies herself with somebody else.

I have suggested that the comic sections of the Swedish gentlemen's magazines can be analyzed as a public arena where a small group of experts performs a weekly story telling session under the direction of the editor. This exchange of erotic stories can be seen as a continuous process where a collective set of values is gradually formed. In summary this set of values expresses a dream of an uncomplicated, irresponsible, animal-like sexuality undisturbed by physical limitations or by psychic problems. This sexuality is preferably satisfied in new, stimulating surroundings together with beautiful but unintelligent girls that don't have to be persuaded and don't demand more of you than you can manage – and they never interfere with the rest of your life.

Jawaharlal Handoo
(Mysore)

FOLK NARRATIVE AND ETHNIC IDENTITY
THE 'Sardarji' JOKE CYCLE

The ethnic and linguistic diversity in India is almost as complex as one notices on the European continent. About 1652 languages[1], belonging to four major language families (Indo-Aryan, Dravidian, Austro-Asiatic and Tibeto-Burman) of the world are spoken on the Indian subcontinent.[2] This linguistic diversity is matched by the ethnic diversity of equal strength which one finds on the subcontinent. The problems of linguistic minorities and smaller ethnic groups as well, have been well discussed academic subjects in Indian anthropological, ethnological, folkloristic and linguistic circles[3].

Under these linguistic and cultural circumstances, it is not unnatural to find ethnic folklore emerging as a dominant form of folklore representing ethnic identity. No other verbal expression can measure this kind of ethnic identity more accurately than folklore in which it finds spontaneous expression. More often than not, this kind of folklore is generated and perpetuated by ethnic stereotypes, i.e., the stereotypes one ethnic group can have about another ethnic group and also about its own group. Dundes writes:

> Part of the reason for this may be that ethnic slurs [jokes] are part of ethnic identity. While many may protest that the slurs are nothing but false caricatures, they may secretly take pleasure in the fact that their group is vital enough to stimulate such traditions. Then again there is also the possibility that the stereotypes may have some basis in ethnographic fact.[4]

---

[1] Cf. *Census of India* (Calcutta, 1981).

[2] Jawaharlal Handoo, "South Indian Folklore Studies: Growth and Development", in *Journal of Folklore Research*, 24, no. 2 (1987), 136-155.

[3] Jawaharlal Handoo, *Folklore: An Introduction*, Central Institute of Indian Languases (Mysore, 1989); cf. also Jawaharlal Handoo and Agarwal, eds., *A Survey of Indian Folklore*, Central Institute of Indian Languages (Mysore, 1982).

[4] Alan Dundes, "A Study of Ethnic Slurs: The Jews and the Polack in the United States," *Journal of American Folklore*, 100, no 332, April-June (1977), p. 220.

So one can see Kashmiri proverbs based on stereotypes about Pangabis, Bengali folktales about Biharis, Tamil folksongs about Kannadigas and similar ethnic folklore in every part of India.

Folklorists in India, surprisingly enough, have not shown any interest in the collection, classification and interpretation of ethnic folklore. One can see two reasons, among others, for this kind of backwardness among Indian folklore scholars. In the first place, ethnic folklore is believed to be offensive in the sense that it hurts the feelings of the members of the ethnic group on whom the joke or any similar item of folklore is based. "Almost all jokes are based on someone else's misfortune".[5] That, perhaps, becomes the basis for humour.[6] Furthermore, it seems that many items of ethnic folklore in India are essentially "erotic" or "dirty" and such scholars prefer to ignore them, because traditionally folklore scholars in India consider it bad and unscholarly to work with such materials. These and other attitudes have kept the fields of ethnic folklore, humour, and the "dirty" joke untouched so much so that there hardly are any foot steps which I could, perhaps, follow in this brief study of the ethnic joke.

Ethnic folklore in India is, as I suggested above, due to reasons of language diversity, geographical and political constraints, forced to remain confined to certain linguistic and geographical regions. So Panjabi jokes and other kind of ethnic folklore are generally current in Panjub and so are Kashimiri jokes current in the Kashmiri speaking area. One does not normally expect a Bengali joke about Biharis being told and enjoyed in a Tamil speaking region. However, the famous and very popular joke cycle about the *Sardarji* (Sikhs) seems to have broken these linguistic and geographical barriers and has achieved the status of a pan-Indian joke cycle. This joke cycle seems to circulate in India on three levels of linguistic communication: (1) it is narrated (performed) in the local language (Tamil, Panjabi, Kashmiri, etc.), if the narrator and the listener share the language. (2) It is narrated in Hindi (Hindustani) – the most popular lingua franca spoken in almost all big towns of India. It is in this lingua franca that this joke cycle is mostly current and has achieved the status of being the most widely shared joke cycle in India. (3) It is narrated in English, more specially the Indian dialect of English, if the narrator and the listener do not share the local language or the lingua franca. For instance, if a Tamil speaker and a speaker of Oriya

---

[5]Cf. Roger Simon, "The Jokes that speak the Unspeakable," *Los Angeles Times*, 23 February, 1986, Pt. iv. P. II. – cf. also Elliot Oring, "Jokes and the Discourse on Disaster", *Journal of American Folklore*, 100, no. 397, July-September (1987), 276-286.

[6]Cf. *ibid.*, passim.

meet in London and want to share a *Sardarji* joke, they will most probably share it in this form of English.

There are no formal or public performances of this joke cycle. Intimate members of a small non-Sikh ethnic group may share the joke "privately". A *Sardarji* joke may be fired and enjoyed even when one of the members of the group happens to be a Sikh. However, on no occasion, I could find the Sikh member or members enjoying the joke. They may, however, pretend to enjoy the humour of the joke by smiling or joining the group laughter. Surprisingly, on many occasions, I noticed that the Sikh member of the non-Sikh group may, under such circumstances, fire a counter joke about a non-Sikh ethnic group, particularly the Baniyas (the business caste of north India) and the non-Sikh members, on such occasion, did not seem to be enjoying such jokes. However, they pretend enjoying the joke about the members of their own larger ethnic group. There is a very fine joke cycle current in India, particularly Panjab, about non-Sikh ethnic groups such as Hindus (Baniyas, RSS activists, and other Hindu groups). This cycle, unfortunately, is confined to the state of Panjab and its surrounding areas, and more so among the Sikhs only; who, however, form the majority in that State and the region. In no way have these "Hindu" jokes attained the status of Pan-Indian joke cycle yet. This joke cycle, therefore, does not form a part of the data I have chosen for this brief study. I am, however, aware that a thorough study of such a joke cycle will be highly beneficial for a complete understanding of folklore and ethnic identity. In this respect, then, my brief study is very introductory and fulfills partly the objectives of understanding the ethnic identity in relations to joke cycles. Let us examine some examples of the *Sardarji* joke cycle.

1. On of the dominant traits of the *Sardarji* joke cycle is that he is always shown as a stupid. The following example serves to illustrate the point:

One *Sardarji* named Malika Singh (in some versions India's fast runner of the sixties) was sun-bathing in some park in England. Asks someone:
"Are you *relaxing*"?
"No, I am *Malikasing*": Says the fast runner.

The stereotype is that a *Sardarji* is not able to distinguish between different words in English. He is not enough "English educated" as the elite of India generally is. The stereotype may lie in the ethnographic fact that most of the sikhs traditionally are associated with jobs that do not need good knowledge of English. For instance, in this case, an athlete whose physical fitness is more important than the proficiency in English language.

2. *"Sardarji* is dirty": is another trait which dominates this joke cycle. The following examples will serve to illustrate the point:

> A *Sardarji* shits in the toilet in a suburban London hotel. He just does not know how to flush the shit down. He rolls the shit neatly in a paper and hurls it out through the window. The roll hits the wall next door. That makes things worse. He befriends the waiter of the hotel.
> Says the *Sardarji* to the waiter:
> "If you remove that thing from that wall, I will give you five pounds".
> The waiter looks out at the wall and is shocked. Says he:
> "If you tell me how you reached up there to do that thing, I will give you ten pounds".

Sikhs of India are identified by their unusual long hair, beards and the headgears. This appearance seems to have generated a typical stereotype among the clean-shaven Hindu majority, that they breed lice in their hair and are therefore dirty and lousy. Consider the following example:

> A *Nihang* (more orthodox) *Sardarji* brings his horse along with him inside a passenger train car. The ticket examiner demands a ticket for the horse. The *Nihang Sardarji* argues that only humans pay for rail journeys, animals travel free. The ticket controller, however, insists on paying the fare for the horse. *Sardarji* removes his headgear, throws his long hair loose and asks the man to see for himself how many animals (lice) he is carrying with him in his hair, and how on earth is he expected to pay for the animals travelling with him.

Yet another example which is more likely an international joke type supports this stereotype:

> There is an aircrash on a rocky island. Three people survive. One Russian, one American and one *Sardarji*. A cannibal ogre appears from nowhere and threatens the three survivors. They beg for their lives. The ogre finally agrees to spare their lives if they pass the following test. He gives one loaf of bread to the Russian, one bottle of wine to the American and a small pig to the *Sardarji*. Then he locks them in three different cave-rooms and says that after one year he will visit them again and one who will still be living will be free to leave the island. After one year he opens the rooms and finds both the Russian and the American dead. But he is shocked to see the *Sardarji* living and healthy. The ogre also notices that his pig, too, has grown very big and healthy. He wants to know from the *Sardarji* how he could manage all this. Says *Sardarji* smiling: "Why, it was so easy. *Piggy eat my shit and I eat piggy shit.*"

It is interesting to note that in this particular joke the last part, "Piggy eat my shit and I eat piggy shit" is always invariably told in English. Moreover, this also seems to be a joke about different nationalities and as such suggests an international type which can be applied to any situation internationally. This may also suggest that *Sardarji* be treated as if representing a nationality rather than a part of that nationality, Indian for example. That Sikhs have been demanding and fighting for a separate country which could give them a separate identity is something which seems hidden in this joke and may, perhaps, justify the application of this international frame to a typical Indian joke. Another interesting feature of this joke is the extension of the fairy tale metaphor in terms of the ogre and the tests. That such types of jokes need to be examined in the context of mass culture or folklorismus hardly needs to be emphasized.

3. Another trait of the *Sardarji* joke cycle is the inaptness and the vulgar sexual habits of the *Sardarji*. Consider the following example:

> A *Sardarji* survives a shipwreck and manages to swim to an island. He is hungry and pretty soon discovers plenty of fruit on the island. After having eaten enough, he thinks if he could find something for sex, things would work wonderful for him. Soon a female donkey appears. *Sardarji* thanks god for providing everything he demanded, and begins to ride the female donkey from behind. She kicks him back. The more he tries the more kicks he recieves. *Sardarji* spends the whole day trying to do the thing with her, but fails every time. Suddenly he sees a very beautiful blonde floating on the ocean. Perhaps one of the other victims of the shipwreck. He rescues her, brings her ashore and helps her in regaining consciousness. Says the blonde:
> "*Sardarji*, you have saved my life. How can I ever repay you? You can have anything I have. Just ask for it and you had it".
> Says *Sardarji*, after a pause:
> "Okay. Can you help me? You just hold the legs of this female donkey."

It is interesting to note that not only is *Sardarji* a victim of the stereotype that he is stupid, but also of another related stereotype that he is vulgar and tasteless in his sexual behaviour. Naturally this stereotype is equally well applied to his family, particularly his wife. Just like the *Sardarji*, she too has vulgar sexual norms devoid of a moral code, as for instance, the non-Sikh women of India are supposed to possess and adhere to. See the following example:

> A bus driver *Sardarji* is sexually aroused by a semi-nude poster of a film actress. He returns home immediately and requests his wife to have sex with him. She refuses on the grounds that she is in between her menstrual periods, and besides it is broadday light. She, however, pities his condition, gives him 50 Rupees and sends him out to do it with some prostitute. *Sardarji* accepts the offer reluctantly. On the way to the prostitute's house, he meets his wife's girl friend. She wants to know why he is looking so upset. *Sardarji* is reluctant to tell the truth. But she insists on telling and somehow manages to find out the whole story. She takes him to her appartment and both have a nice time. She takes only 20 Rupees. A content *Sardarji* returns home. His wife wants to know where he finally did it. He narrates the whole event honestly and truthfully and returns the remaining 30 Rupees to her. Says she:
> "That bitch took 20 Rupees from you. Why, I take only 10 from her husband".

160

There is an endless amount of *Sardarji* humour in India in various forms
such as narrative-jokes, anecdotes, proverbs, idioms, words and even gestures.
The present sampling is merely to delineate various aspects of the stereotype of
the *Sardarji* in Indian folklore. Two important aspects of this joke cycle need
comments before I conclude this short study.

The *Sardarji* joke, obviously in its any generic form, invariably generates
humour. One of the important reasons for this joke cycle to become so popular
and pan-Indian is, in fact, the humour which these jokes carry. The more the power of humour in a *Sardarji* joke, the more possibilities of its being popular. The
question one can pose is what is there in the text of a *Sardarji* joke which creates
humour. Victor Ruskin has sufficiently demonstrated that "for a text to be joke
carrying ... it be compatable with two different scripts that are 'opposites' of each
other".[7] Ruskin's this kind of analysis is of course in harmony with the school of
psychology that sees ambiguity and incongruity as the very essence of humour.[8] I
believe Ruskin's script-based theory is particularly useful in dealing with ethnic
jokes. In this regard, consider the following remarks of Davies:

> ... It is clear that a joke is genuinely ethnic if and only if its main 'opposition' or one of
> its main oppositions involves at least one truly ethnic script. In the case of a truely
> ethnic joke, the removal of the evoked ethnic script would render it incomprehensible.
> At the core of an ethnic joke lies an apposition between pairs of script scenarios that
> are real as opposed to unreal (actual/non-actual, normal/possible, possible/impos-
> sible) and goodness-related as opposed to badness-related.[9]

The other question which deserves scholarly attention is how this ethnic stereotype about the Sikh community might have developed in India. One of the
reasons, and very often put forth by scholars to explain the rise of an ethnic joke
is, "to make a majority feel superior to a minority".[10] This might be true in the
case of *Sardarji* joke cycle as well. Sikhs are in minority and Hindus in majority in
India. But the real questions are 1.) why would Hindus want to feel superior
when in reality they are superior; at least in terms of numbers, and, 2.) why Hindus could not choose some other minority, say Christians, Buddhists or even Muslims as the ethnic group for the joke cycle. Of course there are jokes about these
minorities as well, but they certainly are not so popular and widespread as the
jokes about the Sikhs. I suspect there might be some deeper reason which might

---

[7]Christie Davis, "Taking Jokes (apart) Seriously," *Semiotica*, 66-4 (1987), 452-454. (A review article
of Victor Ruskin's *Semantic Mechanisms of Humor* [Boston, 1985]).
[8]Cf. *ibid.*, p. 451.
[9]*Ibid*, p. 453.
[10]Cf. Alan Dundes, "Polish Pope Jokes," *Journal of American Folklore*, 92 (1979), 219-222.

have generated the "Sikh stereotype" and the related joke cycle. Psychologists believe, and I fully agree with them, that jokes "help people cope with anxieties."[11]

It was Freud who pointed to the significant similarities and dissimilarities between jokes and dreams.[12] People, I believe, joke in order to satisfy some deep, dark urge. So the question is what is this deep, dark urge or anxiety which the majority Hindu community of India has in its subconscious and which generates these stereotypes and the jokes related with them. In my opinion, the "success-story" of the Sikh-community as a whole has taken the form of a deep-rooted anxiety in the collective minds of the non-Sikh majorities especially the Hindus of India. This success-story of the Sikhs is manyfold. Sikhs are very hardworking people. They are a martial community. They dominate the rank and file of the armed forces and are the best truckers. They are also very successful businessmen, able travellers and can be found not only in every part of India but also of the world. The "Green Revolution" that changed the agricultural economy of India in the early sixties took off primarily from the state of Panjab, the home of the Sikh community. Sikh religion is very simple and egalitarian in character. So, unlike the Hindus, the Sikhs do not have a rigid caste system and its hierarchies. Moreover, the Sikhs have played very significant roles in Indian politics, administration, agriculture and economy. In conclusion, Sikhs are a very prosperous and successful people. I suspect this might have threatened the Hindu ego and created the anxiety which in turn seems to have taken the form of various stereotypes and the resultant joke cycle.

[11]Cf. Oring, *op. cit.*, 281 f.

[12]Sigmund Freud, *Jokes and Their Relation to the Unconscious*, Trans. and ed. by James Strachey (New York, 1905, 1960).

ETHNICAL FIELDS

Venetia Newall
(London)

THE SIGNIFICANCE OF NARRATIVE IN MODERN
IMMIGRANT SOCIETY:
THE INDIAN COMMUNITY IN BRITAIN

In Britain today the largest immigrant community consists of people of South Asian origin. According to the 1981 census, a national survey taken every 10 years, it accounts for 19 % of the so-called "foreign-born" population of 3,5 million. Moving into the highly industrialised society of Western Europe was a unique experience for the people of the Indian sub-continent. These migrants brought with them a rich variety of practical skills, languages, cultures, religion, fashions, tastes, food ways, and applied arts. In what one of my informants calls "the fast society of the West" people are exposed constantly to the media and nearly all aspects of life are affected by the process. But the migrants, especially the first generation, came from a highly traditional background and often maintain their cultural links with the rural past of their homelands. There the level of literacy was – again in the words of an informant – very low, and the majority of the people could not afford to buy a radio or television set. Nor were they pressurized to feel that this was necessary.

In the sub-continent today the old tradition of narrative for religious, historical, romantic and moral tales obtains. A highly educated informant comments:

> This attitude had also the reason of keeping the masses from having access to knowledge in written form. Then there is a tradition of a number of people from certain castes engaged in a number of activities and act as teachers, preachers, and some are simply busy in the art of demonstrating their knowledge, experience, and expertise.
> The caste-ridden society had a history of division on the basis of family origin, occupation, region or profession. Each caste protected and guarded itself against anyone joining it. The upper class consisted of highly literate and clergy groups who were educated and enjoyed the monopoly of knowledge, religion, and prestige and was busy in discharging their religious duties. Books were hardly written. Teaching was limited to only a select number of people. They were required to go to their master for lessons and most of the studies consisted of oral lessons. Memorising was usually the main part of the curriculum. Thus a very small fraction of the people had access to only a

tiny amount of available knowledge and nearly all the majority of the population was excluded from literacy. The Indian society developed an attitude of leaving a variety of things apart from the usual essential communication. Stories, music, religion, culture were presented orally. So a small group of people developed a talent for imparting to people religion, stories, music, culture.

Of course the popular book culture is comparatively a new phenomenon in the world. The occupation of India by a number of foreigners did not improve the situation: the grandeur of the moghuls and the British imperialism had a very limited effect. The result was that old Indian tradition was not altered. Oral and aural transmission of all sorts of cultures continued.

The categories which this particular informant singles out for discussion are of interest. They appear to be listed in order of importance:

On the top of it are stories about religions. The story of the Ramayana is well known among Hindus. A variety of personalities and their parts are very well narrated to people. Another is the story of the Mahabharata. Both these stories are very popular. Moral endings are emphasized.

The Muslims of the sub-continent have a number of stories about their important saints, showing their miraculous power. Usually these are described vividly and show the audience the great spiritual position of the faith. The famous battle of Kerbla, where the prophet's grandson and his family were killed is repeated in a number of religious gatherings.

The Sikhs have 10 gurus – masters, whose lives were full of struggle. Stories from Guru Nanak's journeys and preachings are quite often told to all sorts of gatherings. One morning, Guru Nanak went to a lake to take his morning bath. There, in the lake, a Hindu was offering his prayers by throwing the water over his shoulders to the spirits of his departed relatives in the heaven. The Guru also took some water in his folded hands, and threw it behind him, and said loudly: "Let the water fall on the farmland in my friend's village!" The Hindu asked him with surprise: "How can your water reach the farmland?" "If the water you sprinkle around can reach miles and miles away in the heavens, why my water should not reach a few miles away from here?"

Stories about famous heroes and heroines from history are popular with people. In 1857 a number of Indians and some Indian sections of the British army tried to turn the British out of India. Though this attempt failed (the British called it a mutiny and the Indians remembered it as a war of independence), the famous people involved are revered. The story of Fani Jhansi, who fought a battle bravely against the British is quite popular among people.

Romantic stories are very popular. The famous story of Hir Ranjha is about a love affair of a couple coming from the working class of the Punjab. A variety of aspects of this story is related in music and narration to people. Similarly the story of Mirza Sahiban is also based on a similar background. These romantic stories have a great appeal for people. A large number of Indian movies have similar themes. However, the majority of the rural Indian people still have not got access to the modern means of entertainment. Therefore stories have their own value.

A number of narratives are related just to show folk wisdom or folk moral:

(a) *Fox and Crow*

A fox invited a crow to dinner at her house. She offered him a flat plate of milk. The crow would not drink much out of it, whereas the fox drank all the milk. The poor crow went home without any meal. After four days the crow thought of teaching the fox a lesson. He invited the fox to dinner. He put all the milk in a bottle with a narrow neck. He drank it with his beak and the fox was unable to reach it. So this time the fox had to go with taking nothing. Thus she learnt that deceit and tricks do not succeed at the end.

(b) *A Clever Crow*

A crow was very thirsty. He searched for water, but could not find any. At last he found a little jar, which had a small amount of water at the bottom. The crow tried to reach it, but it was too deep for his beak to touch the surface of the water. So, after thinking, he hit upon a plan and found some pebbles. He carried them one by one and threw them into the jar. As a result, the water arose and the crow quenched his thirst. The moral drawn from this story is: work hard and never give up your efforts.

There are funny stories about a comic story-teller, for example:

Tennali Ram, one of the well-known story-tellers of South India in the Middle Ages, is supposed to have walked into a temple of the Goddess Kali, who has six heads and twelve arms. When Tennali Ram saw the Goddess Kali like that, he was least frightened – he began to laugh. The statue of the Goddess became alive and asked Tennali Ram why he was laughing. He said, "The thought crossed my mind that what will you do if you catch cold? I get fed up with my one nose. But you have got six noses!" The Goddess was pleased with the humour and gave him the boon of being comic.

Bombay is known as the Hollywood of Asia. People from all over India, Iran, the Middle East, China, go there in search of jobs, wealth, business, or even a role in the Indian movies. The city is cosmopolitan, with people of many cultures, habits and tongues. Narratives and jokes are swapped by the people in the shade of street trees, sipping cups of tea from roadside tea-stalls, at religious festivities, wedding gatherings, almost everywhere. These are called story-session gossip, coming from street culture.

Most of these narratives in these gatherings usually reflect stereotypes. The Marwaris are the people from the region called Marwar, in between Rajasthan and Gujarat. The region is a desert. So people have to move to other parts of India. Wherever they go, the locals believe that the Marwaris come with nothing but a small brass glass, and soon (with) their money-lending business and habit of not spending even on necessities of life, they become rich and begin to dominate people around:

A Marwari woman was undergoing a lot of trouble before delivering her baby. Doctors, nurses, were trying all their skills but baby was taking a lot of time. Outside the room, the Marwari man was walking up and down, restless, and knocking at the door every hour, and was told by the midwives, "Not yet, but soon ..." Soon, he lost his patience and entered the room with a bag of copper coins. He faced the womb of his wife and talked to his unborn baby, and jingled the bag of money. "If you will not be born soon, I shall have to give the doctors all these gold coins. Doctor, take this gold coin." And he dropped one on the floor with a loud jingling sound. He waited. Everybody watched. Nothing happened. Then he took the second coin out and said in a very painful voice: "Look my baby, I will have to give all my coins to the doctors. Here, take this, Doctor." And he dropped that coin on the floor. The coin made a jingle sound and rolled on the floor. But before it fell flat, up popped the baby from the mother's womb and caught the coin tight in its fist.

There are similar jokes about Gujarati communities, often mistaken for Marwaris because of the Gujarati passion for business:

A Gujarati shop-keeper was obsessed with his shop and kept his shop opened very late and slept in the shop. An inquisitive customer asked him once: "If you keep your shop opened late, then who looks after your wife?" "Well, I have got a servant from home-town, who looks after her well" was the innocent reply.

On similar lines, there are still worse jokes made by the locals. There are a number of people from Uttar Pradesh, who have migrated to Bombay. Some of them are in the dairy business. They are called Bhaiyas – the Brothers or U. P. Wallahs:

One day a Bhaiya was celebrating the birth of his son by giving free glasses of milk to the passers-by. Somebody asked him: "Bhaiya, how is it, that for the last so many years you are here, and your baby was born there, in your home village? There upon the Bhaiya milkman replied: "Well, I've got my brother there to look after our family."

The Bengali people have stuck with the Baboo image since the colonial clerical bureaucracy came to India, two hundred years ago. Baboo means one who works in an office. Usually the image is of someone very slow and full of excuses. A Bengali clerk used to go to his office late. One day his boss said to complete the job in hand and work for an extra twenty minutes as he came late in the morning. The Baboo replied: "You do not want me to be late twice in one day!"

In India there are more than forty-five languages spoken in different states. The language difference between Northern India and South India is more marked. The Northerners think that South Indians speak faster than others. Once, a North Indian returned from his trip to Madras. He cheerfully told his mates that his trip was a resounding success. A friend wondered: "How is it that you can't speak a single word of Tamil, Malayam, or Telegu and South Indians will not speak Hindi and still you claim your trip was successful?" The Northerner replied: "It was easy. I just put some pebbles in a brass glass, and, whenever any South Indian talked to me, I shook the pot. The South Indian seemed all happy with that conversation."

Of all the jokes in India, the Sikh jokes are most popular. However, Sikhs call them "Sick Jokes". The Sikhs are popularly nicknamed by non-Sikhs as Bara Baje ie 12.00 o'clock. There are a number of stories about this. A Sikh went to buy a wrist watch. The salesman showed him many watches. After a lot of questions and arguments, he bought an old-fashioned one with an hour and a minute hand. He asked the salesman to set it to the right time. It was about 11.45 am. The salesman set it right. The *Sardarji* – that is equivalent to nobleman – or Mr to a Sikh, wore it and went around looking at other things in the shop. At 12.00 o'clock he looked at his watch and saw only one hand. He rushed to the salesman and said: "Look, one hand has fallen out! I don't want this watch." Also, it is supposed that, at exactly 12.00 mid-day, the heads of all *Sardarjis* get heated (on account of their turbans) and they go mad.

Kushwant Singh, a well known Sikh author, comments:

They (the Sikhs) not only enjoy anecdotes about themselves, but are also the authors of most of them. This attitude is born out of a sense of confidence in that in any sphere of activity, physical or mental, in any profession, farming, soldiering, medicine, science or art, they can – and do – outsmart their sister communities, the Hindus, Muslims, and the Christians.

The Sikhs see themselves as in constant competitions with the rest of the Indians and they have to outsmart their sister communities all the time. This itself is a very sick attitude. The second is that the rest of the Indians are organised against the Sikhs. The analysers of the Indian social sciences say that the whole Indian society is divided into many caste, languages and cultural groupings. Major religions until recently hardly helped them to organise one against the others, but individuals always faced the competition with the rest; and the competition becomes evil where it is identified with the labelled groupings, but the competition could be the motive and spur behind the rancour in the jokes.

The Sikhs have a very rich tradition of humour. It criticises the social faults and also looks at themselves with a smile. It goes back to the time of Guru Nanak, when the Sikh religion was without complicated rites and rituals, and perhaps that was the main motive Guru Nanak had in mind. The Hindu religion at that time was dominated by meaningless rites and rituals. (The speaker is a liberal Muslim.)

The Pathans are very tall and heavily-built people and, because of the harshness of nature in Afghanistan, many emigrate to various parts of India and earn their livelihood. Tagore wrote a beautiful story on the plight of the Pathans called "Kabuli Wallah." Because of their tall physique, they are often employed as bodyguards or as gate-keepers by the rich Zamindars:

One day, a Pathan gate-keeper goes to his boss and in thundering, aggressive words, says: "If you will not increase my salary, I will have to ..." The boss raises his eyebrows and says "Yes, what will you have to ...?" "I will have to carry on as usual", says he, in a tiny voice.

Women, wherever they are, usually become constant butts for the stereotyped jokes: sexist jokes, frustrated wife jokes, thick-headed wife jokes, silly mother-in-law jokes. Here is one example:

"I don't like that young chap you are going with. He is rough, common, and bloody stupid," said an angy, worried father to his daughter. "No, Dad, he is smart. You know, he already cured that little illness I used to have every month."

Using sex as a topic and man's virility as the major for his achievements, women, too, can make them look small:

A high caste Indian in his loin cloth sat outside his house, carelessly picking his nose. A sweeper woman and her daughter just passed that way. The little girl looked at the man in the loin-cloth and started giggling. That made her mother giggle too. The man stood up angrily, tidied up his loin cloth and with a contorted face, he accosted them. The poor woman said: "Oh Sahib, don't take any notice of her. She'd giggle at any small thing."

But women's humour is miles away from the battle of sexes and stereotypes. It reflects the harsh, domineering sexist world of war, and woman's plight in it:

A visitor to India, at the turn of the century, curiously asked the owner of the house he visited: "Why are there wells in the backyard of every house?" The man was perplexed about the questioner's intelligence, but his wife, who was following her husband from a distance, pulled over her face the hem of her sari and said: "They are there for the women in the household to commit suicide."

Even today, the percentage of women found dead in wells, rivers, lakes is very high in Gujarat, Bengal and many other states of India.

"The black people, whatever part of the world they live in, suffer continuously by the jokes, jibes and insults thrown at them. They are the targets of the worst kind of humour human beings ever think of. In India, a black-complexioned person is hounded by the less dark persons.

"In India black satin silk is very expensive and satin saris are worn by women with great feeling. A man got a proposal from a girl's parents. After seeing her, he said to his parents: 'You must not bother to ask her parents about a dowry. I can put a white sari on her and take her out in the mid-day sun. Soon her sweat will turn her white sari into the black satin silk. I shall sell it and become rich.'

"Indian girls with black complexions are hardly married. Many of them are found dead in various wells, lakes, and rivers. If they are married, they are treated as evil Iblis (devils) by the husbands' relatives.

"Visits of families at the weekends to friends from a similar background are marked activities of South Asia people in this country (Britain).

Similarly, during religious festivals and civic holidays these people invite each other. Weddings of South Asian people are noted for the large number of guests of all ages, however usually from the same region of the sub-continent. In these gatherings, narratives, folk-tales, humour, are a great source of entertainment. These are especially popular for the first generation of migrants. Their experience and knowledge of English way of life have been during their youth and old age. They do feel and appreciate such gatherings, where they can exchange news about friends and relatives. Nostalgic feelings for the sub-continent culture come to the surface with these tales. There are not many South Asian professional story-tellers in Britain. However, volunteers from these groups serve the purpose. These activities have a special significance for the first generation. The new generation brought up in the country have a large choice of European culture and continue to enjoy South Asian contribution at the same time. The large number of Indian movies available in South Asian corner shops have not been able to meet this need of the old South Asian people in Britain. Of course, in spite of all revolution, of TV, radio, video, and cinema, and progress in library or school service, the narrative of all sorts still occupies a secure place in rural parts of South Asia. In Britain this activity looks like waning, though the present popularity is remarkable. It will be a pity if this natural source and resource is allowed to phase out of existence.

The format of this paper reflects the structure of a society within a society, which we find in many Western European countries today. I was fortunate to obtain so full a statement on the topic of story-telling from a Pakistani (Indian) immigrant. In his choice of categories and genres, my informant creates a picture of a society dominated by racial prejudice, stereotyping, inadequate recognition of the dignity and role of women, religious sensitivities, the power of love, and the enduring traditional wisdom of the folk. He is particularly concerned with humour, a topic I shall be considering further in another paper. My informant defines his own position as an immigrant in British society by telling tales, especially, jokes, centred on other racial groups, regions, religions, and languages. By so doing, he makes clear to himself his own identity.

He is, perhaps, premature in his comment, familiar to the folklorist, that storytelling among members of his community in Britain "looks like waning". I say this for two reasons. Firstly, and there are many others like him, because this particular informant did not initially regard himself as a storyteller:

> I don't regard these stories as from a story-teller. Just memories of what I have heard in my life. They are not stories from me. That is your discovery. Since I developed that habit of comparing everything in the present to something in the past, and to describing it in an interesting way, that made me like a story-teller. I regard them as part of my personal experience. Yes, that means they are to me very important. The beauty of my memory is that I enjoy narrating them. I relive my past, because I have such a vivid memory of the past and I enjoy it. The narratives make me feel very good and very happy. When I give examples from my past experience, that's a sign of someone who can recall his experience of his past. It makes me feel good that I can remember my past and that I can recall my experiences as a piece of knowledge and for others.

The second reason relates to remarks by Veronika Görög-Karady in her excellent paper presented to this Congress. She refers to a phenomenon which she sees as part of the protest against consumer society:

> The vast rehabilitation of naive art forms, primitive music, and expressions of oral art ... products of traditional civilisations graced with nobility and taken as models rather than ... suvivals ... the return to the folktale (as) part of a cultural change ... the analysis of myths, ethnolinguistics, and the interpretation of oral literature (as) blooming fields of research.

A similar situation obtains in England and I would, for example, refer you to the admirable work done by Dr. Ruth Finnegan in this last connection. In our country there are now libraries that feature story-telling sessions for children, there are occasional street performers, the BBC has broadcast narratives for children chosen from the major immigrant communities, numerous popular tale collections have been published, and lectures on the topic are well attended by enthusiastic audiences. There is a growing awareness and interest in the phenomenon, which I believe will blossom rather than fade away.

One final, personal, comment. In the course of interviewing this particular informant, he has on five occasions visited friends in hosipital. They were there, not for treatment of natural ailments, but because they had been beaten up in racial attacks. I believe that by helping to make these narratives, and the culture from which they spring, better known, especially among children and the younger generation, we stand a greater chance of helping to eradicate the ignorance which gives rise to racial prejudice. We may sit in our ivory towers and consider genre theory, but when an informant's friend is savagely beaten up, that is a very immediate sort of reality, and we do wrong to pretend that it does not exist. If this is applied folklore, then I am all for it!

Bibliography

Beck, Brenda E. F. and others, *Folktales of India* (Chicago, 1987)

Fyson, Nance Lui, *Multi-Ethnic Britain* (London, 1984)

Görög-Karady, Veronika, "The New Professional Storyteller in France", ISFNR Theory Commission Paper (1989)

Newall, Venetia, "Narrative as an Image of Cultural Transition: Portrait of an Asian Story-Teller", Vol. 26 *Fabula* (1985)

Saunders, Malcolm, *Multicultural Teaching* (London, 1982)

Shaw, Alison, *A Pakistani Comunity in Britain* (Oxford, 1988)

Singh, Khushwant, *A History of the Sikhs*, 2 vols. (Oxford, 1977)

Souza, Allan de, *The Sikhs in Britain* (London, 1986)

Finnegan, Ruth, *Oral Literature in Africa* (Oxford, 1970); and *Oral Poetry: Its Nature, Significance and Social Context* (Cambridge, 1977); ed., *Man* (The Journal of the Royal Anthropological Institute); ed., *Cambridge Series in Oral and Literate Culture* (Cambridge, 1977-)

Veronika Görög-Karady
(Paris)

THE NEW PROFESSIONAL STORYTELLER IN FRANCE

The renewal of storytelling in contemporary France cannot be precisely
dated, nor do the agents of this renewal share identical literary or political inclinations, even if the majority comes from the same generation. Nonetheless, one
can assert that a genuine movement of storytelling in a new fashion arose and
established itself after 1968 and in the beginning of the 1970, inscribing itself definitely in the modes and models of cultural reception which developed during
this period. This exploratory work, based essentially on a series of directed interviews with storytellers, will only examine three aspects of this phenomenon
whose complete study is far too complex to be analyzed briefly. I will attempt to
understand above all the social conditions underlying the emergence of the new
storytellers as well as the functions of the imaginary and the fantastic in our advanced industrialized societies. Secondly, I wish to present the new professional
taletellers, considered as a developing cultural and professional corporation, I
will, however, restrict my analysis to storytellers established in Paris and not consider those who live elsewhere in the country (although the former do perform
outside of the capital). Thirdly, I will briefly consider the texts themselves in order to explore repertorial specifities.

Considerations on the social function of the imaginary:

The folktale is a form of traditional oral literature coming from rural societies. Its historical obsolence is linked to the peasantry's dislocation as a class or
social group with a homogeneous way of life of its own. Nevertheless, the folktale
has survived marginally in industrial society: in "high"-literature which has saved
and made use of certain of its aspects, in the culture destined for child socialization and, finally, as an object of ethnological knowledge. In all cases, it's a preca-
rious survival since in none does the story retain its old function as an autono-

mous literary discourse.[1] The appearance and relative success of a new storyteller undeniably constitutes a return to an expressive form which had lost, for a greater or lesser length of time, all pertinence among the common symbolic products of contemporary society. This revival is obvious even if today's listeners no longer hold the same relationship to folktales as the peasants of yore. The existence of such a movement can be understood in the context of a vast rehabilitation of naive artforms, primitive music and expressions of oral art which began at the turn of the century. This rehabilitation means that the products of traditional civilizations were graced with nobility and taken as models rather than being relegated amongst the survivals. In addition, the specific relationship which one imagines between the creators and users of primitive arts tends to be exemplified and recreated whenever possible, thanks to the actions of spontaneous artistic movements or of activities coupled with official instances of cultural diffusion.

As a result, the return to the folktale is part of a cultural change, or more precisely, an evolution in esthetic taste and the relationship considered normal to art, which more generally includes the renewed favour of all sorts of artistic, or even ancient artisanal practices. These practices have in common the reduction and abolition of the distance established between professional artists and their audience and between symbolic products and their users.

The conditions for the emerge of the new storytellers have not, however, been based solely on esthetic considerations. Orality's rehabilitation is also grafted on to a cultural project which is linked to both regional movements and the ethnological and anthropological sciences, understood broadly. Even if regionalism exceeds the folkloric phenomena characteristic of the different regional units because of its socio-political ambitions, one of the least contested social definitions of a region is that it contains and expresses a traditional culture. Not surprisingly, the past two or three decades have seen the rediscovery of French regions' narrative patrimony – a way of reappropriating a long neglected symbolic treasure. Certainly the exploration of French Folklore is not recent. But the enormous work of collecting, observing and analyzing accomplished through the foundation of the Celtic Academy under the Empire, up to Van Gennep and Sébillot (authors who were outside of the University) was confined to a narrow disciplinary ghetto. Surviving popular traditions or those unearthed by scholars needed the impetus of regional studies in order to attain a new "political" function and to achieve in this manner a wider audience. Thanks to its new public legitimacy, derived in part from its regional use, the new ethnographic field – that

---

[1]Currently in the French countryside, the most commonly practiced oral forms are jokes and more or less lengthy anecdotes, close to facetious tales.

of regional units – succeeded in imposing itself in higher education and research, parallel with the exotic ethnology which had heretofore cast a shadow over it. Because of this success, scholarly folklore has contributed more and more to the popularization of its own research object. Within the ethnological sciences, the taste for oral traditions is also nourished by the shifting of interest towards studies of collective representations and acts of language. As a result, the analysis of myths, ethnolinguistics and the interpretation of oral literature are blooming fields of research. Rapidly at that ethnology, social and cultural anthropology, semiology and linguistics have become the leading fields in the social sciences in France. Such a public response to specialized research generates in the desire to know more about the object of this research, both in its traditional forms and in its present forms as they are proposed, for example, by the new storytellers.

As a result, the rehabilitation of traditional and naive artsforms, the regionalist movement and scholarly folklore collectively brought forth, although latently, a new demand. At the same time it was necessary to have a sufficiently large and receptive audience for the practice of storytelling to develop. These conditions were progressively better met in the 1970s and 80s. With the general extension of leisure time, the proportionally larger number of older people, the growth of schooling, the changes in the structure of the working population (growth of the tertiary sector, part-time work) and social laws which diminished the number of working hours, the size of the potential audience of all kinds of cultural consumption – both new and old – grew considerably. Traditional genres such as the folktale had the advantage that they did not presuppose any acquired cultural competence. Nonetheless, since industrial society had eliminated the customary occasions for storytelling, the encounter with the potential audience had to be organized, occasions had to be reinvented through the existing structures for cultural diffusion. This was all the more necessary in that, henceforth, any new cultural practice must encounter, or at least avoid, the weighty hegemony of audiovisual means in order to succeed. The role of public libraries, Youth Houses (Maisons de la Jeunesse), senior citizen clubs, and schools, etc. proved to be capital in the launching and maintenance of the movement of new storytellers because they offered concrete opportunities to what had previously been merely a virtual interest in listening to folktales.

One is better able to understand this participation of the different cultural instances if one recalls that the social project from which they are derived – the democratization of culture – responds directly to the more or less consciously pursued objectives of the new storytellers: to reinvent or bring to life messages which address themselves to everyone, which require neither specific gifts nor previous qualification because they rely on the imaginary and, perhaps, the unconscious. As such, storytelling is certainly one of the most democratic forms of esthetic experiences, because of the intimate complicity established through its peculiar sociability of participatory listening.

Everything leads one to believe, in fact, that the canalization of an audience towards the "simple words" of storytellers as well as the search for an audience of "simple people" by the latter, are all part of an ideological project which aims to reestablish a close relationship to symbolic artefacts. This project, with which all protest movements against consumer society share in some respects (be they ecologists, model communities, biological food adepts, anarchists, etc.) underlies the actions of both cultural organizers and storytellers because public narration, even in an institutional context, appears to approach the closest to the ideal of an immediate esthetic relationship. There is no screen between the storyteller and his public (no stage or separation), the content of the messages comes from common and accessible stock, the artists use relatively few specific skills which should lock them into the role of a particular "artist" and, above all, the folktale deals with a different world, an "otherness" which is controlled by a different logic than that of the real social world.

This logic can easily transgress the rules of "alienating" reality. The fantastic is the locus of symbolic space where men can perhaps communicate the most directly because everyone maintains a reference to personal experience, which is by definition inexpressible. A new, intimate, active, even participatory relationship develops between creators and their audiences that calls out to an imaginary world which adults generally repress (in dreams, games, the unconscious). The storytellers and their audience experience narration as a break with consecrated artistic expressions.

The public is often mixed by age, education level and social class. There is no privileged space: folktales can be told in theaters and in the street, in libraries and in vacation houses. The audience possesses an exceptional liberty to listen or to leave, to participate, and even to take the place of the artist and tell stories in turn. For certain storytellers, narration is the means of breaking down the barrier of genre. Evocative images and objects can be integrated into the narrative spectacle. The enacted text is mobile, transformable, and adaptible to the place, the audience and the moment.

Such a vast potential for spontaneity in oral literature is opposed by definition to written texts, but the folktale offers improvisation in a specific range of action. Exempt from conventional constraints aside from those voluntarily accepted, even the most traditional folktale can acquire new meaning by articulating new messages. The disruption of forms and means of expression in narrational genres has virtually no limits, and the literary act upon which it is based can still evolve considerably, as many other types of artistic performances have during the twentieth century.

Psychoanalysis and other psychological therapies have contributed for their part to the cultural legitimation of the fantastic and the supernatural. Not only have the terrifying aspects of magic tales been reinterpreted as the acting out of suppressed desires, but even the idea that they are harmful to children's socialization has been revised. The current tendency is to defend a certain disjunction, or disharmony, between socialized reality and the apparently uncontrolled world of the imaginary as necessary for a child to construct his or her personality. Be that as it may, even among pedagogues, the fantastic and the supernatural no longer suffer from the discredit they bore for a certain period. This change, founded on the authority of scientific technique, can only reinforce the general acceptance of the imaginary's and even the irrational's place in the symbolic field of our societies. The slogan that covered the walls of Parisian universities in 1968: "Power to the imagination!" was probably political, calling for greater liberty in innovation. Still, in negative counterpart, this attitude also expressed a radical distrust of the rational codes proposed by science, social norms and the accepted arts. In the Latin Quarter and on certain university campuses, anarchistic ideologies aiming at the subversion of the symbolic order also paved the way, be it indirectly, for certain elements of educated classes to be more receptive to the new storytellers.

Professional storytellers

Although no survey of the practising new storytellers established in Paris exists, one can estimate that the number of these "professionals" (those who live by telling stories) does not exceed fifty. A large number of them belong to the generation which began its adventure with oral literature after 1968. For many, the years between 1968 and 1978 are explicitly considered to be the critical years of their development. Clearly, significant breaks with other forms of classical artistic professions occurred during this period.

1977 is an important date because at that time nine of the very first storytellers gathered for a community training session. Ties were made, vocations were encouraged, techniques were shared and audiences were tested. This date also marked progress in the hunting out of allies who held power within the institutional audiences for narration: librarians and cultural animators.

Bruno de la Salles's career, probably the best-known and one of the first storytellers, is exemplary in this respect. He began initially as an amateur in 1969 at the *Theatre de l'Epée de Bois* at the Avignon and Belfort festivals. Then he established contact with children's librarians who invited him to tell tales and play with their youthful clientele. In this way he got to know the association "La Joie par les Livres" which has a documentary center and exerts considerable influence over the distribution of children's literature. This association soon spread the demand for folktale and encouraged the (re)introduction of l'"Heure du conte" in libraries.[2] One-day training sessions were organized to train the librarians in charge of this program. As Bruno de la Salle quickly realized an isolated storyteller could not easily mobilize the naturally extensive folktale audiences. He got into contact with other storytellers and helped new ones to assert themselves.

Naturally, the biographical itineraries which lead to narration and the storytellers' individual motivations are extremely varied. In their development most of them experience a sudden break in their careers: they may abandon studies or a regular job, or – more dramatically – they may "make contact with oral literature" as opposed to written culture. Although not all of them begin as outsiders in established artistic professions, most have generally gone through some sort of conversion experience to find their vocation. There are no typical cases. For some, beginnings in theater – and particularly musical theater – or in film, led them directly to folktales. Others will reject the written constraints in literature. Still others are librarians or cultural animators for whom storytelling seemed to expand their professional lives. It enabled them particularly to extend the didactic, even political, dimension of their vocation. And even others, launched into narration as the inheritors of an extant oral tradition in order to reclaim an ancient social role. Sometimes they began storytelling by accident, having come into contact with an available juvenile audience in the library they were in charge of. The degree of professional interest in folktales varies a great deal from case to case but the possibility of speaking simple and universally accessible words is a fundamental motivation for all of them.

The social backgrounds of storytellers are also extremely diverse. Indeed, it is difficult to relate them directly to the birth of vocations. However, certain connections – both negative and positive – do appear when storytellers evoke their social trajectory. Often they refuse aspects of the "bourgeois culture" in

---

[2]Following the Americans, as early as 1924, *L'Heure joyeuse* was introduced into children's libraries (in Paris) and *L'Heure du conte* in youth sections in other libraries. In these programs, librarians either read or told stories according to their taste. Since then, this practice has survived more or less depending on the location.

which they were raised, even if elements of this culture (such as the acquisition of particular artistic skills) will be profitably used in the chosen career.

But social background can also play a positive role when the family served to preserve and transmit a traditional cultural patrimony. Three groups of storytellers, Jews, North and Black Africans established in Paris, owe their vocation to this familial setting. African trajectories are relatively simple since they often pursue in public an existing familial narrative tradition, even if they perform before a foreign and cultural dissimilar audience.

Jewish narrators offer a more ambiguous case, not only because they come from two very different cultural sources in French Judaism (Sephardic and Ashkenazic), but also because their relationship to their referential tradition is far more distended. They are more concerned to reconnect with a partly or almost completely lost oral culture or at least with a culture of which their families have lost the trace. If there is direct heritage it is diffused and transformed. It reveals itself more through a less constrained relationship to the spoken word (which offers the possibility of verbal games and spontaneity) than in the knowledge of a traditional narrative repertory. It appears obvious, nevertheless, that Judaism is a non-negligible factor in the birth of vocations, given that Jews are over-represented among the best-known new storytellers, especially between 1968 and 1978. One recognizes here the voluntary return to the sources of a rich oral tradition, but one which reaches our contemporary generations through underground networks and mixed with other traditions. It is rare, in fact, for storytellers from ethnically allogeneous but assimilated families to hark back to a single tradition, that of Judaism, which is capable of expressing a strong particularist identity whose call may occasionally appear irresistible.

Beyond the direct effect of social background and the cultural patrimony transmitted by the family, narrational vocations owe a great deal to certain forms of artistic training received during the educational period and the taste for performances inculcated from an early age. Elementary esthetic training cannot be reduced just to literature or performances (musical or theatrical) but also extends to drawing, painting and calligraphy. Many professional narrators recall memories of a grandmother or a devoted relative who told stories, whether or not they come from milieus which possess a particular cultural tradition (such as Sephardic Jews). This sort of short or long range vocational determination occasionally explains the relationship the storyteller maintains with his practice, the social function he gives it and the way in which he experiences it. For Black or North African storytellers, for example, who consider themselves to be guardians of traditional cultural heritage, narration is always a means of preserving (within) and affirming (without) a collective identity. Other less traditionalist narrators and those who revolt against their "bourgeois" origins tend to invest their folktales with political or cultural significance (protest against the war – in Vietnam or in Afghanistan – the recreation of an itinerant culture). One would have to consider each case individually in order to discover general themes, which is beyond the scope of this article.

One must, however, say a word about the organized nature of this form of storytelling. It may be misleading to have referred several times to a "movement" when describing the new storytellers. Even if most of them know each other and maintain continous relationship, through listening, encouragement, reciprocal criticism and even rivalries and jealousy, they only rarely act collectively as a professional corporation. Nonetheless, because of the specific nature of their practices, they are collectively distinct within the subculture of innovational and marginal artistic enterprises which have come to light in the last decades and within which they seem to fit because of their life-style and the market which they exploit. One folktale performance brings forth another, and the success of one storyteller gives rise to interest in others. It is probably the market rules which explain at least in part the efforts storytellers make to distinguish themselves from each other. Originality can not be reduced to its market value: it is the justification of all artistic enterprises. Even so, originality has no meaning unless models of professional practice exist, if – even potentially – standards of excellence, norms, a deontology exist along with a public image which enables one not only to identify the members but which also gives the latter the possibility to claim to belong, to refer to it and to distance themselves from it. It is in this sense, that one can refer to a professional corporation of new storytellers.

It also appears that storytellers' remuneration is established according to the type of performance expected, that is to say, according to an abstract collective norm and not according to the performer's fame or to the individual performance. Even if every storyteller maintains his right to bargain, in practice, they tend to accept the conditions which are offered to them. Few have sufficient personal notoriety to enable them to dictate – like a movie star – their own conditions or to monopolize a fraction of the public, even when they address themselves preferentially to a specific audience. In contrast to the way in which the market functions in classical artistic professions, narrational demand is addressed generally to "storytellers" rather than to a specific storyteller, no matter what the originality or the diversity of the market supply.

All storytellers depending solely on their profession experience differing degrees of insecurity – that may change with the years – concerning their artistic career. If, under certain circumstances, they are able to benefit from National Healthcare (for instance in schools or vacation centers) not all fees are systematically declared. In this respect, as in the importance they attach to the audience before which they perform, the market is highly hierarchical. While radio and television coverage offers both the highest fees and a reputation, storytellers rarely achieve this and do not always accept it; on the other hand theater gives them access to a cultivated audience and to critics. Municipal youth cultural centers (*Maisons de la Jeunesse et de la Culture*) are appreciated for their regular financial resources and their frequently motivated audiences.

Obviously the audience and institutions chosen vary from one storyteller to another. Librarian storytellers, in particular, perform more frequently before the young clientele of libraries. Others perform more frequently in public festivities or offered street performances after 1968. Repertoires, ways of storytelling and the techniques or accompanying performances all depend enormously on the audience and the context of performance.

Repertories

Repertories and their evolution would require a separate study, if it were possible to compare complete inventories. One can, nevertheless, make a few general observations.

The case of traditional, especially African, storytellers appears the simplest because it is most often limited to the cultural transmitted heritage. They seek to perpetuate a tradition received as infants, although their relationship to this tradition may vary a great deal between them. An Algerian storyteller, for example, uses – either faithfully or with variations – traditional tales heard in familial evenings, but he also tells Grimm tales and others. He uses few gestures and no music. A Tunisian storyteller presents traditional stories and intermingles them with musical and gestual accompaniment. Another storyteller of mixed Egyptian and Tunisian background employs classical Arab texts to create a theatrical performance set to music. A native of Black Africa (Ivory Coast) tells his tales freely in the customary fashion with an interlocutor (répondeur). He intermixes his tales with songs and willingly calls the audience into his performance.

French storytellers, as a rule, do not limit themselves to traditional French repertory. They are genuinely eclectic, no matter what their social backgrounds, to the point of making at times eclecticism a matter of faith. "Nowadays because of travel and business being transacted on a world-wide basis, the storyteller is no longer obliged to root himself in a territory" (Donagan). In many interviews,

182

storytellers explicitly refuse the function of "perpetuating a tradition corresponding to a now-vanished rural civilization" (Zvitka, Couterau, Théâtre à Bretelles). Nonetheless, a classical and traditional patrimony continues to furnish the essential materials for their inspiration: popular folktales, in a broad sense, whether they be *The one Thousand and one Nights*, Grimm, Andersen or Perrault tales, or else, African, Asiatic, Yiddish and Indian oral texts of more recent collections. If there is a form of traditional inspiration it is less from a traditionalist concern than from a concern about accessibility, democratization, even anti-intellectualism. The French new storytellers want to speak directly to today's people. Most often they learned their narrative patrimony through reading. For some, the choice of repertory was initially made to convey political messages. More recently, it seems that esthetic preoccupations mostly determine the choices made in the creation of a repertory where the influence of classical narrative sources remains strong. Indeed, the new storytellers connect with their audiences through a more or less shared childhood culture that of the traditional European folktales. Nonetheless, repertorial diversity is considerable.

Librarian storytellers are perhaps the most faithful to the traditional repertories and ways of telling tales. They rarely use anything but the spoken word. They represent the classical pole of storytelling amongst the new storytellers. The "Théâtre à Bretelles" illustrates the opposite and most reworked pole since its avowed objective is to link up with another tradition of tale tellers who show images (conteurs-montreurs d'images). Concretely, the "Théâtre à Bretelles" is an accordeon-sized box carried as such within which lies a large band of drawn and painted paper. A handle pulls the band along like a barbary organ of images and at the same time the story is told and musically illustrated (accompanied by a flute, an accordeon and a horn). Sketches and different songs may also form part of the program. This performance appears to be particularly adapted to public places, addressed to unprepared audiences, since its message belongs to that of everyday existence.

Other professional storytellers may be situated between these two "extremes". They may present traditional tales, personal transpositions of popular tales, but also stories they invent and accompany with musical instruments and gestures.

It would be premature to attempt even a circumstantial answer to the question which begs nonetheless a response. Where are the folktale and the new storytellers headed? Their audience is expanding even if folktales remain a marginal form of art in contemporary France. It is still possible that the success of the folktale and of that of the storytellers as well changes in the longterm the spontaneous relationship between storytellers and their audience. Recuperation by the theater and audio-visual means is a risk which most, if not all, storytellers would consent to take. But will the folktale which is spoken on stage or on television be the same? Will it be received in the same manner? And above all, will it address itself to the same audience as today?

Toshio Ozawa
(Tokio)

STORYTELLING IN CONTEMPORARY JAPAN

In its traditional sense storytelling has almost disappeared today. There are old people, however, who can memorize about ten, fifteen or twenty fairytales, and who can narrate them by heart. It is not too difficult to find these people if one enquires in such regions as northern Japan and Okinawa.

However, the custom of telling stories to children in the evening, sitting in front of the fireplace, hardly exists anymore. Television seems to attract much more interest, and, in general, the lifestyle has changed completely.

But there are mothers today, or nursemaids in kindergartens and librarians, who simply tell fairytales or other stories to the children by heart. These narrators, "narratrices" for the most part, may reasonably be described as contemporary storytellers.

When speaking of everyday storytelling one should focus on these contemporary narrators. Their occupations and professions usually create a challenge for telling stories again, either in schools or kindergartens, and, last but not least, within their families.

I. The place where stories are told

1. Children's library in the family: There are, nowadays, many families who own hundreds of children's books in their private libraries, which are borrowed and lent by neighbours and friends. Mothers who organize narrating groups and meetings gather here and there in order to tell stories or to discuss new editions of children's literature. The children of the area form the listeners.

One may find associations of family-libraries in larger cities. The mothers then organize several educational dates, for example a "storytelling afternoon", where mothers tell each other fairytales and stories they have learned by heart. Through this they gain experience.

2. The children's house: In Japan there are public children's houses, especially in recently-built areas. The children usually meet here after school or on Saturdays and Sundays in order to play there at will or to take part in several entertainments. Mothers living in the neighbourhood, whose children take part in these activities, organize several such, among others, for example in the so-called "story-telling afternoons". Those mothers who have acquired some skill in telling or those who are still learning have the chance to try their skills there.

3. The kindergarten: There are many nurses today, who have learned to tell stories from books by heart, and you may find an increasing number of them in Japan. They are happy to have listeners for their skill.

4. The school: For some reason it seems to be difficult to tell stories in elementary schools. The timetable demands much of the children and the teacher has only a little time to tell fairytales and stories out-of-class. In addition, the teacher himself usually had no chance to listen to fairytales in his own childhood. For a long period I have personally tried in vain to motivate teachers to tell stories in school. For two or three years, however, reports of different schools in various cities have arrived in my archive, dealing with storytelling by women, by "narratrices" in the classes; these reveal that schoolchildren always listen intensively to the tales. They do not lack concentration, as many teachers feared. This seems to indicate that children still do love fairytales in spite of their passion for television.

II. The female story-tellers ("narratrices")

Mostly, the narrating person is a woman, aged approximately between 30 and 50 years. Of course, a young mother reads stories to her little ones. Still, she may not have too much leisure-time to learn the stories by heart. Only when her own child has grown a little, will she have some leisure hours, then will probably recognize the importance of storytelling and, finally, learn some tales by heart.

III. The content

Because in most cases she has not had the chance to listen to fairytales in her childhood, the mother of today knows no other way to learn than through the written word and therefore she does not know which narrative style would be suitable and adequate for a genuine folktale.

Orally transmitted fairytales are usually recorded in dialect and they are used by folklorists directly in dialect. Becoming texts for children's books, however, these stories are transmitted by male or female authors into comprehensible standard language. Unfortunately, the majority of these authors doesn't know anything of the original style of orally transmitted tales. Consequently, story-tellers, who know nothing about the typical style of the folktale, acquire their knowledge from books, written by authors, who know nothing from dialect either and thus having transcribed and violated the original. By these means the danger of destroying the peculiar folk-style arises.

On the other side, however, there is the urgent demand for preserving this very style. Therefore, many contemporary story-tellers try to acquire the original, orally transmitted tone of the folktale.

IV. The children

Children love to watch TV. But as far as we know, this does not mean they do not love to listen to directly told stories either. Children do enjoy this a great deal, a fact we can prove from a large number of empirical examples. Children, then, do not only comprehend the tale "as such", but also the voice of the narrator, the atmosphere of the surroundings etc. However, they do not learn the means of dramatic expression which traditional narrators in general have.

V. Traditional male and female story-tellers

As mentioned before, there are many old people in Japan who can tell ten, twenty or even more than one hundred folktales by heart. Toshiko Endo, a (female) specialist from northern Japan is said to know more than five hundred folk- and merrytales or legends by heart, whereas the (male) narrator Koichi Sato, also from the north of Japan, knows more than five hundred tales. Satsu Suzuki told 157 fairytales and jokes. My students have recorded her entire repertory on tape. But these people do not only tell for tapes, but chiefly for the kindergartens and schools of the places where they live.

For a long period these traditional story-tellers have not told stories at all, believing their oldfashioned themes held no fascination for youngsters. Perhaps they feared they would be despised for their old, stupid ideas. Recently, however, they have been influenced by the activities of the narrating mothers, nurses and librarians and, therefore, began to tell anew. They are quite often invited by workshops and educational associations of all sorts to join a meeting. They listen eagerly to them and thus learn what might be called traditional storytelling. One may therefore speak about an interchange or a reciprocal effect.

Whether such activities lead to new traditions remains questionable. However, I would like to call it a new wave of storytelling in our country. Children of today, who, as little ones, have experienced the world of fairytales as a narrated one, would rather – as adults – tell oral stories by themselves to their own children and grandchildren, because they one enjoyed these tales as a happy experience of listening.

Giovanni Battista Bronzini
(Bari)

FROM THE GRIMMS TO CALVINO:
FOLK TALES IN THE YEAR TWO THOUSAND

1. The *American Lectures* which Italo Calvino should have delivered at Harvard University during the years 1985-86, have recently been published after his death by his wife Esther.[1] Not only do they represent *Six Proposals for the Next Millenium*, as the subtitle says, but also a sort of probable hypothesis about the survival and the adaptation of narrative literature in literary society in the year two thousand. The most probable outlet for folktales is outlined on the basis of the very principles themselves to be saved. We can foresee that the next millenium will bring our society towards more advanced technologies and, as a reaction, towards a more and more feverish search for a kind of 'humanism of machines'. This will determine a radical decontextualization of the traditional concept of 'folk' in the field of literature together with its progressive impoverish-

---

[1] Italo Calvino, *Lezioni americane. Sei proposte per il prossimo millennio*, (Milano, 1988). – Amongst Italo Calvino's works see: *Le fiabe italiane. Raccolte dalla tradizione popolare durante gli ultimi cento anni e trascritte in lingua dai vari dialetti* (Torino, 1956). The introductory essay has now been republished together with other important essays written by Calvino about folk tales in a posthumous booklet entitled: *Sulla fiaba*, a cura di M. Lavagetto (Torino, 1988). The entire literary production of Calvino has to be regarded for the tendency to telling and the references to the stylistic features of the folk tales. The production itself was inspired by. In the present contribution there is only an explicit reference, that is to his last theoritical, unfinished work with the draft of *Lezioni americane. Sei proposte per il prossimo millennio*. They were published posthumously (see above). The critical bibliography about Calvino, still rich during his living, has become richer in the last years, after his death (1985). The most important contributions I referred to are: Italo Calvino, *Atti del convegno internazionale* (Firenze, palazzo Medici-Riccardi, 26-28 febbraio 1987), a cura di Giovanni Falaschi (Milano, Garzanti, 1988); Italo Calvino, *La letteratura, la scienza, la città*. Atti del Convegno nazionale di studi di Sanremo (Genova, 1988); *Inchiesta sulle fate. Italo Calvino e la fiaba*, a cura di Delia Frigessi, Prefazione di Cesare Segre, Illustrazioni di R. Fiumana (Bergamo, 1988); F. Bernardini Napoletano, *I segni nuovi di Italo Calvino. Da 'Le Cosmicomiche' a 'Le città invisibili'*, (Roma, 1977). – Amongst the written sources Calvino referred to, cf. D. Comparetti, *Novelline popolari italiane* (Roma/Torino/Firenze, 1875); A de Nino, *Usi e costumi abruzzesi III. Fiabe* (Firenze, 1883); V. Imbriani, *La novellaia fiorentina* (Palermo, 1877); G. Nerucci, *Sessanta novelle popolari montalesi* (Ferenze, 1880); G. Pitré, *Fiabe, novelle e racconti popolari siciliani*, 4 vol. (Palermo, 1875).

ment. No doubt computer memory will limit the use of human memory. Also the field of vision, understood as the visual memory of one's own experiences, will be overcome by the artificial point of view from the outside (e.g. by television) or by prefabricated images. The latter appear to be non-conductive to an active reception on the part of the masses, in contrast to collective 'imaginary', which is varied and open, as it includes someone who narrates and someone who listens to tales. The increasing literacy of the popular classes and the fragmentation of everyday life will put an end to oral tales and sign the triumph of literary writing together with its visual projections. But the loss of oral tradition as a way of narrating does not necessarily involve the loss of the qualities and values conveyed by it. As we come to cross the threshold of the year two thousand, it may be opportune to take up the stylistic features from oral tales into written tales.

2. The significance of the elaboration performed by the Grimm brothers on the *Kinder- und Hausmärchen* (henceforth cited as KHM) has to be evaluated according to this point of view. A point of view that was recovered a century and a half later in Italy by Italo Calvino, who edited a wide chrestomathy of *Italian Folktales* for the publishing house Einaudi in 1956. They were translated and elaborated from regional collections (and will subsequently be cited as FI).

The idea of such a work arose from editorial need of placing side by side a collection of Italian folktales and other collections of national folktales being published in the series *I Millenni* a short time before. The *Millenni* had already included the *Russian Folktales* together with the *African Tales*, the *Norwegian Tales* and so on; in primis the Grimms' *Fireside Tales* had been published, the title of which reminds us of their original destination for adults and not only for children. The commissioned work was to be an anthology of folk narrative for educated readers, following Croce's aesthetic principle of 'maggiore poeticità' together with the politically unifactory principle of representing the literature of all the Italian regions. The latter criterion was particularly important in the climate of the Italian national reestablishment of democracy following the second world war. Calvino subordinated both principles to an elaboration which could assure the reception in an educated milieu of folktales in a written form.

He intentionally took the Grimms' work as his model even though he was aware of the cultural and ideological gap which separated him from them. Like many other intellectuals, Calvino was driven to recover national folk culture by a Gramsci-influenced motivation, which was not the Grimms' romantic and nationalistic one. In fact they had reinterpreted the ancient inheritance of German popular literature on ethnical and political bases. Nor did Calvino share the scientific motivations of critics and scholars in the nineteenth century, who continued to follow in the Grimms' footsteps (more in Jacob's than in Wilhelm's, I should say) to study folktales from a philological, mythological and historical point of view.

At the present time, a comparative motives- and themes analysis judged by the criteria of the Finnish school together with a morphological analysis of the texts according to Propp's methods represent different but converging ways of searching for an *Urform* and an *Urstruktur*.

Calvino, on the contrary, deemed important the leavening of the traditional folktales subject-matter which had been set in motion by the Grimm starting from Jacob's conservative, theoretical and philologically rigid projects and attaining to Wilhelm's rather free literary elaboration, which was orientated towards the didactic and pedagogical purposes of society in those times. The dynamic vitality of folktales struck Calvino, who started from a glacial detachment and, in the end, was totally pervaded by their world, as he stated in his *Introduction*. In those years his inclinations as a writer had been freed from realism and turned towards a fabulistic tone, in perfect sintony with it.

We will dwell upon the problem of orality, in relation to the process of de-mythologization of 'folk', a process Germanist critics are also discovering in the KHM-writing.

3. Starting from the question of style Calvino laid the foundations for the destiny of folktales in the second millenium, that of being absorbed into the sphere of writing. Every form of culture belongs to a particular age. The oral handingdown of folktales belongs to the first millenium, in which its end had already been foreseen. But what was effectively the degree of orality of the Grimms' sources? The latest German critics have dismanteled the myths of the 'alte Marie' and 'Frau Viehmann'. Calvin took pleasure in believing in those romantic conceptions of folk and folklore even though his appeal in favour of oral collecting and the study of that material seemed rather a forced tribute to science, because of the use which he actually made of written sources. Gramsci was the great absence from the *Introduction* to FI, and even though his conception of a national-popular literature was taken up, it was not used in the sense of a subordinate culture. If we consider the proselitism of Gramscian thought in Italy during the fifties, Calvino is seen to have a greater strength of personality, impervious to ideological fashions.

Calvino carried his growing negative opinion about popular creativity to the point of decreeing its end, sacrificing the orality of folktales for the writing of literary tales, whose milieu was popular or at least pseudo-popular. The passage from the oral to the written form had to be based on an idea which could bring the world of tales to the same level of the rational minds of adult readers. The previous task of orality had been to create the conditions for reconstructing "the great collection of Italian folktales, which has also to be a book pleasant to read, popular in its destination and not only at its sources." Thus, the listening public is replaced by a reading one.

Calvino therefore revived, though unconsciously, the Italian romantic concept of 'active folklore', deriving from a middleclass milieu. He also recovered the idea of a book for the masses according to the directions prefigured in 1846 by Cesare Correnti in the *European Review*. As he got nearer and nearer to the mysterious subject-matter of tales he felt all the combinatory potentiality of motives and images, seeing in the literary writing a sort of escape-valve. Tales came about through it, revitalized and fit to circulate in literary circles with an expressive and receptive fluidity, equal, if not superior to that of the masters' tales.

4. The passage from oral to written form had to be based on an idea that could put the world of tales up to the same level than the one of the rational, adult reader. In Calvino's opinion the link between life and tales was that "tales are true" as "they represent, alltogether, a general explanation of life through their always repeated and always varied casuistry of human events, which began in ancient times and has been brought down to us in the slow pondering of peasants' consciousness. They form a catalogue of destinies a man or a woman might have, most of all because of that piece of life in which the making of a destiny consists." Here we recognize the aesthetic aspirations to recover deep values like order, harmony and perfection which tales tend to re-establish through balancing fatal events and those which restore the hero. Being thus over-turned, the world of tales makes room for the human element, the natural, spiritual and rational element we deduce from Calvino's writing on tales, in that it represents the defeat of the enemy who symbolizes the hostility of the external world.

Calvino's work concerning this pattern is "comparable – in reality – to the second part of the Grimms' work as a type of intervention," as he wrote.

The following are the points in his programme:

a) "always choose the same versions from among this mountain of narrations, the most beautiful, original and rare ones, which can be reduced more or less to fifty variations,"

b)   "translate them from the dialect they had been gathered from (even when unfortunately they have been handed down to us only in their Italian translation, often lacking any vivid authenticity) try to narrate them once more – a difficult task – trying to regain some of their lost vividness,"

c)   "possibly enrich the selected version with the help of its variants, keeping its character and its inner unity untouched in order to make it as rich and articulated as possible,"

d)   "complete the points which seem suppressed or cut off with a light touch of invention,"

e)   "keep everything at the level of a language which is never too personal nor too colourless, which has its roots as much as much as possible in dialect, without any jump into 'educated' language. This language should be nimble enough to welcome and incorporate images from dialect, together with the most expressive and unusual round-about expressions."

Point a) gives us the criterion of a choice based on not always compatible parameters, being the first an aesthetic parameter and the other two corresponding to the 'lectio difficilior' in textual criticism. Point b) involves the most difficult task, that of translating from dialects, aiming at the preservation of the "freshness of authenticity" in the dialectal text, which often has not been handed down to us. Point c) seems to aim at a text which summons up all the variants and keeps their "inner unity". Point d) contains the most meaningful and innovatory principle, which is that of the degree of invention admissible in order to fill in empty spaces in popular memory, reestablishing the unspoken links which have been substituted in oral narration by gestual language. Point e) demands the search for a literary language which is able to absorb dialectal images and circumlocutions without being oppressed by them. It is in particular by applying points c) and d) of this programme that we can judge the significance of Calvino's folktale literary writing. Furthermore, by comparing KHM and FI, we can point out the peculiar correspondence between some procedures of the Italian writer and those of the Grimms'.

5.   From the first edition in 1812 to the last in 1857, many tales gathered in KHM show almost always improving textual modifications, some of which can also be found in the proceding private versions. Thanks to Lüthi's studies[2] we

[2]Max Lüthi, *Volksmärchen und Volkssage. Zwei Grundformen erzählender Dichtung* (Bern/München, [2]1966); – The Grimms' tales were published for the first time in 1812 while the seventh edition appeared in 1857. The following is the latest reprinting of the last edition: *Kinder- und Hausmärchen*.

may recognize know that Jacob's intervention in *Rapunzel* (KHM 12) succeeded in giving a more refined form to Fr. Schulz's text. The latter in term was derived from M.lle de la Force's *Persinette* and revealed the style peculiar to fairytales introduced in the Sun King's court. The corresponding Italian versions chosen by Calvino were the Sicilian *Prezzemolina* and the Tuscan *La vecchia nell' orto*. The transposition made by Calvino while translating from the oral into the written form is evident. He suppressed the narrator's interjections and the final rhyme formula of the Sicilian version, which had been published by Pitrè: *iddi arristaru filici e cuntenti / e nuatri semu senza nenti* (Those lived happily and glad / and we were left with nothing). Nevertheless, he considered the Sicilian version to be the most original one, both for the initial motive of the mushroom-ear and for the cross-fertilization with two themes (or types) of German folk-tales: *Rapunzel* (KHM 12) and *Hänsel und Gretel* (KHM 15). As regards the Tuscan version, which had been published by V. Imbriani, Calvino intervened in order to make the form slighter and the structure more simple. In his translation he eliminated the syntactic and stylistic schemes deriving from oral narration, i.e. historical present, iteration, direct speech and so on, which were not necessary and sometimes cumbersome, in order to make its reading more comfortable. The content, too, has been expressed in a more direct way through the elimination of secondary characters and events. Memè remains the only magic assistant and he puts an end to the tale intervening with deeds and words of advice. The fairytale does without the final motive of the fairies thrown into a hot cauldron: it is a cruel sort of revenge which the rational minds of modern readers would not have accepted.

As we can see, Calvino behaved differently in relation to the source of the text. As a matter of fact, orality has specific and distinct features varying between different areas and regional cultures. Sicilian orality more than any other has in-

---

Ausgabe letzter Hand mit den Originalanmerkungen der Brüder Grimm ed. Heinz Rölleke (Stuttgart, 1982); also compare with Jakob and Wilhelm Grimm, *Die Märchen der Brüder Grimm*, (München/ Zürich, 1985); there is also a translation into Italian of the entire collection of tales made by C. Bovero. It was edited by Calvino, who wrote the introduction: Grimm, *Le fiabe del focolare*, Prefazione di Giuseppe Cocchiara (Torino, 1951); amongst the critical essays about the tales collected by the Grimms see: J. Bolte und G. Polívka, *Anmerkungen zu den Kinder- und Hausmärchen der Brüder Grimm*, 5 vol. (Leipzig, 1913-32); *Die älteste Märchensammlung der Brüder Grimm. Synopse der handschriftlichen Urfassung von 1810 und der Erstdruck von 1812*, ed. and comm. by Heinz Rölleke (Cologny/Genève, 1975); K. Schmidt, *Die Entwicklung der Grimmschen Kinder- und Hausmärchen seit der Urhandschrift* (Halle, 1932); W. Schoof, *Zur Entstehungsgeschichte der Grimmschen Märchen. Bearbeitet unter Benutzung des Nachlasses der Brüder Grimm* (Hamburg, 1959); for critical accounts of the history of art tales in modern Europe I referred to Volker Klotz, *Das europäische Kunstmärchen. Fünfundzwanzig Kapitel seiner Geschichte von der Renaissance zur Moderne* (Stuttgart, 1985).

herited the literary tradition of chivalry epic, which has been kept alive by ballad-singers and the puppet theater. Some typical formulas of connection belong to the same tradition (like *Lassamu a stu Re ... e pigghiamu a un medicu, lassamu a idda chi dormi e pigghiamu a sò patri* = Let us leave this King ... and take a physician, Let us leave she who sleeps and take her father). In this way, the narrator keeps the listener company and brings him, as if holding his hand from to one place to another, inviting him to pay attention to one character then to another. Tuscan orality, on the other hand, has more the flavour of a wordy and prolix chronicle. Calvino juxtaposes the geometrical essentiality, which the homogenious scheme of all the folktales relies on, to its descriptive and often affected overabundance, to its biting immediacy, to its fluidity. Not only is the substitution of the historical present by the aorist functional to the passage from orality to writing but it aims also at a temporal ordering of actions. The aorist is "the expression of an order" (Roland Barthes).

If we compare the first edition, which was sent to Brentano in 1810 and attributed to the mythical "alte Marie" with that of 1812, then *Der Räuberbräutigam* (KHM 40) shows the passage from an immediate transcription from the oral to a smoother, linguistically and stylistically retouched one. The corresponding Italian tale is *L'assassino senza mano* (FI 89) which had been translated from the Florentine version entitled *Il Re avaro*. The changes made by Calvino regarded style and content and had all been inspired by the aim of making the tale's development coherent and precise, so that some incoherent passages were eliminated, thereby attenuating the over-bloody and less than decorous ones, and making believable unlikely events.

6. If we try to isolate the most specific elements of Calvino's selective and creative elaboration of FI from the above-mentioned examples, we have to remark how they coincide with those that have been noticed throughout the Grimms' writing of KHM.

The constitutive elements of Calvino's elaboration prove themselves to be the basic structures of his poetics. Translated into values, they can be found concentrated and codified in those of an aestethic and stylistic order, which Calvino synthetized into the six aphorisms contained in the *American Lectures*:

1. Lightness
2. Swiftness
3. Rapidity
4. Exactness
5. Visibility

6.   Consistence

All of them have educated (explicit) referents and popular (implicit) ones, which have been brought back to their common anthropological origin.

Lightness takes its form from the sorcerer's power of annulling his body's weight, raising it above the world during his tribe's hard times (droughts, illnesses, evil influences). His aim is to defeat evil forces from a position of physical superiority or to restore the order which had been disturbed. The protagonist's venture into the unknown in tales is provoked by an initial injury and aims at its final redressing and at the protagonist's rehabilitation after having passed the tests. The relation between privations and elevations makes the search for lightness in tales a reaction to the burdens of life. We can say that literature will have an existentially liberating function in a near future dominated by technologies. There is the example of *Der Kübelreiter* (The Knight of the Bucket) in the conclusion of the first lecture, which is one of Kafka's short stories; as in tales, in the end the bucket "becomes so light that it flies away with its knight, till it looses itself beyond the Ice Mountains". "So, riding our bucket we will face the new millenium – Calvino wrote – looking for lightness and swiftness", which is the subject of the second lecture.

In the folktale-world, the horse is the symbol of both a noble and a peasant life and acquires the meaning of a swift riding, equal if not superior to the swiftness of Cape Canaveral missiles in our reality. Swiftness is a functional necessity. The Sicilian narrator advises the listener that *lu cuntu nun metti tempo* (the tale does not consider time) "when she wants to jump some passages or indicate intervals of months or years". Speaking in dramaturgical terms, we can say that tales do not respect the Aristotelian unities of time and space. But perhaps it is not a matter of time-cancelling but of transference into another temporal dimension, set apart from the technical one. The hero's flight into another world, on a horse or a bird or in the devil's carriage, takes place in a flash. The venture into the beyond is likewise swift, even Dante's, which should – when viewed with our eyes – have taken an eternity instead of one week.

There are also other devices which satisfy the need for a direct approach suited to the structure of tales. The omission of details extraneous or superfluous to the plot and the insistence on the repetition of the obstacles to overcome and the corresponding expressive forms function as anticipations of the familiar and are, therefore, pleasurable. ("The childish pleasure of hearing tales consists also in the expectation of what is repeated: situations, sentences, formulas"). Everything, including the geometric symmetry of the actions, which have the same function as the rhymes in verse narrations have, is part of the technique of oral narration in folk tradition and can be partly saved through its writing inasmuch as it can produce sensations of swiftness also in the reader.

Exactness, which the third lesson deals with, apparently stands in contrast to swiftness. As a matter of fact it expresses the need for a precise vivisection of the various aspects of the 'imaginary', aspects which are summoned up and confused into vagueness and indefiniteness. Both concepts are like two lights of aesthetic pleasure which light up in their various possible combinations, as Leopardi stated in the *Zibaldone* and demonstrated in the *Idilli*. Calvino's combinatory technique is based on the search, at times maniacal, for precise particulars. The accuracy of particulars can determine a progressive growth of images in his tales as in his literary works.

Imagination is always visual, in Dante's as well as in popular narrators, who are bound to visualize what their characters see in reality or think or dream they have seen by means of metaphors and similes. Visual imagination comes together with oral narration, following and setting in motion its writing. It cannot but be anthropomorphic as it represents what is different, what it could be. As regards to both the functions tales must fulfil, tales are destined to be received, produced and reproduced in a continual recycling. But the visibility Calvino deals with in the fourth lesson, is seriously exposed to risks if separated from imagination, because of the "wild growth of prefabricated images". These risks can be avoided when starting from the 'writing degree zero' (using a concept of Roland Barthes, that reestablishes the connection between vision and image sent haywire by the eccentricity of mass media; or, when letting the 'fancyful' enter into literature, because it overcomes the 'everyday' whilst at the same time arising from it. The last proposal has not been explicitly stated by Calvino, but it can be added as another solution to the problem he pointed to, concerning the possible ways-out for fanciful narrative in the year two thousand.

The fifth lecture deals with multiplicity, which includes the absorption of several narrative systems in a story, even a short one. It is typical of mythical and fabulous compositions to be amenable to multiplicity as regards characters and voices even beyond the human repertoire, like the speaking trees or birds. The structure of tales is multiple because of the quantitative conception they are based on, as for example plural numbers, the first of which is number three, ruling the systems of the tests to be overcome.

But the numerical structure goes beyond the magic value of number three and its multiples. It is the key to understand the tale's *Kettentechnick* opposing the novel's *Episodentechnik*. The first is a technique followed by Calvino and the

198

Grimms, which allows them to distinguish the abstract from the functional meaning of motives.

The text of the sixth lecture which Calvino had planned on the theme of consistence is missing, because he had not yet written it. The same applies to texts of at least two further lectures on themes, he said, he had already gathered materials for. Only one title was written in his notes: *On the beginning and ending* (of novels or tales?). It confirms the potentialities of the values Calvino projects into the year two thousand after having experimented with them, like the stylistic features of folk- and high literature, following in the spirit and the footsteps of the Grimms.[3]

---

[3]Translated by Chiara Simeone, Bari (Italy).

Patricia Lysaght
(Dublin)

A TRADITION BEARER IN CONTEMPORARY IRELAND

Introduction

Scholarly assessment of the repertoires of individual tradition bearers has been a feature of Irish folk narrative scholarship since the 1930s. The tradition bearers who have received special attention and whose repertoires have been scientifically collected, assessed and published, in whole or in part, have been, and invariably are, native Irish-speakers from *Gaeltacht* – or Irish-speaking areas – or recently *Gaeltacht* areas in Ireland.[1]

Individual non-*Gaeltacht* tradition bearers and their repertoires have, on the other hand, received little scholarly attention.[2] This situation is to be regretted since such attention would contribute substantially to a better understanding of traditions and tradition processes in Ireland generally in earlier and in recent times. In an attempt to widen the focus of Irish storytelling scholarship the following introductory analysis of the repertoire of a tradition bearer from the midlands of Ireland is presented.

The tradition bearer is fifty years old Mrs. Jenny McGlynn, a housewife from Mountmellick, Co. Laois. Unlike her *Gaeltacht* counterparts, she was born and still lives in an area of Ireland which experienced English influence from an

---

[1] Considerations of space make it impracticable to list the published or partly-published repertoires of individual tradition-bearers here. However, an indication of what has been published to date can be gleaned from the bibliog. in Séamus O Duilearga, *Leabhar Sheáin I Chonaill* (Dublin, 1948), 3 ed. (Dublin, 1977), 399-407; English translation by Máire MacNeill, *Seán O Conaill's Book* (Dublin, 1981), pp. 363-72 and Caoimhín O Danachair, *A Bibliography of Irish Ethnology and Folk Tradition* (Cork and Dublin, 1978), pp. 36-39, 43-52. For delination and discussion of the *Gaeltacht* areas in Ireland, see Brian O Cuív, *Irish Dialects and Irish-Speaking Districts*, Dublin 1951.

[2] Very many items from individual English language tradition bearers have appeared in a wide variety of publications during the last century and a half. (See Caoimhín O Danachair, *idem*). However, no scholarly study of an individual English language tradition bearer and repertoire has yet appeared.

early period. By the middle of the sixteenth-century, during the reign of Mary Tudor, the area (together with neighbouring Co. Offaly) was partly 'planted' with English settlers and was known as Queen's County. Its principal town (now called Portlaoise) was called Maryborough, a name still used by old inhabitants of the county.[3] Laois was also one of the counties in the eastern part of Ireland which became English-speaking at an early date.[4] By the middle of the nineteenth century only a small pocket of native Irish speakers, mainly old people, remained in the south of the county and these represented only one per cent of the population.[5] Mrs. McGlynn was brought up in an English language milieu, but she learned the Irish language at primary school which she attended until the age of fourteen years. Although she uses the odd Irish word in speech, she has effectively forgotten her school Irish, and that language has essentially no place in Jenny's life, either in general terms, or in her capacity as an active bearer of tradition.[6] She is, therefore, an exponent of folk traditions known and transmitted through the medium of the English language in Ireland, and especially of such traditions in the eastern midlands of the country.

In addition, Mrs. McGlynn was not born until 1939, four years after the foundation of the Irish Folklore Commission, an institution which concentrated the work of its folklore collectors mainly in the Irish-speaking areas.[7] Jenny's exposure to the oral tradition, therefore, occurred initially as recently as the 1940s, and continued in her home environment during the 1950s. She only became an active bearer of tradition after her marriage in 1961, a little over twenty-five years ago. In such circumstances, it is reasonable to assert that knowledge of the chains of transmission of her oral narrative genres should contribute to our understanding of the processes of oral transmission of traditions in the English language in Ireland from about the turn of the century[8] and in recent

---

[3] V. Rev. John Canon O'Hanlon, and Rev. Edward O'Leary, *History of the Queens's County*, vol. 1 (Dublin, 1907), pp. 436-9; Theodore W. Moody, Francis X. Martin, *The Course of Irish History* (Cork, 1967), p. 190.

[4] Brian O Cuív, *op. cit.,* pp. 17 ff.

[5] *Ibid.,* pp. 23-4.

[6] The concepts of *active* and *passive* bearers of tradition as used in this paper are from Carl W. von Sydow, "On the Spread of Tradition", in *Selected Papers in Folklore*, ed. Laurits Bødker, Copenhagen 1948, pp. 11-43.

[7] The Commission was unable to concentrate personel in the English-speaking areas of Ireland due mainly to the lack of resources. But collection work in the *Gaeltacht* was always considered more important and urgent. For a discussion of the Irish Folklore Commission and its work see Bo Almqvist, *The Irish Folklore Commission. Achievement and Legacy* (Dublin, 1979), (pamphlet). Also in *Béaloideas*, 45-7 (1977-79), pp. 6-26.

[8] As is evident from the text of this paper, Jenny names her grandmother, and her mother (born 1897), as sources for some of the legends.

times. Although the following aspect cannot be dealt with in any detail within the scope of this paper, it seems likely that a comparison of our findings in relation to Mrs. McGlynn's repertoire with those already established for some tradition bearers in the *Gaeltacht*, should further enable us to achieve a fuller understanding of oral narrative transmission processes in Irish tradition generally.

Genre analysis of Jenny's repertoire is likewise of importance since it should indicate oral narrative categories – though by no means all such categories – current in the English language in Ireland at, and indeed before the turn of the century, and also in modern times.[9]

Jenny McGlynn and her traditions are products of an English-speaking environment. However, in order to get a proper perspective on this modern tradition bearer from the midlands of Ireland and on her repertoire, it is necessary to consider also – albeit only briefly here – the Gaelic storytelling[10] tradition and all its variety of genres and performance, as it was, and as it still remains to some extent, in Irish-speaking areas of Ireland. It is thus to the world of Gaelic storytelling that we now return.

Gaelic Storytelling Revisited

A story about storytelling, or rather about the decline in appreciation of a certain form of oral narration, tells that a mysterious voice in the chimney exclaimed three times 'faid saoil chugat, a fhiannaí!' (long life to you, storyteller!) as if paying due (and expected) tribute to an old man who had just told a tale in the traditional fashion while those present had paid no heed to him and had not thanked him at the end. Clearly the storyteller (*scéalaí*)[11] had told a long tale in the Irish language; perhaps he had narrated a version of one of the most popular of all oral folktales in Ireland, the folk version of the classical tale of Perseus entitled 'The Dragon Slayer' and designated Type 300 in the Aarne-Thompson

---

[9]Mrs. McGlynn knows no examples of the legends described in international folklore scholarship as Modern (Urban) Legends. And Intermediate type list of Dublin modern legends has been prepared by Eilís Ní Dhuibhne, "Dublin Modern Legends: An Intermediate Type List and Examples", *Béaloideas* 51 (1983), pp. 55-70.

[10]Storytelling or *scéalaíocht*, refers to the narration of folktales and heroic romantic tales in the Gaelic language, by the *scéalaí*, the "Gaelic story-teller, properly so-called". See James H. Delargy, *The Gaelic Story-Teller* (London, 1945).

[11]See previous note.

catalogue of international folktales: *The Types of the Folktale*;[12] or he may have
narrated a long hero tale, perhaps Conall Gulban,[13] a tale which was possibly the
most popular of heroic romantic tales and had great vogue among traditional
storytellers in Gaelic-speaking Ireland and Scotland; or indeed the storyteller
may well have recited a Fenian tale, even 'The Boyhood Deeds of Fionn',[14] one of
the most enduring tales of the great mythic hero Fionn Mac Cumhail and beloved of Gaelic audiences down the centuries.[15] Whatever genre the storyteller
performed, the story leaves us in no doubt but that the storyteller, in the performance of his art, was worthy of respect and praise. But no cries and murmurs
of appreciation arose from the unappreciative 'audience'. Only the voice in the
chimney acknowledged his performance with the traditional exclamation of
appreciation as though some dead narrator or appreciative listener had come
back to pay him due respect.

This little story aptly sums up the situation in which the founding fathers of
the movement to collect and preserve the folklore of Ireland in the 1930s,[16] found
the storyteller who knew and was capable of telling long elaborate Märchen or
hero tales in the Irish language – genres intimately connected with, and preserved in, that language. This tradition specialist, *an scéalaí*, so vividly described by
James H. Delargy in his celebrated lecture *The Gaelic Story-Teller*[17], was alone
with his tales in a changing society largely uninterested in, and perhaps no longer
capable of fully understanding the language of the tales, or indeed appreciating
his performance of them. Storytelling involving such long tales was no longer a
familiar feature of the social life of the people, and at least one storyteller, described by Delargy, felt compelled to repeat his long tales to inanimate
'audiences' such as stone walls lest they slip from his memory.[18] Another storyteller maintained, and indeed, regretted, that his storytelling had been spoiled by

---

[12]FF Communications No. 184, Helsinki 1961, sec. rev. 1973. Irish folktales are classified in, Seán O
Súilleabháin and Reidar Th. Christiansen, *The Types of the Irish Folktale*, FF Communications 188
Helsinki 1963, 1967.

[13]See Alan Bruford, *Gaelic Folk-Tales and Medieval Romances* (Dublin, 1969) (= *Béaloideas*
XXXIV, 1966 (1969), especially pp. 72-9). Also published in book form (Dublin, 1969).

[14]For a study of the Boyhood Deeds of Finn in Gaelic narrative tradition see Joseph F. Nagy, *The
Wisdom of the Outlaw* (Los Angeles, 1985).

[15]For a study of the corpus of legend and tradition associated with Fionn Mac Cumhaill, see Dáithí
O hOgáin, *Fionn Mac Cumhaill. Images of the Gaelic Hero* (Dublin, 1987).

[16]See note 7.

[17]See note 10.

[18]James H. Delargy, (*op. cit.*) p. 12, tells how Seán O Conaill, the Cillrialaig storyteller was observed
telling his stories to "an unresponsive stone wall, while herding the grazing cattle".

being forced, through love of the tales, to tell them in English to young people who did not know Irish.[19]

The storytellers, mainly men[20] who could perform the wonder- and hero-tales and compel the attention of an audience, were growing ever fewer in number by the turn of the century.[21] Thus the collection work in the 1920s, and the 1930s especially, was in effect the Indian summer of such storytelling. In the last flush and flowering of the narration of the folk- or hero- or Fenian-tale in the Irish language, in its time-honoured setting before an appreciative audience, the outstanding *scéalaí* performed tales which were by no means the debris of native hero tales or international Märchen dredged up from the deficient memory of an inactive storyteller. Rather they were, by and large, outstanding examples of long, elaborate and demanding tales, and in performing them, the storyteller emerged from the shadow of his twilight years and became once again an individual with status and prestige in his own family and community.[22]

Although the gifted old time storytellers have passed away, the genres which were their precious stock-in-trade and which were also known to many passive bearers of tradition, have not yet died out in Ireland. While it is true that the narrative occasion now, as in the earlier decades, is mainly the recording session with the professional folklore collector, nevertheless, long Märchen and heroic romantic tales in the Irish language are still performed by a few storytellers in some *Gaeltacht* or Irish-speaking areas in Ireland. They are thus still part of the storytelling environment in Ireland.[23] To what extent these elaborate genres ever prospered in the English language in Ireland, is a matter that needs investigation.[24] It is clear, however, that such genres were never part of

---

[19]Delargy, *op. cit.*, p. 16. In his preface to *Beside the Fire* (London, 1910), pp. xlii-xliii, a collection of folktales translated from Gaelic, Douglas Hyde mentions in particular the effects of the decline of the Gaelic language on the storytelling tradition.

[20]Delargy, *op. cit.*, p. 6, Seán O Súilleabháin, *Storytelling in Irish Tradition* (Cork, 1973), p. 11. The telling of Fenian or native heroic romantic tales by women was usually frowned on by men and was considered unlucky –, A woman *fiannaí*, or a crowing hen!, – as the proverb states (Delargy, *op. cit.*, p. 7).

[21]Delargy, *op. cit.*, pp. 6, 12, 14 for example.

[22]For example, the Co. Clare storyteller, Stiofán O Ealaoire who was much sought after when he became an active bearer of tradition (Delargy *op. cit.*, p. 15). Of relevance here is the application and discussion of Roger D. Abraham's ideas about storytelling as a means of personal power, by Inta G. Carpenter in *A Latvian Storyteller* (New York, 1980), pp. 40-42.

[23]See Séamas O Catháin, *Scéalta Chois Cladaigh* (Dublin, 1983), p. XIV with reference to the Mayo storyteller Seán O hEinirí whose repertoire extends from brief anecdotes to long hero tales ... There are still a few storytellers who can relate the Fenian tales, but rarely more than one or two each.

[24]See Delargy's comments on this question in Delargy (*op. cit.*), p. 6-7.

repertoire, and it is thus unlikely that they were ever part of the repertoires of those tradtion bearers from whom she learned her lore. Thus in order to get an indication of Jenny's store of tradition, an outline of her repertoire follows.

Outline of Repertoire Content

While some outstanding Gaelic storytellers were known to scorn narration of short items of traditional lore,[25] the published repertoires of other prominent Gaelic storytellers, such as Seán O Conaill of Cillrialaig, Co. Kerry,[26] show that these storytellers knew and related shorter tradition categories also. It is probable that they continued to do so even more after their more exclusive narrative genres were no longer in demand. But the tellers of local tales, prayers, songs, social-historical tradition and short realistic narratives about fairies, ghosts and other supernatural beings, were always more numerous, even in *Gaeltacht* areas, and these genres were told by women as well as men.[27] The tradition bearer I am concerned with in this paper belongs to this latter category in terms of her repertoire content. She has a large store of folk beliefs about the supernatural world and a corresponding wide range of legends of the supernatural. Some of these are local legends, others are found over the greater part of Ireland, while others still are international migratory legends as we shall see presently. Some legends such as 'The Changeling' and 'The Three Sneezes' are set in the domestic sphere while others are concerned with 'reserved' areas of the physical landscape associated in popular thought with beings such as the fairies, for example. Mrs. McGlynn's repertoire also contains a large and important body of socio-economic material; here, however, we are concentrating on a selection of her supernatural legends. We will investigate the source or sources of these legends, and if possible the circumstances in which she learned them, how, and when, she became an active bearer of them and other traditions, and the effect, if any, her new role as an active tradition bearer had on her status in her home and community.

---

[25] Delargy, *op. cit.*, p. 16 tells of an outstanding Co. Kerry storyteller who had "no regard for oral material other than long folk-tales..."

[26] See note 1 *supra.*

[27] Delargy (*op. cit.*, p. 7) states that women excelled men in these areas of tradition.

Thereafter we will discuss briefly whether her repertoire can be characteris-
ed in terms of *active* and *memory* repertoire,[28] the ways in which she has maintained her audiences' interest in her narratives to the present day, and to what
extent, if any, she believes them herself, or expects her audiences to believe them.

As a first step in this proposed investigation we will briefly survey Jenny's
life history and the factors which were material in the formation of her particular
repertoire.

Life History and Repertoire Formation Outline

I visited Mrs. McGlynn for the first time in June 1976 when I was collecting
up-to-date source material about belief in the banshee.[29] It was obvious to me
then that she possessed a large store of diverse beliefs and legends about the supernatural world. Since that time I have recorded her on a regular basis, often
alone at New Year and sometimes in the summer with students as part of their
field-work programmes.[30] Initially, the interviews were on specific topics connected with my own research work. My interest in her own life history at that time
was primarily for the purposes of context formation in order to understand the
mechanics of her repertoire especially in relation to its genre content. As time
went on, however, I realised that her life story was an important social document
providing much socio-economic and socio-historical information about life for
the men, women and children of a working class family in a small rural town in
the midlands of Ireland for the better part of a century. In addition, this biographical information, which was recorded by means of open-ended, in- depth
interviews, sometimes in the presence of family members, also provides inval-
uable data about the formation of her repertoire and the tradition bearers and
the narration situations which were part and parcel of the formation process.

Mrs. McGlynn learned her traditions essentially in her home area. She has
lived all her life in her native Mountmellick, originally a Quaker town situated
some fifty miles westwards from Dublin city. She was born into a working class

---

[28]See Carpenter, *op. cit.*, pp. 37-8.

[29]Jenny is by far the best exponent of the banshee tradition that I have met. The banshee complex
has been studied by Patricia Lysaght, *The Banshee. The Irish Supernatural Death-Messenger*
(Dublin, 1986).

[30]In addition to c. 17 hours of taperecording, I have also made three video recordings of c. 2 hours
duration of Mrs. McGlynn.

family living in Manor Lane, an area slightly outside the town where there were ten labourers, cottages for working class families. The family lived with her maternal grandmother, and, as was so often the case, Jenny, the grandchild, learned some narratives from her grandparent. It was from her that Jenny heard a version of the following well-known Irish treasure guardian legend about the Leipreachán's pot of gold.[31] When I asked her if she knew this legend she replied:

> I heard that years and years ago. My granny used to tell the story that if you caught a leipreachán or fairy you'd have to ask them for their wealth. And they usually had a crock of gold and it was buried under a *buachalán* [ragworth]. And there was a lot of *buachaláns*, but this one was the biggest *buachalán* in the field. And the man dug it up and saw that it was the fairy gold. He tied a piece of his red handkerchief around the *buachalán* and went home for to get a spade for to dig down deeper to see if there was anymore of them there ... And when he came back with the spade every *buachalán* in the field was tied up with red string.[32]

Jenny's mother and father also told stories to the children, especially on rainy days when very little else could be done. She told me this quite spontaneously one day when I asked her if she had ever heard the story about the devil playing cards. She replied: "Time and time again, when we'd be sitting at home with nothing to do, on a rainy day especially, we'd start telling the stories and we'd hear about it."

The Cardplayers and the Devil (ML 3015)[33]

> It happened not too far away from here, really, about the playing of the cards. There was a few men that were in [town] on a fair day and they had a few drinks too many and they used to stay out too late. And one night they were going home and there was this man sitting at a table at the bull corra gate[34] playing cards. And a candle on the table, and he invited them to play with him. So they got into the game and were playing away. He let them win. There was a whole lot of sovereigns flying every way. About twelve o'clock one of the men sneezed and a card fell. And when they stooped down to

---

[31] Migratory Legend-Suggested Irish Type (MLSIT) 6011 under the title "Capturer of Fairy Shoemaker Outwitted" has been suggested by Bo Almqvist in *Crossing the Border. A sampler of Irish migratory legends about the supernatural* (Dublin, 1988), p. 45 for this legend. See also Diarmaid O Giolláin, "The *Leipreachán* and Fairies, Dwarfs and the Household Familiar: A comparative study", *Béaloideas*, 52, esp. pp. 85-91.

[32] Patricia Lysaght, Tape VIII, 25 July 1981.

[33] The migratory legend numbers used here are those in Reidar Th. Christiansen, *The Migratory Legends. A Proposed List of Types with a systematic catalogue of the Norwegian variants*, FF Communications No. 175, Helsinki 1958. For a study of this legend in Irish tradition see É. Ní Anluain, "An Cearrbhach agus an Diabhal: Ml 3015 in Éirinn", *Sinsear* 5, 1988, pp. 75-87.

[34] A field-gate near where Jenny lived.

pick up the card they saw that this man had a cloven foot. Of course, everyone broke up. The next morning they found that the sovereigns they had won were only leaves.[35]

In her time the family house was also a rambling house. It was the 'middle' cottage in Manor Lane and the people rambled in from the cottages at both sides. She says "We'd be in bed at six when we were young, but we'd be listening to them. And every Friday night there was a card game; the men played the cards and the women chatted." Of course children are also influenced by situations outside the home. It was in her father's home-place in Co. Offaly that Jenny picked up this version of the 'Changeling Legend':

The Changeling (ML 5085)
> J. McG.: A changeling, that's a child that has been taken, and a fairy put back in its place. And the only way to get rid of it is to use violence.
> P. L.: Could you tell me a story about that?
> J. McG.: There's two or three stories.[36] One is about the child the mother used to put up in the room as soon as it was fed its last feed. And she'd hear terrible strange sounds coming out of the room. The child was all the time crying and keening. And she'd go up and the child would stop. She was nearly wore out. So her uncle came to visit her and noticed that the child wasn't right. It looked old for its age, wrinkled and old. And she thought that was because the child was crying so much that it had de- formed itself. So he decided that he'd take over one night and give her and the hus- band a break. And as soon as the child started to keen he went in with a needle on the top of a stick and prodded the child. And it went through the window. And the next thing there was a child crying out in the yard and they found that the baby had been left back, a nice healthy good-looking child. It had been a changeling that had been in the cot for four or five months that was breaking the mother's heart.[37]

As Jenny grew up many other types of situations had a bearing on the contents of her repertoire; for example, the years she spent in service in houses in the town when, as a schoolgirl, she worked for two hours before school began and did like- wise in the evenings after school, her work in the peat-bog saving peat for family use and also for pay, and her work with the local farmers. The inclusion of the well-known legend of the milk stealing hare (or the hag in hare-form) in her repertoire is probably due to her familiarity with farm work and milch cows and also to the fact that it was her task in her early years to collect the butter and milk for household consumption which her family bought from a local farmer.

---

[35]Patricia Lysaght, Tape VI, 16 April 1981.

[36]Mrs. McGlynn has two other somewhat dissimilar versions of The Changeling Legend which she got from other informants. For a study of the Changeling Legend in Ireland see Séamas Mac Phi- lib, *Iarlaisí: Símhalartú i mbéaloideas na hÉireann* (MA thesis in Dept. of Irish Folklore, Univer- sity College Dublin).

[37]Patricia Lysaght, Tape VI, 16 April 1981.

The Milk-Stealing Hare[38]

P. L.: Do you know a story about a hare which was believed to steal milk from the cows out in the field?

J. McG.: Yeah! Well, that's one of the stories that Mammy used to tell us too.

The cow would be out in the fields and every morning when the man would go to get the cow to milk it, she'd be dry. They had the vets* with them and they couldn't find out what was wrong. Then an old man came; he was a tramp of the road, and asked them did they ever notice was there anything at the cows at night? So the old man and the farmer went out and they sat out all night long. And this hare came on the scene and no matter how they tried to catch it, they couldn't. So they decided anyway that they'd lay a trap for it. And 'twas a big she-hare. And they met this old woman in the mornings: she used to be walking up and down the roads. They were telling her and they said they were going to catch the hare and she asked them not to, 'don't kill it'. They said they had to because it was leaving them without any milk for the children.

It was going on anyway for three or four weeks at a time. This night the farmer and his son went out and his son had a gun. As soon as the hare saw them coming, she ran away. And as she did, the young lad let off with the gun and shot her. And with that she let an unmerciful scream and staggered away, anyway. So they followed it on to see where it would go, to make sure it was dead. It went into a little old hut. And when they got to the hut there was no hare, but there was an old woman lying on the ground and her ribs all shattered with pellets from the shotgun. It happened that she was after being enchanted in some way and she was able to change into a hare at night, something to that effect.[39]

* vet = veterinary surgeon

The legends mentioned so far are all from Jenny's pre-marriage days. On her marriage in 1961 at the age of twenty-two years she moved to the Bay Road at the other side of the town. She was very lonely initially but gradually began to feel part of the community. There is no doubt that her move to the house on the Bay Road on marriage was a most significant factor in the later enrichment of her store of traditional knowledge. The 'Bay' house was also a rambling house, a house where people were always coming and going – not only neighbours, but also family and other relations. These people, together with her husband and brothers-in-law, all played a part in the further formation of Jenny's repertoire and indeed their influence became greater as the years went by.

It is obvious from Jenny's altogether spontaneous attribution of so many items of tradition to her mother-in-law, that old Mrs. McGlynn greatly influenced, and was responsible for, many additions to Jenny's stock of supernatural lore. She described quite naturally in the course of my very first interview with her the

---

[38]A common legend in Ireland for which SIT 3056 has been put forward by Almqvist, *op. cit.* (1988), p. 60. Jan Wall, *Tjuvmjölkande väsen*, I-II, Studia Ethnologica Upsaliensia III, 1977, 5, 1978, Uppsala, deals with the Scandinavian traditions of milk-stealing.

[39]Patricia Lysaght, Tape VI, 16 April 1981.

domestic setting in which her mother-in-law told her about the death coach, an omen of death in Irish tradition, and how she felt she herself heard it on that occasion and her reactions to the experience. Here is an extract from her personal narrative on that occasion.

> I have heard the coach ... sitting down by the fire. One night I heard it. I heard it my-self, yeah; me mother-in-law and I were sitting, one at either side of the fire. She didn't be well, you know, and I used to sit up with her. It was before Catherine was born. That's about fourteen year ago and a ... the time was half past one. Our men was work-ing in the bog at the time and they were on the night shift and we were waiting for them to come home. She was sitting by the fire. She wasn't too well with an old heart attack coming on her. And she thought that when she heard it first that it was her time [to die] and, she said 'bless yourself, for that is the dead coach'. And I listened: I could only hear the wind first and then I heard the noise. It was the very same as a pony's trap ...
> P. L. And how did you feel?
> J. McG.: Well, I went very cold and I thought 'if it is the dead coach it is one of us that are going to go,' especially like when we were in bad health and me having ... being ex-pecting the child and that, you know?
> P. L.: Did anybody die at that time?
> J. McG.: A woman further up the road died that time, Mrs. Geoghan.[40]

Although her father-in-law lived for only ten months after her marriage, he in-fluenced her in two significant ways; firstly, she learned much from him. She says "Chaps would ramble in and the old man would be talking about what happen-ed ..." It was from him that she picked up a version of the international migratory legend 'The Legend of Pan', which she described as "an old one that was going around in the family for years."

The King of the Cats (ML 6070B)[41]

> There was a man coming home from work late at night, it was in the winter nights and those times he used to work until maybe ten or eleven o'clock. And the man was ma-king his way home and the road was completely blocked with cats. He had to step through them. And just as he was going past the last cat one shouted "When you go home tell Muggins that Juggins is dead. We have to elect a new king."
> So he went home, and he was a bit frightened over it. And the wife was sitting at the side of the fire and he says "I'm after getting the fright of me life", he says, "I thought I heard a cat saying 'When you go home tell Muggins that Juggins is dead'."

---

[40]Patricia Lysaght, Tape 1 side 1, 28 June 1976.

[41]A study of this legend in Irish tradition is Eoghan R. O Néill, *"The King of the Cats is Dead" in Irish folk tradition* (Student essay in Dept. of Irish Folklore, University College Dublin). The classical study is Inger M. Boberg, *Sagnet om den store Pans død*, (København, 1934)

And the minute he said it the cat that was on the hearth let a roar' "Let me out, that's me uncle!"[42]

Secondly, it was with her father-in-law's encouragement that she became an active bearer of the traditions which she herself already knew: "... the old man would be talking about what happened and anything I heard up at home I'd tell down there ... when I told the story of the big black dog[43] in Manor Lane he said that did happen ..." So with the benign influence of her father-in-law she felt able to relate what she knew.

She became an active bearer of tradition.

This was an important social and psychological achievement for Jenny. Her emergence as an active tradition bearer gave her confidence and a sense of belonging in her new surroundings after her marriage and helped her to integrate into the Bay Road community. In a family situation in which the extended family-in-law control network maintained a high level of conformity in behavioural patterns, Jenny gained, and maintained, a special position and identity, by virtue of her abilities as an active bearer of tradition.

But how are we to characterize her repertoire? Why do people still wish to hear her narrate? And does she believe the legends she narrates? These are questions which we will now address briefly.

'Active' and 'memory' repertoire and the belief criterion in legends

While still in her twenties then, Mrs. McGlynn became an active bearer of the traditions she then knew. She has continued to relate legends from her home environment prior to marriage and has also added legends learned from her in-laws and others to her repertoire over the years.

In describing Mrs. McGlynn as an active bearer of tradition,[44] I do not mean to assert that she has been active with regard to all of her traditions all of

---

[42]Patricia Lysaght, Tape VI, 16 April 1981.

[43]The black dog apparition is a common theme with Jenny and tradition bearers in general in Ireland.

[44]See note 28 above; also von Sydow, *op. cit.*, note 6 above, and Kenneth Goldstein, "On the Application of the Concepts of Active and Inactive Traditions to the Study of Repertory" in América Paredes and Richard Bauman, eds., *Toward New Perspectives in Folklore*, (Austin and London, 1972).

the time. Her repertoire consists of an *active* repertoire and a *memory* repertoire. Certain themes have a continuing fascination for Jenny and her audiences. She has been, and still is, particularly interested in supernatural lore and performs[45] this genre very well. That supernatural traditions have been, and are, part of Jenny's active repertoire, are well attested by the legends quoted so far. On the other hand, narratives such as the international migratory legend entitled 'River Claiming its Due', 'The hour has come but not the man', ML 4050[46], which she heard many years ago and has told only infrequently in the intervening years and consequently tells rather badly, belong to her *memory* repertoire.

Circumstances in which items belonging to the *memory* repertoire may become part of a tradition bearer's *active* repertoire are also illustrated by reference to Mrs. McGlynn. She had been a passive bearer of marriage traditions for many years until the marriage of her daughter brought them to mind again. Then she began to tell the legend of the attempted abduction of a bride by the fairy host with the initial help of a human. The legend has been titled 'The Three Sneezes' and is fairly common in Ireland.[47] The following is Jenny's version:

> Well, they had this man helping them for to get at the bride so that they could take her and he was there and they were having high tea the evening before the wedding. And she was to fit on her clothes and let them all see her – the family that is – before she went to church next day. And the little people, you see, got in while the old man [the human helper] was making his greetings and they were up in the rafters. And they used do terrible funny things, you see, to distract the neighbours and family from the bride so as to be able to take her. And one of them was moving over and seemingly there was dust and she sneezed and the fairies vanished. So they couldn't take her; you see, they wouldn't take her unless she was perfect. They couldn't have anyone that was sickly in their tribe because otherwise they'd all get sick. So they had to have everyone perfect especially the humans they had taken.[48]

---

[45]For a discussion of *performance* as a central concept in folklore communication see Mihály Hoppál, "Genre and Context in Narrative Event", in L. Honko and V. Voigt, eds., *Genre, Structure and Reproduction in Oral Literature* (Budapest, 1980), p. 118, and works by American scholars such as Del Hymes, Don Ben-Amos, Kenneth Goldstein, Linda Dégh and Andrew Vázsonyi, mentioned there.

[46]Patricia Lysaght, Type VI, 16 April 1981. For a discussion of this legend in Irish tradition see Barry O'Reilly, *"The River Claims its Due"* and *"Fód an Bháis"*: Two Irish Legends of Fate (Student Essay in Dept. of Irish Folklore, University College Dublin).

[47]This is a frequent rescue-type legend in Ireland told about a bride. Dumbness as result of the abduction occurs in some versions. See for example legend No. 11 in Seán O hEochaidh, Máire Ní Néill, Séamus O Catháin, *Síscéalta O Thír Chonaill / Fairy Legends from Donegal*, (Dublin, 1977), pp. 52-3.

[48]Patricia Lysaght, Type VII, 16 April 1981.

In the more usual version of this legend the attempted abduction takes place during the wedding meal. It is foiled by the pious exclamation of the human helper who says, *Dia linn!*, God with us!, when the bride sneezes, and the fairies must then vanish. But Jenny has given a more modern setting and rationale to the legend and perhaps we can learn something about the so-called belief criterion in legend definition from a short discussion of this one.

The legend is set in the context of a pre-marriage party for the bride during which she shows off her wedding clothes. Such parties are quite common nowadays and this realistic modern-day setting is suitable for her younger family audience. The bride's allergy to dust which causes her to sneeze has also a modern-day health-conscious ring to it.[49]

Jenny also tends to add explanatory riders to the legends. But this is not as a result of distance from her legends,[50] rather it is partly due in the first instance to her own personality since she thinks a lot about the various beliefs and tries to rationalise them for herself. It may also be partly a reaction to some scepticism on the part of her family and their friends. For Jenny not only uses details in the setting of the legend to make it, as it were, more realistic, but she adds these 'explanations' as if to evoke belief in her audience.

But it is not vital for Jenny as a narrator that her audience should believe the story of the legend. Jenny has told me that she herself does *not* believe that brides ever were stolen or that human children were exchanged for fairy children. She believes rather, that belief in the abduction of brides – like the changeling belief – was held by people "years and years ago". This is what she sees as the essential point of the legend. Thus, the apparent lack of subjective belief on Jenny's own part (and perhaps also on the part of her audience) does not in any way invalidate the legend for Jenny or cause her to reject it, because the essential message of the legend, as she understands it, remains. This is also her position in relation to religious legends.[51] Thus the legend structure, which seems to incorporate a compelling momentum on its own, enables her, as a good narrator, (and without the requirement of subjective belief on her part) to make her case as

---

[49] Jenny also very often uses modern day setting and refers to modern day practices and requirements in her narration.

[50] This concept of 'distance' from the tradition, in relation to Anglo-Irish folklore collectors, such as T. Crofton Croker, is discussed inter alia by Neil C. Hultin in "Anglo-Irish Folklore from Clonmel: Thomas C. Croker and British Library Add. 20099", *Fabula* 27, H. 3/4 (1986), esp. pp. 294 ff.

[51] Jenny will also tell legends with religious themes which she does not believe. She says: "...the fact, that I don't believe them doesn't mean I won't tell them..."

convincingly as possible to her audience – and it is for the audience members themselves to form their own opinions about matters of truth and belief.

It is thus quite clear from the supernatural belief legends presented here that Dégh's and Vászony's assertions that subjective belief on the part of tellers and audiences is not a necessary criterion in legend definition, and that it is unessential in the process of its creation and communication, but that the *"general*[52] reference to belief is an inherent and outstanding feature of the folk legend", are borne out.[53]

Conclusion

This paper consists of an introductory analysis of the repertoire of a tradition bearer from the English-speaking areas of Ireland. It is an attempt to achieve a more balanced approach to repertoire studies in Irish folk narrative scholarship, since to date only the repertoires of native Irish-speaking tradition bearers have received full attention as the published works show.

The tradition bearer whose repertoire is analysed is a fifty-years old housewife, Mrs. Jenny McGlynn, from Mountmellick, Co. Laois, whom I have visited and recorded at intervals over the last twelve years. She is the product of an English language environment both in terms of domicile and cultural milieu.

Genre analysis of her repertoire shows that she has a large store of traditional knowledge of several different kinds. Apart from her wide ranging socio-economic and socio-historical knowledge, she has a particularly rich store of supernatural lore since this is, and has been, an area of special interest to Jenny, to her own family, and to her family-in-law.

In this paper we have concentrated on legends dealing with the supernatural since the transmission channels are known and we can, through them, follow Jenny's progress from being a learner and passive bearer of tradition to becoming and remaining, an active bearer of tradition.

Like so many of the Gaelic-speaking tradition bearers, Jenny never left her home area for any significant period of time. She learned her narratives in her local environment, in her own home initially and after her marriage in 1961 in

---

[52]Author's italics.
[53]Linda Dégh and Andrew Vázsonyi, "Legend and Belief", *Genre*, vol. 4, no. 3, Sept. 1971, pp. 281-304.

the home of her parents-in-law, situated across the town from where she had lived. This house, like her grandmother's in which the family had lived, was also a rambling house and large storytelling sessions continued there until the nineteen sixties and seventies. From her family-in-law and those who visited the house at night, she added to her store of narratives, particularly in relation to the supernatural. With the encouragement of her father-in-law she became an active bearer of tradition and performed for seasoned adult audiences while still in her twenties. This was an important social and psychological achievement for Jenny because in so doing she achieved acceptance, status and position in her new family and community.

It became clear during the course of my recording work with her that her repertoire consisted both of an *active* repertoire and *memory* repertoire. A legend about the attempted abduction of a bride was part of her *memory* repertoire until her youngest daughter got married. It then became part of her *active* repertoire.

Jenny does not believe the story of this legend. Nevertheless, it is quite clear from considerations of the structure and style of this legend, its painstaking selection of setting as she adapts it to modern tastes and modern times, and its explanatory conclusion, that her aim is to convince her audience of the truth of the legend, whether she succeeds or not does not affect the validity of the legend for her. Consequently, we are in agreement with Dégh and Vászoni that subjective belief is not a necessary criterion for legend definition and is unnecessary for the formation and communication of the legend. What is of basic and inherent importance is the relationship of the legend to belief systems.

The fact that Mrs. Jenny McGlynn was only learning her traditions in the 1940s and 1950s, and that she only became an active bearer of them from the 1960s, is evidence of the continuing vitality of the oral tradition, even in modern-day English-speaking Ireland, and of the enduring appeal of the legend, as a narrative genre, to Irish audiences.

Isidor Levin
(Leningrad)

FOLKLORISTIC DOCUMENTATION, TEXTOLOGY AND EDITORIAL PRINCIPLES: METHODOLOGICAL PATHS FROM FIELDWORK TO COMPUTER-AIDED CORPUS

1. Orality in the usual sense of this modern and philologically superfluous, vague concept, as is common knowledge, is perceived in vivo (i.e. directly) only accoustically or visually, with the result that it receives rather impressionistic treatment. To the best of my knowledge more profound descriptions or experimental studies of orality are extremely rare.

1.1. Although there has existed (from time of sound films) reliable and discreet equipment to construct a comprehensive documentation as such, albeit woefully inadequate, which recently has been technically much refined, it has been much neglected in Europe. Therefore, the criticism of the lack of correspondingly developed means of analyzing phenomena which are on the face of it only partially detectable is indeed justified.

1.2. The verbalization of orality – just as attempts to describe painting or music in words – is hardly reliable as a means of scientific description, particularly since no consensus exists over the terminology used to describe what is heard.

2. *General* statements about orality on the basis of *written* individual, unsystematic, i.e. indirect evidence (which in any case is iconographic and there with static) are ipso facto inadequate and conjectural.

2.1. Case studies and verbalized reports by participatory observation which are bound up with the individual as informant (storyteller, singer and poet) or as observer, and which have a tendency to proliferate of their own accord, sometimes rather too facilely, are higly subjective as proof of ad-hoc theories linked to them, such as in the case of the gestures of a fairytale narrator or of a singer of folksongs.

2.2. The value of statements on manifestations which ostensibly or seemingly are determined by orality (e.g. the transcription of a composition whose original is lost, or notations of oral performances) will always remain in principle restricted in respect of the composition, style, or creation of the existing text or copy (let alone of an anonymous work à la *oral poetry* which claims to be an independent scholarly discipline), which must be reconstructed by textual criticism. Orality, in my opinion, can be investigated if one differentiates between *notation* (or "text" – a term which is only applicable in this philological, and not in its philosophical, sense) and *work* (Oeuvre, opus), type, as a category containing genetically related descriptions or oral activations. Those who think that they can ignore this distinction need read no further.

3. On the basis of historical sources (before the mid-20th century) orality can paradoxically only be investigated in so far as it can be made transparent in writing. This orality, once determined and thus investigated, is perhaps the only and quintessential object of folkloristic research, which regards itself as the one academic discipline dealing with variants that emerge from oral reception of traditioned works of whatever compass.

4. However orality is understood, as something else and more than creativity or personal style, as far as orality is concerned two distinct *levels* really count if folkloristics claims to be a precise discipline – first: the level of the quantity or totality of notations (of "testimonies") of *one work* (one "type", even if it is as long as a Homerian epic or as short as a saying or metaphor), no matter how, by whom or for what purpose composed, and where or when recorded; a preventative selection of references in terms of prejudice or value judgement should be avoided at all costs. – Secondly: the level of the restricted repertory, i.e. of the totality of references for several or discrete works of ostensibly oral origin or provenance. There are theoretically established means, which have been in practice extensively tested, to comprehend these totalities (such as the identification of genetically related contents and the verification of their representativeness).

4.1. From the point of view of folkloristics each individual notation (i.e. each primary text) is regarded as pars pro toto, that is to say, understood within an existing but yet to be determined synchronic totality – sometimes, however, as a diachronic component of an ideal sequence of *transmission*. Every possible *variant* in the (individual) *text* (which may not be identified in its totality as a "variant"), only makes sense, therefore, as the expression of orality as a process, in short, as a witness to the reception as an event in the transmission of a work.

4.2. Only the totality of notations (behind which even much larger number of persons is concealed) is capable of comprehending not only the work transmitted (often in the original, genuine turn of speech), but also implies that registers of variations within necessarily restricted (in terms of content and dispersion, chronologically as well as socially) yet also unconsciously formed repertories which at the same time to a great extent objectivizes the orality and therewith render it succeptable to analysis in the first place.

4.2.1. With this verifiable totality scholarly deductions become possible on the quiddity of each variant and the text which contains them, on the value of the variant as part of the text as well as that of the concrete text as a whole in its transmission, likewise in the transmission, likewise also in the genesis of a work and in the repertory of a people.

5. A precondition for the comparative interpretation of the process of reception and therewith by implication for the hermeneutics of orality is the ready accessibility of variants which have been systematized according to their provenance and typology. That means recognizing the register of variants chiefly as the consequence of numerous, variators whether they be of epochal (typical of their times) or possibly social (group-specific) or even individual character. One has to recognize variability as the consequence of *variators*.

5.1. It has to be recognized, however, that neither space nor time, not even community should be responsible for directly determined variants (or forms thereof) in the transmission of a work. The variation in the corpus of vocabulary (perhaps also of material culture such as maybe held to exist within a cultural landscape) is decisively influenced by mental, i.e. psychical parameters, and is rarely determined monocausally. For that reason if for no other the register of variants, implied orality, offers rich material with which to trace the mentality of its exponants.

5.1.1. In this regard the living exponent of variants can only claim our interest as the creative or distorting source of the variant (and/or of a work) in his supposed quality as the transmitter of a variant (variator). It remains to be proved, however, that this particular person has actively created specific variants (which must therefore in themselves be singular) in the transmission or genesis of a work. Since it is not even possible to determine that in the generative process of numerous reproductions of one and the same work, archival research is the order of the day.

5.1.2. "Creativity" does not have to imply alteration of tradition, as devotees of the romantic cult of the *originalgenie* believe. There are many highly differentiated types of narrators and singers, who insist on being reproduced passively and word-for-word (even if that should fail). Others, however, try to participate actively and improvise in the light of the given situation. Some others, again, seek to play a narratively defined role. All of these can lead to artistically successful as well as deplorable results.

5.1.3. The enhanced importance vouchsafed to the person of the storyteller over against the story told, or of the singer over against the song, or of the once-and-for-all performance over against the process of reception cannot but in the end lead to a mystification of orality. The one-sided preoccupation with the variator, i.e. with the transmitting person, has of late become more widespread as an instrument of political manipulation, or at least as an easy available substitute for philology. That is to be regretted.

5.2. Admittedly, whatever is *unique* about a work and/or the repertory, be it archaism or innovation, may provide a certain aesthetic fascination, just as the personality of the informants themselves, but in terms of folklore studies and indeed for research into orality (just as the "old person" and the "original genius" occupy sociologists) of no consequence.

5.2.1. At this point folklore studies touch upon the realms of psychology of reception and memory, whose methodology and insights may also be applied to orality research as well as the investigation of topoi. What matters is to explain the *mechanism* whereby particular exponents of transmitted works (but also of patterns of behaviour and mentality) have themselves undergone change er else have become stabilized. This is a genuine issue of great theoretical and, alas, on account of the mass media, also practical consequence.

6. The task of any folkloristic, i.e. also cultural-historical research, which cannot ignore the considerable written collections or originally oral stories assembled in the course of the centuries in which they were eagerly collected, but which the same time seeks to investigate them properly, can only be accomplished step-by-step and in a deliberate strategy of computerized research. The immediate goals of such research are in themselves worthwhile and susceptible to development.

6.1. Let us begin with a rational and formal pagination (0001-9999) of the sides of paper. 10,000 pages form on *section* (the sections are numbered consecutively [numbers 01-99]). If necessary, i.e. if the series of sections (should there be more than 99x9999 pages) or the "fonds" shall be identified by two letters (according to the abbreviation of the documentary institute): for example FA 01:0001 for the first page of the material. Since several "texts" may be contained on one page, they should be numbered (with commas) seratim (from 01 to 99): e.g. FA 01:0001,01 (for the first notation on the first page of the first section in the first "fond" of the archive). Thereafter no further enumeration of the texts is necessary.

6.2. Each text (to be identified by the aforementioned 12 digits) should be *classified* by means of an agreed codificatory (or classificatory) system into five further categories:

according to *place* (following global sections on the map of the world, to be subdivided in three by three blocks (1 to 9) and each "field" in four by four squares (01 to 16) – one small area can yet again be subdivided into smaller squares identified by a cross (a,b,c,d), so that the localization of the notation can be determined by six digits (three of which are already internationally fixed for the global sections: instead of the last three digits it is desirable to use readily understandable abbreviations consisting of three letters for large cities in contrast to villages in the same field where the population is more stable.

according to *year (or the complete date* of the notation), personal provenance, i.e. according to *collector* and *informant* (each with fore- and surname, and sex and age group (1 to 9), and finally according to the type of archival *text* (which determines the *extent* of the individual text within otherwise connected reports (three digits are sufficient for this).

6.3. The simple archive unit (text) which has been *classified* and *registered* in terms of content through possible supplementary information in four respects (to be determined strictly according to the codificator), i.e. to specific *communities* (groups, collectives, peoples), to *times* (e.g. in the course of lifetime or year), to several *existential types* (e.g. form, function, circumstances, technique of presentation). The final tenth digit provides *documentary information* (i.e. notes on the technical character of the reference – e.g. paper, tape, etc. as well as the condition of the document and its language).

6.4. These ten codified parameters in the classificatory system (including their ramifications – in effect circa 5x5x9 columns –) make possible the rapid localization of the relevant reference in terms of its problem-oriented single document and reveal the internal statistical *correlations* of their fundamental characteristics (e.g. type of text, human community, time etc.). Therefore, they also provide a fundamental qualitative and quantitative insight into genesis, geography, history and sociology of the source basis in whole or in part.

By means of this code the texts required can be called up either manually, by punch-card systems, or by computers. Similarly, catalogue can be printed out by these means. Therewith the first step towards achieving an analysis of an archive is completely done.

7. Consequently, the second step of an analytic documentation of raw material organizes as technically as possible the fundamental textforms (in excerpted copies) in terms of *content* (that means in material folklore, folkart etc.):

according to relevant *objects* (in the case of so-called rites, customs, games etc.), according to *stereotypes of communication*, i.e. processes of communication, but also in the case of many different types of linguistic material (such as proverbs, narrations, songs), according also to *written works*, that is to say according to real research oriented entities. By this means texts may be grouped according to their contential identity.

7.1. Within the more or less invariable, stable totality of a subgroup of notations the *variability* becomes transparent not only in terms of content, it also lends itself, almost mechanically (and therewith objectively) to the *differentiation* of the *works* themselves.

7.2. Such a differentiation in the repertoire (i.e. entire source basis) of a fundamentally arbitrary plethora of notations, which documents the reception of any optional work in question (which previously possibly has remained unknown in terms of size, content and form), leads necessarily to a critical analysis of the variants in their diverse relations (to space, time, community, etc.), and subsequently to a *synthesis* of invariability. Each should have regard to the possible construction of the problematic archetype and the illumination of the variative factors which have deformed or meaningfully redefined the original text. The point is to organize *motives* according to numerous carto-, chrono- and sociograms on the level of the work itself. The coordination of spatial locations and other points of reference, particularly when many of them occur within several works, itself contains a cultural geographical value. In addition, it is a question of immanent synthesis and criticism: only from an archival, technical point of view should every notation be regarded as of equal value in the preliminary stage of research, but once comparative analysis has been completed, the expressive quality of one variant or of an entire group of notations turns out to be highly distinctive.

7.3. The immediate goal of this well established historical-philological text-analysis is the factual depiction of the references of a single work (e.g. of every severally transmitted song or fairytale) as the testimony of a reception which had really occurred in the form of a printable, critical book (*corpus*), which comprehends, renders and also makes superfluous the individual, local archives for researchers world-wide, just as editions of "critical texts" accomplish.

7.3.1. For this I have elaborated a specific editorial synoptic technique, which I have frequently tested also in teamwork.

7.4. Only a considerable quantity of such corpora is capable of objectivizing the characteristic features of a previously oral and local repertoire by means of a mapped pattern of variation on its synchronic or diachronic level.

It also makes these corpora hermeneutically reliable for any research into *mental history* of its transmitters, which is, indeed, the ultimate goal of every documentation and, supposedly, of each academic discipline in the arts either in the present or the future.

7.4.1. The chief historical question, which – mutatis mutandis – is also valid for natural phenomena, runs thus: *how* and *why* have transmissions of individual oeuvres and their orality become that which we encounter in our source material?

8. Meanwhile, even before the corpora are printed, it becomes clear that (in terms of quality and quantity) an abbreviated and typical definition of the repertoire of several textual genres (e.g. proverbs, songs, even motif-indices for prose narrations) is possible.

8.1. For this purpose, one should excerpt those heuristically detected (and afterwards more closely defined) *key-words*, which previously well served to classify *types*, separately, in isolation form the text (in the case of prose one will probably isolate elementary motives). In addition, one should note the frequency of each key-word (according to the amount of source material). The provenance of certain registers should also be noted by means of abbreviations (sigla).

8.1.1. On both levels one has to distinguish in principle between two different kinds of frequency; on the one hand a key-word (e.g. a motif) can only derive from *one* text in the repertoire and can, therefore, recur as often as hundred times, because the text in question has been recorded one hundred times. On the other, a certain key-word can similarily recur one hundred times because it is mentioned ten times within ten different recordings. The meaning of the number 100, can imply very different values. In the first case it testifies to an archetypical stability of a very high order, but is certainly irrelevant for the *repertoire*. Vice versa, however, in the second case (cf. in the first case 100:1, whereas in the second 100:10, – or even e.g. 100:100)!

8.1.2. The proportion of the number of texts in a repertoire (which contain a significant key-word) to the number of texts (in which the word occurs identifiably) has to be taken into account in every interpretation. Whoever neglects quantity (for whatever reason) will never achieve an interpretable quality defining a repertoire or even a single work.

9. As catch-words for the differentiation only *meaningful* words should be marked, a procedure which has been supported by statistical-psychological experiments (in prose narratives these words consist mainly of subject-forming motives). These catch-words cover a relatively high percentage of the thesaurus of one single repertoire.

9.1. The once excerpted thesaurus contains (in terms of frequency) not only well-known topoi but also innovations, which occur precisely in unusual variation. On the basis of extensive concordances of complete texts selective registers of realia and their epithets, of metaphors etc. can be produced.

9.1.1. For an interpretation of the repertoire according to its content (and of individual works consecutively) it is not the grammatical form of the words, but the *lemmata* which are relevant and, consequently, their related groups. Synonymity – however important for the genesis of variants – does not count here, because words which are related in terms of meaning and content must be collated with regard to their frequency. The frequency of *one* word outside its semantic field is hermeneutically largely irrelevant, just as the formal, arbitrary fables in a frequency-dictionary are. The priority of content for interpretation as such requires that the excerpted thesaurus should be structured not according to an ABC but rather by problem-oriented headings. I am well aware of the difficulties of such a method, when seeking to thematize a language in toto, but here I am applying it to a restricted number of units only, and that is obviously practicable.

9.2. In order to tame the arbitrary nature of this division by subject headings one should proceed in a problem-oriented way by always paying attention to the frequency of the terms when evaluating their importance within the repertoire. A list of subject-headings alone, as well as for instance a frequency-dictionary can often result in casual misinterpretations. As is well known, therefore, one has to combine both approaches.

9.3. For the characterization of the repertoire the absolute frequency and that of the principal subject-heading do not really matter. It is only the *relative* frequency of the "pure" subheadings which is of interest. More precisely, this means that the internal (quantitative and qualitative) *correlations* are of relevance, specifically with expert regard to the parameters of the given language ("parole") and to comparable repertoires, so that significant deviations may be recognized. Eo ipso, characterization begins.

Only under these conditions can a partial thesaurus in the form of a "dictionary of imagery" – ordered by subject-headings and frequency – be interpreted, separated from the fabula of the texts.

9.3.1. Theory and methodology of the relevant hermeneutics (as of textual criticism) can be learned and are certainly capable of elaboration. (Examples cannot be discussed here. They are available in numerous dissertations which have been written under my supervision in Tadjikistan and Armenia.)

9.4. A dictionary of imagery (on the basis of written documentations of *variability*) represents the quintessence of a repertoire, but at the same time enabl-